June 2011

Welcome, Dr. Stroble!
From the Space Coast
alumni, faculty,
students & staff!

Cape Canaveral,
Cocoa Beach &
Florida's Space Coast

A Great Destination

W9-BVQ-117

Cape Canaveral, Cocoa Beach & Florida's Space Coast

A Great Destination

Dianne Marcum

with photographs by the author

The Countryman Press   Woodstock, Vermont

Suggestions and comments are welcome. Please email the publisher at countrymanpress@wwnorton.com or visit www.DianneMarcum.com.

Second Edition

Cape Canaveral, Cocoa Beach & Florida's Space Coast: A Great Destination

ISBN 978-1-58157-120-2

Interior photos by the author unless otherwise specified
Book design by Bodenweber Design
Page composition by PerfecType, Nashville, TN
Maps by Mapping Specialists, Ltd., Madison, WI, and Erin Greb Cartography
© The Countryman Press

Published by The Countryman Press, P.O. Box 748, Woodstock, Vermont 05091

Distributed by W. W. Norton & Company, Inc., 500 Fifth Avenue, New York, NY 10110

Printed in the United States of America

10 9 8 7 6 5 4 3 2 1

For my mother, Harriette, who understood that when your heart
is your compass you will always find your way.

EXPLORE WITH US!

Florida's Space Coast is long and narrow, with 72 miles of Atlantic beachfront. Eastbound travelers cross several bridges that span intracoastal waterways flowing like liquid ribbons down the length of the county.

In the beginning of the book you'll find "What's Where," an alphabetical listing of highlights and important information that you may want to reference quickly. There follow comprehensive descriptions of the region's history and recreational opportunities, plus a guide to traveling to and within Brevard County.

The next four chapters zero in on specific locales. "Cape Canaveral and Cocoa Beach" includes Port Canaveral and a nearby section of Merritt Island. "Central Brevard" includes historic Cocoa Village and the newer community of Viera; "North Brevard" is anchored by the city of Titusville; and "South Brevard" stretches from Eau Gallie and Melbourne to Sebastian Inlet.

Finally comes some suggested itineraries to help you custom-tailor your explorations.

Listings within each chapter are in alphabetical order. In general, most facilities and activities have some degree of wheelchair accessibility, and this is noted. However, the specifics vary considerably, and those with special needs should call ahead.

PRICING CODES

The information in this book is as timely and accurate as possible, but like a beach landscape, the terrain is always shifting. Dining prices are based on the cost of a dinner entrée with appetizer and dessert. Lodging prices are a per-room, double occupancy rate, during the peak season. Rates usually drop 20 percent or more during nonpeak times. Not included is a 6 percent Florida sales tax on dining and lodging and a 5 percent countywide resort tax on lodging.

	Lodging	**Dining**
Inexpensive	Up to $100	Up to $15
Moderate	$100–150	$15–25
Expensive	$150–200	$25–35
Very Expensive	Over $200	Over $35

KEY TO SYMBOLS

✎ **Child-friendly.** With a casual atmosphere, miles of beaches, and a multitude of outdoor recreation spots, the Space Coast is an ideal child-friendly vacation spot. The crayon symbol appears next to lodging and activities of special interest or appeal to youngsters.

🐾 **Pets.** The dog-paw symbol appears next to venues that accept pets, although some lodgings may only accept small dogs and have a limited number of rooms available. When dogs are allowed at a dining establishment, seating is always outdoors.

⚘ **Waterfront Dining.** The umbrella symbol highlights restaurants that offer waterfront seating or a spectacular ocean or lagoon view.

⚭ **Weddings.** The wedding-ring symbol appears next to lodging venues that are experienced in hosting weddings and offer a beautiful setting.

Brevard County has one area code, and it's easy to remember: 321—blast off!

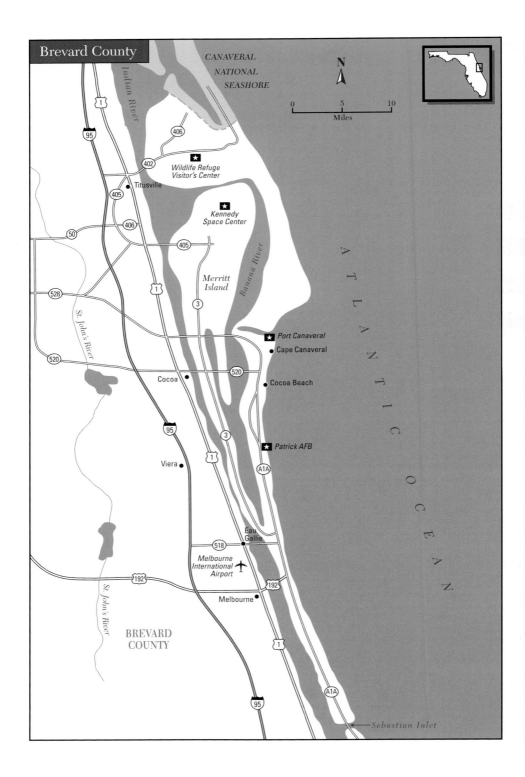

CONTENTS

11 ACKNOWLEDGMENTS
12 INTRODUCTION
14 WHAT'S WHERE
26 HISTORY
39 TRANSPORTATION
46 RECREATION

1 Cape Canaveral, Cocoa Beach, and Port Canaveral / 63

2 Central Brevard / 135

3 North Brevard / 161

4 South Brevard / 185

217 SUGGESTED ITINERARIES
222 BIBLIOGRAPHY
229 INDEX

LIST OF MAPS

8   BREVARD COUNTY

40   FLORIDA'S HIGHWAYS

51   NATURE PRESERVES AND PARKS

64   CAPE CANAVERAL AND COCOA BEACH

72   PORT CANAVERAL

138 CENTRAL BREVARD

164 NORTH BREVARD

167 VIEWING A SPACE LAUNCH

188 SOUTH BREVARD

Wildlife Profiles

38   SEA TURTLE

42   BOTTLENOSE DOLPHIN

60   BALD EAGLE AND OSPREY

130 ROSEATE SPOONBILL

160 PELICAN

183 GREAT BLUE HERON

212 MANATEE

214 ALLIGATOR

ACKNOWLEDGMENTS

It takes a community to write a travel guide. The stories and enthusiasm of the people who live in and love Brevard County are woven through every page of this book.

Thank you to the entrepreneurs and artists I met who care about strengthening the community as much as growing their own business, and were eager to share information and pass along the name of the next person who might help me; and the nature lovers who prove that eco-tourism really works and were generous tutors on surfing, fishing, paddling, birding, and other pursuits.

I appreciate the support of friends in the Space Coast Writer's Guild and Cocoa Beach Writer's Workshop, especially Mary May Burruss who generously shared her expertise. *Florida Today,* our local newspaper, does a great job of reporting on current activities, and I have benefited from the talents of writers Chris Kridler, who does restaurant reviews, and John Kelly, who covers space events.

I am grateful to the many individuals that provided information and ideas. Talented photographers Jim Angy and Roger Scruggs contributed to the images that illustrate the beauty and diversity of this area. Bonnie King with the Space Coast Tourism Development Commission was a wealth of information. Roger Dobson and Laurilee Thompson are Brevard County pioneers who inspired me with their love for the area.

To everyone at The Countryman Press, especially Kermit Hummel, Lisa Sacks, and Doug Yeager, thank you for your valuable advice and support, and a toast to Sandy Rodgers for her editing talent and the sunny outlook she contributed to these pages.

My love and gratitude go out to friends and family who joined me on field trips, contributed ideas, and celebrated every small success, especially Maggie Megee and John Anderson who were always ready to head out on a new adventure. A huge, appreciative hug to my grandchildren—Cassidy, Jessica, Colin, Alyssa, Carson, and Shay—who hit the sand running when they visit and remind me of the absolute joy of a day at the beach.

INTRODUCTION

H ow would you like to live in a place like this?" writes a visitor describing the beauty and wildlife of the Indian River on the back of a postcard. The message was penned nearly a century ago but could just have easily been sent yesterday. Brevard County is one of those rare vacation spots where people picture themselves living one day, an extraordinary blend of sunshine, beaches, pristine natural resources, and space-age technology.

The Space Coast moniker is not just hyperbole. Brevard County is the birthplace of America's space program and the world's most active spaceport. From along the coast or across the river in north Brevard, the sight and sound of a launch is breathtaking. A tour at Kennedy Space Center Visitor Complex takes you right onto NASA property and close to all their facilities. You can even have lunch with an astronaut. (See "North Brevard" for a summary of aerospace offerings that explore that past, present, and future of space exploration.)

MONUMENT TO MERCURY 7 ASTRONAUTS AT SPACE VIEW PARK.

The waterways of the Indian River Lagoon estuary flow the entire length of the county and host an abundance of marine life, birds, plants—and, of course, manatees and dolphins. The mix of fresh and salt water creates an idyllic spot for wildlife and a wonderful recreational playground.

Planning should be the easiest part of your vacation. This book is designed to provide all the information you need to have fun along Flori-

A CONVERTIBLE IS A GREAT WAY TO CRUISE THE ISLAND ROADS.

da's Space Coast. In addition to suggestions on where to stay, eat, and shop, you'll find listings for cultural and recreational activities. Everybody can enjoy outdoor adventures—novices and experts, children and adults.

So come visit. Bask in the sun, ride a wave, dive in the pool, paddle through quiet waters, reel in a fish, laugh at pelicans, marvel at dolphins, be mesmerized by manatees. Just don't forget to text friends back home: "How would U like 2 live IA place like this? L8RG8R."

WHAT'S WHERE

AREA CODES AND CITY HALLS

The area code for all of Brevard County is 321. For metropolitan Orlando the area code is 407, and you must dial all 10 digits to place a call. An elected board of commissioners governs Brevard County, which has a population of nearly half a million. Many services are provided at the county level, but individual municipalities retain local controls and are the best resource for specific community information.

City Hall	Phone
Brevard County	633-2000
Cape Canaveral	868-1230
Cocoa	639-7550
Cocoa Beach	868-3235
Grant-Valkaria	951-1380
Indialantic	723-2242
Indian Harbour Beach	773-3181
Malabar	727-7764
Melbourne	608-7000
Melbourne Beach	724-5860
Melbourne Village	723-8300
Palm Bay	952-3400
Palm Shores	242-4555
Rockledge	690-3978
Satellite Beach	773-4407
Titusville	383-5775
West Melbourne	727-7700

BANKS

The following are banks in the Cape Canaveral and Cocoa Beach area. Most have links to national or regional banking systems and are part of automatic teller networks.

Bank of America, 82 N. Atlantic Avenue, Cocoa Beach 32931; 321-783-2444.

Bank of America, 4300 N. Atlantic Avenue, Cocoa Beach 32931; 321-783-2455.

Coastal Bank, 1701 N. Atlantic Avenue, Cocoa Beach 32931; 321-868-3580.

RCB Centura Bank, 4350 N. Atlantic Avenue, Cocoa Beach 32931; 321-868-6060.

Sunrise Bank, 5604 N. Atlantic Avenue, Cocoa Beach 32931; 321-784-8333.

SunTrust, 150 Galleria Center, Cocoa Beach 32931; 321-799-2203.

BEACHES

The most often asked question by first-time visitors to the area is "Where's the beach?" The answer is: "Everywhere." Cross the bridges to the barrier islands and a beach with public access is always just a few blocks away. To be sure you are close to parking, rest rooms, life-

carved through thick palmetto and fought off insects and reptiles. In *A Land Remembered,* **Patrick D. Smith** follows three generations of the MacIvey family as they go from dirt-poor Crackers and cowboys to land barons. *Canaveral Light,* by **Don Argo,** centers on the conflicts and interactions of Florida pioneers and Native Americans during the Seminole Wars. **Zora Neale Hurston** lived and wrote in Eau Gallie for a time. *Their Eyes Were Watching God* is the story of a proud, independent black woman and a classic look at Florida from the eye of a hurricane.

Space is the final frontier and the men and women of Brevard County have paved the way for this exciting journey. In *The Right Stuff,* **Tom Wolfe** takes a look at the first astronauts, space pioneers, and heroes who "were willing to sit on top of an enormous Roman Candle" and wait for the fuse to be lit. John Glenn was the first, and later oldest, American to fly into orbit. His story is personal and

guards, and other amenities, settle at one of the beach parks listed in each regional chapter under *Green Space and Beaches.* There are beach parks in every community, lining the shore like a string of pearls—each similar when seen from a distance, but distinctive in color and texture upon closer inspection. Every park is a jewel, but some might be more to your taste than others. Two great choices in the Cocoa Beach area are **Jetty Park** and **Lori Wilson Park**.

BOOKS Adventure, nature, and technology merge in Brevard County and several books bring the area to life. Florida's colorful and surprising history is captured in the easy-to-read and informative *Florida: A Short History,* by University of Florida professor **Michael Gannon**. In *Land of Sunshine, State of Dreams,* writer **Gary R. Mormino** weaves the influences of citrus, land development, tourism, technology, and Americans' continuing fascination with the beach into an entertaining social history of the state.

Three local authors have penned captivating and award-winning historical novels about early pioneers who

anecdotal in *John Glenn, A Memoir,* by **John Glenn and Nick Taylor**. For 50 years veteran NBC News reporter and local resident **Jay Barbree** has covered America's manned space flight. He shares his inside stories about the astronauts and the evolution of the space program in the very entertaining *Live From Cape Canaveral.*

Relax and reminiscence with *Cross Creek,* by **Marjorie Kinnan Rawlings**, a Pulitzer Prize–winning novelist who left New York to settle a homestead in a wild stretch of central Florida. In 1955 **Anne Morrow Lindbergh** gave us *Gift From the Sea*. This timeless classic of reflection centers on her solitary stay along a Florida seashore and a collection of seashells, and has been enjoyed and shared by generations of women. To appreciate the timeless wonder and beauty of the state, paddle along with **Bill Belleville** in *River of Lakes: A Journey on Florida's St. Johns River*. Photographer **John Moran** has captured the best of Florida through images, essays, and philosophical observations in *Journal of Light: The Visual Diary of a Florida Nature Photographer.*

What's a day at the beach without a fun read? *The Old Man and the Sea* by **Ernest Hemingway** remains the definitive fishing tale; *The Barefoot Mailman* by **Theodore Pratt** traces a mail carrier on a mid-19th-century walk along a 100-mile route on the sands of Florida's Atlantic coast. Vampire-lit fans—or anyone looking to escape into a great story—will enjoy the three-book series by Cape Canaveral writer **Susan Hubbard**: *The Society of S, The Year of Disappearances,* and *The Season of Risks*. Any book from **Tim Dorsey** is a laugh-out-loud look at the seedier side of Florida. Expect murder, mayhem, drugs, and a side dose of the fun parts of Florida's history. His latest is *Gator a-go-go*.

Several wonderful children's books showcase the state for young readers. *A is for Sunshine: A Florida Alphabet* by **Carol Crane** introduces the wonders of Florida, like the alligator, which can stay underwater for an hour. Little ones love the board book, *Good Night Florida,* by **Adam Gamble** and **Red Hansen**. Melbourne Beach residents **Mara Uman Hixon** and **Steve J. Harris** have written and illustrated *Turtles Way: Loggy, Greeny & Leather,* an accurate and delightful story of sea turtles perfect for toddlers and preschoolers. For children of all ages interested in birding, the field guide *Birds of Florida* by **Stan Tekiela** sorts our feathered friends by color, making them easy to identify.

CAMPING AND RVING Year-round pleasant weather and the stunning natural environment make the Space Coast a perfect spot for camping. Expect higher demand and higher rates during the winter months and holidays. Both the sun and the insects grow stronger in the summer, so be prepared with sunscreen and bug repellent. See the listings in each chapter under *To Do*.

CHAMBERS OF COMMERCE **Cocoa Beach Area Chamber of Commerce,** 400 Fortenberry Road, Merritt Island 32952; 321-459-2200; www.cocoabeachchamber.com. **Florida Puerto Rican/Hispanic Chamber of Commerce,** 2293 Aurora Road, Melbourne 32935; 321-752-1003; www.fprhcc.org. **Greater Palm Bay Chamber of Commerce,** 4100

Dixie Highway NE, Palm Bay 32907; 321-951-9998; www.palmbaychamber .com. **Melbourne–Palm Bay Area Chamber of Commerce,** 1005 E. Strawbridge Avenue, Melbourne 32901; 321-724-5400; www.melpb -chamber.org. **Titusville Area Chamber of Commerce,** 2000 S. Washington Avenue, Titusville 32796; 321-267-3036; www.titusville.org.

EMERGENCIES In Brevard County, three phone numbers connect you to assistance, information, and referral to the appropriate agency. **Dial 911** for medical and other emergencies, and an operator will immediately route you to ambulance, fire, local police, Brevard County Sheriff, Florida Highway Patrol, or Coast Guard Search and Rescue. **Dial 211** to reach the Brevard County Help Line, where trained counselors are available 24 hours a day to provide information or referral on local governmental, health, or social services, including disaster planning information. **Dial 511** for traffic reports. Other important numbers: **Poison Control:** 1-800-222-1222. **Sexual Assault Victim Services Rape Crisis Hotline:** 321-784-4357.

FAMILY FUN AND FITNESS No matter what your age or fitness level, there are lots of convenient and exciting outdoor activities, many perfect for children. Visit the Port Canaveral locks or take a walk in the park at sunset. Stop by the Cocoa Beach recreation complex for an afternoon of swimming or tennis. The more adventurous might take a spin on a Jet Ski or windsurf. Everyone will enjoy a trip to the zoo or a baseball game. Activities are listed in each chapter under *To Do*.

GALLERIES Along the Space Coast you'll discover works of art ranging from fanciful to elegant. Many of the galleries and studios showcase the incredible talent of local artists, and many works reflect the natural environment or the culture of space exploration. The galleries tend to cluster, so within a few blocks of the same neighborhood you'll find several choices. Pop into the studios that appeal to your taste, or perhaps take a detour and discover something new. See *Selective Shopping* in each chapter for a comprehensive list of galleries.

HANDICAPPED SERVICES Space Coast hotels, restaurants, and recreational providers do a great job of catering to those with special physical needs. Florida law requires that dogs assisting disabled visitors be allowed in restaurants. All businesses must provide handicapped parking, so remember to pack your permit. When making reservations or planning an outing, call ahead to confirm what's available. There may be some limitations, especially in older buildings, but in general, disabled visitors will find themselves able to enjoy every facet of a fun vacation. Here's just a small sample of what to expect. **Travelynx** (321-783-2112) has a minibus with a motorized wheelchair lift; all Space Coast Area Transit buses are similarly equipped. Kennedy Space Center Visitor Complex (321-449-4444) is set up for full accessibility for mobility-, hearing-, and seeing-impaired guests. Lori Wilson Park and the Johnnie Johnson Nature Trail have ADA-compliant parking, rest rooms, playground, boardwalk, trail, and dune crossovers. Specially designed beach wheelchairs are available at Canaveral National Seashore, Jetty Park, and Sebastian Inlet State Park. Boat and fishing tour guides are happy to accommodate the needs of all passengers, but let them know in advance.

HISTORIC PLACES Although the area's Native American roots reach back centuries, most local historic sites date from settlements beginning about 150 years ago. A tour of historic places, still existing or captured in memory, provides a close look at the challenges and adventures inherent in taming this small stretch of Florida wilderness. In this book, you'll find historic sites listed under *To See.*

HOSPITALS AND CLINICS ABC Urgent Care (321-799-7777; 275 W. Cocoa Beach Causeway, Cocoa Beach 32931) Adults and children receive prompt treatment for illness or injury, including X-rays and lab work, at this clinic located in the Banana River Plaza near the intersection of SR A1A. No appointment is needed and most insurance is accepted. Open daily 8 AM–7 PM. **Cape Canaveral Hospital** (321-799-7111; 701 W. Cocoa Beach Causeway, Cocoa Beach 32931) Emergency room is open 24 hours. Part of the Health First system, which provides a medical referral line at 321-434-2300. **Health First Physicians Walk-in Clinic** (321-784-4211; 105 S. Banana River Boulevard, Cocoa Beach 32931) Minor illnesses and injuries are treated at this clinic, conveniently located just off A1A about 1 mile south of FL 520. They participate in many insurance plans and accept several major credit cards. Open Monday through Friday 8 AM–7:30 PM, Saturday 9–3:30, and Sunday 9–12:30. **Holmes**

Regional Medical Center (321-434-7000; 1350 S. Hickory Street, Melbourne 32901) Physicians are on duty at this 24-hour emergency room, which has a level II trauma center and air ambulance service. Part of the Health First system. **Palm Bay Community Hospital** (321-434-8000; 1425 Malabar Road, Melbourne 32907) Emergency room open 24 hours. Part of the Health First system. **Parrish Medical Center** (321-268-6111; 951 N. Washington Avenue, Titusville 32796) Emergency room open 24 hours. **Wuesthoff Medical Center–Melbourne** (321-752-1200; 250 N. Wickham Road, Melbourne 32935) Emergency room open 24 hours. Part of the Wuesthoff Health system. **Wuesthoff Medical Center–Rockledge** (321-636-2211; 110 Longwood Avenue, Rockledge 32955) Emergency room open 24 hours. Part of the Wuesthoff Health system.

LODGING Early motel development in Cocoa Beach was fast and furious, trying to keep pace with the overnight demand created by space workers, media, and curious tourists. Expectations were simple—clean, comfortable, and inexpensive. Over the years modern, spacious chain hotels have replaced most of the small motels. Surprisingly, many of the new facilities are owned and operated by the same families who built the original motels. They love it here and want you to feel the same way.

Cape Canaveral and Cocoa Beach are the closest beaches to airports and highways, so most of the recommended lodging is in that corridor. Expect friendly small-town service and reasonable rates. Pay attention to definitions when you make your booking:

Courtesy Crowne Plaza Oceanfront

Oceanfront rooms face the ocean, some with a balcony. Beach view suggests that the property is on the beach, but the windows may point north or south—which often offers a great panoramic look at the coast. Beachside properties are on the east side of A1A and within a block of the ocean, but not directly on the beach. Prime real estate is upper floors, oceanfront.

In this book, properties are divided into Hotels and Motels, and Vacation and Condo Rentals categories. Because this is a family beach community, many of the hotels and motels stock standard rooms with microwaves and mini refrigerators for the convenience of their guests. In general, condominiums are more appropriate for longer stays and family groups, where the per-person, per-day rate may be lower. They are more spacious, but sometimes lack expected amenities like daily housekeeping, restaurants, and on-site management, and may require a minimum weekly rental.

Most properties have ADA-accessible common areas and a small number of rooms with limited or full wheelchair accessibility. Roll-in showers are not common. Each information block provides basic information, but if you have special needs, it's best to inquire when you make your reservation. Unless noted otherwise, facilities have free Internet access and do not permit smoking or pets.

Rates are for a standard room, double occupancy during the December–April peak season. If you upgrade to a premium room or best view, the cost will increase. Rates drop by about 20 percent during less busy times. Inquire about discounts for AAA, AARP, Florida residents, and Internet bookings.

MAIL AND SHIPPING U.S. Post Office, Cape Canaveral (321-783-3163; 8700 Astronaut Boulevard, Cape Canaveral 32920) Open 9–5 weekdays, 9–noon Saturday. Lobby open 24 hours. **U.S. Post Office, Cocoa Beach** (321-783-2544; 500 N. Brevard Avenue, Cocoa Beach 32931) Open 9–5 weekdays, 9–noon Saturday. Lobby open 24 hours. **Pak Mail** (321-799-9905; 8501 Astronaut Boulevard, Cape Canaveral 32920) Open: Monday through Friday 9–5:30, Saturday 10–3. **The UPS Store** (321-799-3030; 2023 N. Atlantic Avenue, Cocoa Beach 32931) Open Monday through Friday 8–6, Saturday 9:00–2.

MEDIA, MAGAZINES AND NEWSPAPERS *Florida Today* (321-242-3500; www.floridatoday.com; P.O. Box 419000, Melbourne 32941) Brevard County's primary newspaper publishes daily. The Friday edition includes a special supplement showcasing activities during the upcoming week. *The Flame Trench* on their Web site provides space launch updates, including a journal detailing progress during the final countdown hours. *Hometown News* (321-242-1013; www.myhometownnews.net; 1102 S. US 1, Fort Pierce 34950) Informative weekly newspaper offers timely information about community events. The edition featuring the beaches is available on racks in local stores. *Orlando Sentinel* (407-240-5000; www.orlando sentinel.com; 633 N. Orange Avenue, Orlando 32801) This daily paper is available at most outlets in Brevard County and is a good resource for central Florida news, as well as information on activities and events in the Orlando area. *Space Coast Business* (321-622-5986; www.spacecoast business.com; 6767 N. Wickham Road, Melbourne 32940) Monthly publication provides insight and information about Brevard business and professional activities. Subscriptions available online. *Space Coast Living* (321-622-5986; www.sclmagazine .com; 6767 N. Wickham Road, Melbourne 32940) Monthly magazine celebrates the arts, interests, and activities popular with residents of Brevard County—a great way to get to know the area. Subscriptions available online.

MEDIA, RADIO STATIONS
ESPN-FM 95.9 (321-984-1000; Melbourne) Sports talk and events. **WAIA-FM 107.1** (321-953-9942; Melbourne) Contemporary music and current hits. **WBVD-FM 95.1** (321-733-1000; Melbourne) R&B, hip-hop. **WFIT-FM 89.5** (321-674-8140; Melbourne) Jazz, blues, folk; NPR programming and local programming. **WHRK-FM 102.7** (321-984-1000; Melbourne) Country. **WLOQ-FM 103.1** (407-647-5557; Winter Park)

Jazz. **WLRQ-FM 99.3** (321-632-5483; Melbourne) Light rock favorites. **WMEL-AM 920** (321-254-1199; Melbourne) Talk radio, news, and sports. **WMFE-FM 90.7** (407-273-2300; Orlando) News, NPR programming. **WMIE-FM 91.5** (321-632-1000; Cocoa) Christian contemporary music. **WMMB-AM 1240/1350** (321-821-7100; Melbourne) Talk radio, news, and sports. **WPIO-FM 89.3** (321-267-3000; Titusville) Christian music, jazz, and talk. **WTKS-FM 104.1** (407-916-7800; Maitland) Edgy talk radio and rock. **WWKA-FM 92.3** (407-298-9292; Orlando) Country.

MEDIA, TELEVISION STATIONS
Cape Canaveral, Cocoa Beach, and most of Brevard County are served by cable provider Bright House Networks. Channel references indicate location on cable listings. **NASA TV Channel 49** (202-358-0001; Washington, D.C.) Space launches and news; science and technology programs. **NEWS13 Channel 13** (407-513-1300; Orlando) Twenty-four-hour local news and weather. **WBCC Channel 5** (321-632-1111; Cocoa) Operated by Brevard Community College; cultural and educational programs; selected PBS offerings. **WESH TV Channel 2** (407-645-2222; Winter Park) NBC affiliate. **WFTV TV Channel 7** (407-841-9000; Orlando) ABC affiliate. **WKMG TV Channel 6** (407-455-1431; Orlando) CBS affiliate. **WMFE TV Channel 20** (407-273-2300; Orlando) PBS affiliate. **WOFL TV Channel 3** (407-644-3535; Lake Mary) FOX affiliate.

PERFORMING ARTS In Brevard County, the **King Center for the Performing Arts** in Melbourne is the star of professional productions, featuring the Brevard Symphony Orchestra and Space Coast Ballet, as well as an array of world-renowned musicals, plays, and headliners. A talented and entertaining supporting cast includes several community theaters with deep roots and a reputation for excellence, and other local groups that appear in smaller venues. Check out the performing arts listings in each geographic chapter under *Entertainment*.

REAL ESTATE Visitors to the area often decide to invest in vacation property or relocate as year-round or seasonal residents. Single-family homes are available, but condominiums will be more affordable and require less maintenance when buying in the beach areas. As a reference, new residents must apply for auto registration and tags within 10 days after starting work or enrolling children in school, and obtain a Florida driver's license within 30 days after the beginning of such employment or enrollment. **Melbourne Area Association of Realtors,** 1450 Sarno Road, Melbourne 32935; 321-242-2211; www.maar-fl.org. **Space Coast Association of Realtors**, 105 McLeod Street, Merritt Island 32953; 321-452-9490; www.space321.com.

RESTAURANTS Dining on Florida's Space Coast is a culinary mix of simple and gourmet dishes. Seafood is often the specialty, but there are lots of choices for landlubbers. Savor ethnic flavors from around the world, or sample a uniquely Florida dish such as fried gator or Key lime pie. The atmosphere is almost always casual, but a summer dress or sport coat may be appropriate for fine-dining restau-

rants. The community is a haven for musical talent, and many places feature live entertainment on the weekends. Dinner seating is usually available with a short wait or none at all, unless it is a holiday or special-event weekend, but it never hurts to make a reservation if you're going at a prime time. Most restaurants recommend you call ahead when you have a group of six or more so they can prepare the table.

The best eateries for everything from a quick sandwich to a leisurely dinner have been summarized and reviewed in this book to help you navigate through the vast sea of choices. The lists are weighted toward locations in the beach communities and favor local establishments rather than chain operations. Many exceptional establishments are in south Brevard and are well worth a drive. Restaurants are listed alphabetically within each geographic chapter, and they are recapped in the Dining Index by price and cuisine. Florida's reputation

to take home as mementos. On the Space Coast, expect to discover resort fashions, bathing suits, and souvenirs, along with some unexpected finds, such as a shark's tooth in a dinosaur shop and a 6-foot-tall Mai Tiki carved from a cabbage palm.

The shopping venues in this book (found under *Selective Shopping*) are generally are small and locally owned. Artists often sell their works in cooperatives or other locations such as hotels and coffee shops, making it easy to find original art, jewelry, music, books, and decorative items. If you need to ship your purchases back home, see *Mail and Shipping*, above.

SPACE Welcome to America's spaceport. From these shores rockets soared into orbit, astronauts flew to the moon, and the Space Shuttle ferried building materials and supplies for the International Space Station. The Hubble Telescope launched from here, along with communication and other satellites.

for early-bird specials is well earned, so inquire about reduced rates for early seating. Restaurants are open daily unless otherwise noted. Smoking is banned inside all Florida food establishments. Establishments have wheelchair access unless noted otherwise.

ROAD AND MARINE SERVICES
Call these numbers for emergency service 24 hours a day. **Automotive: A Beeline Towing & Auto Service**, 321-799-9893. **AAA Membership Emergency Road Service**, 1-800-222-4357. **Atlantic Towing & Service**, 321-452-3377. **Spaceport Amoco in Cape Canaveral**, 321-784-5228. **Marine: Sea Tow Port Canaveral**, 321-868-4900. **Towboat US Port Canaveral**, 321-783-5600.

SHOPPING For many, a vacation is not complete without the pleasure of unearthing unusual and fun treasures

In 1919 Brevard County was a community centered around agriculture, cattle, and fishing. Folks took no notice when Robert Goddard, a physics professor from Massachusetts, published *A Method of Reaching Extreme Altitudes*. Goddard had just erased the thin line separating science fiction from science. Until his death 25 years later, this reclusive and determined rocket scientist chased his dream of proving to the world that space travel was more than just a fantasy.

Brevard County was isolated and sparsely populated in 1958 when the

RARE FINDS

The most amazing shopping gems are sometimes hidden like one perfect pearl in an ocean of oysters. Museums, nature centers, and other attractions usually have shops that feature topical, educational, and unusual gifts, including wonderful choices for children. Proceeds from most of these shops support the operations. In all cases, access to the shopping area is free. Here are some of my favorites.

The **U.S. Space Coast Walk of Fame Museum** (321-264-0434, 4 Main Street, Titusville) has astronaut costumes and shuttle models that can be assembled. The **U.S. Astronaut Hall of Fame Museum** (321-449-4444, 6225 Vectorspace Boulevard, Titusville) focuses on space books and memorabilia, including a selection of patches from every shuttle launch. At the **Brevard Community College Astronaut Memorial Planetarium and Observatory** (321-433-7373, 1519 Clearlake Road, Cocoa) the choices are centered on out-of-this world home décor items and gifts that feature the stars and the universe.

The **Brevard Museum of History & Natural Sciences** (321-632-1830, 2201 Michigan Avenue, Cocoa) tells the story of the settlement of Brevard and carries items focused on early Indians. **Florida Books and Gifts at the Florida Historical Society Library** (321-690-1971, 435 Brevard Avenue, Cocoa) has an extensive collection of fiction and nonfiction books for all ages, with a particularly expansive section of children's reading and activity books. **Brevard Art Museum** (321-242-0737, 1463 Highland Avenue, Melbourne) features artistic books, art education materials, and gifts themed to special exhibits.

Most of the nature centers have wonderful shops with jewelry, books, artwork, and artifacts that highlight their area of interest. The **Merritt Island National Wildlife Refuge** (321-861-0667, N. Merritt Island) carries different species of small, stuffed birds; each makes their recognizable call when squeezed. At the **Enchanted Forest Sanctuary** (321-264-5185, 444 Columbia Boulevard, Titusville) they have games and puzzles that talk about protecting our natural resources. The **Barrier Island Sanctuary** (321-723-3556, 8385 S. Highway A1A, Melbourne Beach) has videos that tell the story of the giant sea turtles that nest along Brevard's beaches.

newly formed National Aeronautics and Space Administration (NASA) chose Cape Canaveral as the dock from which new-age captains would launch powerful ships skyward. Engineers and technicians enlisted as the crew for this great adventure. "Go for launch" became the Space Coast mantra. The dedicated and spirited men and women of Brevard County continue to build a path from the earth to the sky, transforming vision into works of art that carry explorers to the ever-expanding edge of the universe. There's no better place to tag along on the journey.

The best places to explore the history of man's adventure into space are both in north Brevard: the **Kennedy Space Center Visitor Complex** and the **U.S. Space Walk of Fame Museum**.

WEATHER AND SEASONS Traveling to the Space Coast should be as relaxing as, well, a day at the beach. Pack for pleasant weather and casual dress. Temperatures average in the 80s during the summer, and a comfortable 60s in the winter. When rain falls, it often arrives in a deluge. After an hour or so, the downpour stops as suddenly as it began, and beachgoers return outside to bask in the warm rays of the sun. Travel to the area is heaviest during the winter months, over holidays and school breaks, and when a launch is scheduled, so reservations for those times should be made as early as possible. Visit in late spring or in the fall for a triple treat of small crowds, remarkable weather, and bargains.

Mean Temperatures (Month Max/Min.)

January 71.7°/50.0°
February 72.9°/50.8°
March 77.2°/55.2°
April 80.5°/60.1°
May 85.0°/66.3°
June 88.6°/71.2°
July 90.5°/71.9°
August 90.0°/72.7°
September 88.1°/71.9°
October 83.3°/67.4°
November 78.3°/60.0°
December 73.3°/53.0°
Source: National Weather Service, Melbourne, Florida

WILDLIFE Brevard County is teeming with wildlife—from the expected, like pelicans and dolphins—to the unexpected, like the occasional peacock wandering the neighborhoods of Cape Canaveral. The temperate-tropical climate and abundance of water create an ideal habitat for year-round residents and migrating winter birds. This book includes profiles and photographs to help you identify the most

visible and popular birds and marine mammals, and tips on the best places to see them. As you cross paths with our wild friends, please remember to keep your distance and not to feed them so they will remain wary of people and capable of taking care of themselves.

ZIP CODES .

City Hall	Zip Code
Brevard County	32940
Cape Canaveral	32920
Cocoa	32922
Cocoa Beach	32931
Grant-Valkaria	32949
Indialantic	32903
Indian Harbour Beach	32937
Malabar	32950
Melbourne	32901
Melbourne Beach	32951
Melbourne Village	32904
Palm Bay	32907
Palm Shores	32940
Rockledge	32955
Satellite Beach	32937
Titusville	32796
West Melbourne	32904

HISTORY

reams are written in the sands of Florida's Space Coast.

On what may have been the first official spring break, Spanish explorer Juan Ponce de León led a flotilla of ships away from the safe harbors of Puerto Rico. The crisp sails of the *Santa Maria, Santiago,* and *San Cristobal* rose tall against the vast baby blue sky. Two hundred dreamers were on a quest for gold and the mythological fountain of youth. In a serendipitous twist, Ponce de León and his men discovered instead a land of natural riches and warm, flowing waters. On April 2, 1513, near the time of the Pascua de Florida or Feast of Flowers, La Florida was claimed for the kingdom of Spain.

TIME FLIES: THE 1970 *ATLAS CENTAUR* SOARS SKYWARD JUST 67 YEARS AFTER THE HISTORIC WRIGHT BROTHERS FLIGHT.
Courtesy NASA

The fleet first made landfall near a cape halfway up the east coast of Florida. Surprised natives, who had not yet grasped the value of tourism, sent the explorers rowing quickly back to the mother ship amid a barrage of arrows made from natural canes that grew near the beach. Back home, mapmakers dubbed the place Cabo de Canaveral, Place of the Cane Bearers, as a warning to future sailors. At the time, many different Native American tribes populated the eastern coast of Florida, but it was probably the Ais (Eye-es), fierce and unfriendly warriors, who discouraged the Spanish visitors from coming ashore. Their victory was short-lived; they would not

PONCE DE LEÓN LANDING

On April 2, 2005, a park in Melbourne Beach was named for Spanish explorer Juan Ponce de León, and a historical marker was dedicated at this spot where historians now believe de León first landed on Florida's eastern shore. Professional historian and navigator Col. Douglas T. Peck made the discovery. In April 1992, Peck left Puerto Rico in a sailboat and retraced de León's path. His journey ended on these shores, and contradicted legend and lore that de León landed farther north. A three-dimensional mural of 380 copper tiles painted by Brevard County students depicts the landing.

survive the relentless waves of weapons and germs brought onshore by European explorers. For more than 300 years the Spanish, French, and British colonists took turns flying their flags. Florida became a territory of the young and growing United States in 1822; in 1845 it became the 27th state. "Not until the year 2055 will the American flag have flown over Florida as long as did the flag of Spain," points out Michael Gannon in his book *Florida, A Short History*.

Fast-forward nearly 500 years from Ponce de León's landing. Visitors traveling by car, bus, motorcycle, and sometimes by boat follow in his wake, searching for a golden tan and a dip in the restorative waves of the fountain of youth that is the Atlantic Ocean. The natives are much friendlier and more likely to offer a fruity drink overflowing a cane mug. The sharp spit of land jutting from these sandy shores was once a welcome landmark for weary sailors after a long journey across a seemingly endless ocean. Today, new-age explorers embark from the same distinctive cape, climbing aboard shiny rockets and blasting off on a voyage into the infinity of space. One tourism tagline labeled this stretch of paradise "the edge of the universe." Settle your chair in the shallow water at low tide, look out toward the sun-speckled horizon, and you'll agree.

NATURAL HISTORY

A KINDER, GENTLER EVOLUTION In the millennia of time, as continents shifted and oceans spilled into rocky crevices, Florida was an afterthought. Small and disconnected islands dotted the shallow waters circling the southern coast of North America. The canvas changed as soft strokes from the artist's brush slowly connected the dots into a peninsula, a finishing touch that dangled from the continent like an emerald teardrop earring.

Surrounded by ocean, the width of Florida's exposed land grew and shrank every 100,000 years or so as ocean temperatures fluctuated. Today the state is half the size it was when the first settlers migrated here more than 12,000 years ago. Scientists believe American Indians descended from wanderers who crossed the Bering Strait. We can only imagine that with each harsh winter they moved just a little farther south, eventually discovering Florida, the edge of their known world. The temperate climate and abundance of flora, fauna, and sea life offered an attractive alternative to these nomadic hunters and gatherers.

An archaeologist's treasure trove found in the midst of Florida's Space Coast yielded solid evidence of the existence and lifestyle of Florida's early inhabitants. In 1982, during a brush-clearing excavation, skulls and skeletons were spotted embedded in the ground. Bulldozers were lowered and engines shut down. Researchers unearthed a world buried under the sands of time. Eight thousand years ago a community existed in this idyllic spot situated between saltwater lagoons stocked with mollusks and green turtles, and the crystal clear, fish-filled currents of the St. Johns River. A hammock (an Indian word meaning shady place or little island) covered with oak, pine, dogwood, and ash supplied more than enough wood for shelter and fires. Palms and palmettos were stripped and woven into fabrics and baskets. During most of the year, trees and bushes offered an abundance of berries and nuts. The people were healthy—some living into

Courtesy Vera Zimmerman

AIS INDIANS ON BEACH.

their 60s. When they died, their bodies were carefully wrapped in a blanket and anchored to the bottom of what today is Windover Pond, just outside Titusville. One young girl, perhaps three years old, was discovered thousands of years later with her arms still tenderly wrapped around her favorite toys. Under a protective cocoon of peat and muck, the remains of these early settlers bear witness to their remarkably ordinary lives.

NATURE'S THEME PARK Every architectural plan begins with a footprint, the basic design of the project. As oceans receded during the last cooling period, the landscape of Florida's central east coast evolved into a primordial patchwork of water and land—the Indian River Lagoon.

When is a river not really a river? Because of the length and width of the waters bordering Florida's Atlantic coast, early settlers incorrectly labeled them as rivers. In fact, the Indian River Lagoon is an ecosystem of three separate estuaries stretching 156 miles from New Smyrna in the north to Jupiter in the south. The Indian River is the longest and most inland of the lagoons. Mosquito Lagoon sits just east of the northern section of the Indian River—originally connected to it by a shallow ditch. The wide, waist-deep Banana River is an offshoot of the Indian River and separates the barrier island from Merritt Island.

The Indian River Lagoon is a calm mixture of fresh and salt water. Breezes, not tides, create current and motion. Originally, ocean access was limited to natural openings at each end of the barrier island. Today, six inlets act as revolving doors connecting the lagoon and the ocean, keeping the brackish mix in place and moving marine life between the two systems. The living conditions are stressful—salinity levels frequently change, coastal sediments limit visibility, and the usually warm waters are intermittently cooled as ocean tides rise. Resilient marine creatures able to acclimate to this dynamic locale don't just survive. They thrive.

At the river's edge a graceful blue heron stands tall and still as a statue. A parade of pelicans swoops overhead. Suddenly one bird breaks from the formation and nose-dives below the blue gray surface to snag a surprised fish. Mullet flip into the air, slow-moving manatees graze in thick grasses, and dolphins arc gracefully across the horizon. You'd never guess that beneath the surface a vibrant community flourishes. According to biologist Kathy Hill, with the St. Johns Water Management District, "The Indian River Lagoon is the most biologically diverse estuary in the continental United States. The lagoon spans both temperate and subtropical zones, creating a welcoming environment for over 4,300 species of animals, plants, and birds."

The lagoon is also the largest marine nursery in North America. Many inhabitants, like shrimp, are spawned at sea and then travel to the estuary, where they settle in a soft cradle of grass and take their place near the beginning of the food chain. Vegetation lines the river bottom and offers refuge to small newcomers. Young fish wander in for a meal and end up playing hide-and-seek with fast-moving tarpon. A sharp-eyed osprey patiently circles the sky waiting for a chance to clutch the larger fish in its talons and carry it away. Lush mangrove forests dot the Banana River; their thick roots a secure home for small fish and crabs. When their protein-rich leaves fall, larger animals and crustaceans munch on them. What about those babies? The ones that survive and mature return to the ocean, reproduce, and the cycle begins again.

Nature protects this fragile ecosystem with the barrier islands, soft sand blankets buffering the powerful waves of the Atlantic Ocean. Long ago, ocean breezes nudged sand, shells, and natural debris into protective embankments. Marine hammocks blossomed into islands of self-sustaining vegetation and a beachside habitat for wildlife. This beautiful and diverse community, with residents like primrose, wild coffee, and cabbage palms, is an irresistible draw for birds and small animals—a chance to frolic under a canopy of live oaks and furry, gray green moss.

The isolated and scrubby Indian River Lagoon was among the last settled areas of Florida, but a century of technology has made this paradise more approachable. Walt Disney may have been inspired by nature when he talked about his dream of a family theme park. "It's something that will never be finished . . . It will be a live, breathing thing that will need change," he said. On the evolutionary teeter-totter, plants, animals, birds, fish, and all other manner of creatures adapt and adjust to maintain a symbiotic balance. Human beings are welcomed to the game, invited to enjoy the abundance of the area while respecting the fragile resources that are the magic and wonder of nature's theme park.

SOCIAL HISTORY

THE FORGOTTEN FRONTIER Florida was not easily conquered. Panthers, mosquitoes, rattlers, alligators, and black bears instinctively defended their territory. In his prizewinning book of historical fiction, *A Land Remembered*, Patrick Smith writes of "too much palmetto" and "snakes as thick as skeeters." The Ais Indians may have been the first tribe to plant deep roots along the central east coast, where plentiful resources helped offset their difficult struggle against the elements. The tribe dominated the area by the time European sailors discovered Florida. Many of their settlements sat near the banks of the large inland river, so the Spanish called the waterway Río de Ais.

Traveler Jonathan Dickinson was taken captive by the Ais when his ship wrecked off the Atlantic coast in 1696. His journal gives us a look at this Native American culture that fished with spears, cooked in clay pots, and drank from conch shells. Small round huts with poles tied together and covered with thatch provided shelter. Gatherings were held in the *cacique*, or chief's house, a wood frame covered on the sides and top with palmetto fronds and that accommodated as many as 300 attendees. Benches along the sides provided seating during the day and beds at night. By the start of the 18th century the noble warriors had disappeared from the area—memories of them lingering in the early mist of a river that once carried their name, now known simply as the Indian River.

Under European rule, settlement of La Florida concentrated along the waterfront, including St. Augustine and Jupiter at either end of the Indian River Lagoon. Foreign adventurers were encouraged to come and help populate the new territory. Many emigrated from the new country to the north, the United States, and when they were here in sufficient numbers they banded together to claim part of Florida for themselves. Spain settled the rebellion by ceding Florida to the United States in 1822. The new government immediately engaged in

OLD HAULOVER CANAL, CIRCA 1854.

Courtesy Brevard County Historical Commission

the Indian Wars, and for two decades, Floridians lived in a land of uprisings and skirmishes. When a truce was finally called, the Seminoles were the only Native Americans remaining in the state. They were ordered to move south, but a few stayed in Brevard—living, trading, marrying, and surviving alongside their neighbors.

THE *MERCHANT* DELIVERED SUPPLIES ALONG THE INDIAN RIVER IN COCOA.

Florida was growing, but only a few hardy souls pushed through to the wild and desolate Indian River Lagoon. In his book *History of Brevard County*, historian J. H. Shofner describes them as "persons with limited means but enterprising spirits and indomitable courage." To reach the area, newcomers sailed from the New Smyrna inlet to a small body of water identified early on as Mosquito Lagoon; then they hauled their vessel and cargo over a short strip of land to reach the Indian River, where they continued their journey south. It would be 1854 before the aptly named Haulover Canal was cut across upper Merritt Island to create a continuous water path from the Atlantic Ocean to the Indian River.

In 1848, the U.S. government commissioned a lighthouse on the cape at Canaveral, a landmark for an ever-growing number of ships that plied the coast. Seven years later Captain Mills Burnham, who had migrated to Florida a decade earlier to improve his health, moved in to man the tower. A few miles inland Burnham discovered citrus trees planted and abandoned by the Spanish. Soon his 15-acre grove produced basketfuls of juicy, sweet oranges. It was Burnham who gave the Banana River its name, suggested by the wild bananas growing along its banks.

Gradually, a sprinkling of folks found their way to what was first called Mosquito County. Settlers built crude houses and made a living from cattle, citrus, and water delicacies, like the green turtles found throughout the lagoon. Isolated homesteads grew into trading posts that also served as regional gathering spots for picnics and parties. Titusville, closest to the Haulover Canal, was a bustling town in 1877 when Captain T. J. Lund piloted the steamboat *Pioneer* into the city docks—blowing her whistle and proudly announcing the start of a new era. An area that once thrived on fishing and agriculture now had a new business, tourism. The word was coined by the French, meaning a turn or circuit, as in *Tour de France*. Welcome to the *Tour de Indian River*.

Soon 200 boats navigated the river every day, carrying passengers and freight. Cruisers stayed in small cabins during the two-day trek from Titusville to Jupiter. Or they could disembark along the way at towns like Cocoa, Rockledge, Eau Gallie, and Melbourne, where hotels and merchants waited to host them. The first luxury liner was christened the *Cinderella*. Tourists crossed the gangplank and set out on a journey through an enchanted land. Letters sent home brought

Courtesy Joe Carbone

INDIAN RIVER HOTEL, ROCKLEDGE.

to life a wilderness teeming with unusual and colorful birds, never-before-seen flowers and greenery, and exotic animals. Alligators sunned along riverbanks; manatees bobbed alongside the boat. Egrets and ibises dotted mangrove islands, and majestic white pelicans swept across a blueberry horizon. Days were spent sportfishing for trout, snapper, and redfish. Nights offered card games and dancing. On deck, passengers were mesmerized as the boat churned through dark water tipped with bright, phosphorescent sparkles. One traveler wrote, "On our left a new moon hung its crescent in the sky, and above it shone the evening star. One by one the stars came out, 'til the firmament was all aglow with the celestial fires."

THE COCOA BEACH RESORT WAS LOCATED ON THE BEACH AT THE END OF WHAT IS TODAY KNOWN AS THE MINUTEMAN CAUSEWAY.

Courtesy City of Cocoa Beach

The frenzy peaked in 1888 when President Grover Cleveland and his new bride, Frances, cruised south from Titusville on the *Rockledge*. This sleek and fast-moving lady (the ship, not the president's wife) was dubbed "queen of the Indian River steamboats."

By the turn of the 20th century, steamboats were passé. The railroad was the new kid in town. The gilded age tumbled onto the shores of the Indian River as America's northeastern upper class packed their trucks, donned their plumed hats, and headed south. Guests lunched on the verandas of modern, waterside hotels.

In the evening drinks flowed and music filled the air. Business was booming, and Brevard County's population accelerated like a slow train gradually picking up speed and barreling down the tracks.

REAL ESTATE AND ROCKET SCIENCE In 1917, the first bridge to span the Indian River was built to connect Cocoa and Merritt Island. Those wishing to cross the 1-mile-wide waterway could now choose between a ferry and a horse-drawn carriage. Then came the automobile! Imagine the first brave soul who got behind the wheel of his Ford Model A Roadster and puttered slowly across rickety wooden planks. Soon a parade of cars was headed east. Businessman Gus Edwards spotted an opportunity, purchased land on the barrier island, and

THE PRICE OF FREEDOM

African Americans were among the original pioneers of Brevard County, first as slaves and later as free citizens struggling alongside their neighbors to carve out a living in the hostile environment. As settlements grew into communities, blacks gravitated to their own neighborhoods, schools, and churches. In 1925, Harry Moore, a well-educated black man from Jacksonville, arrived in rural, segregated Brevard County. For two decades, he served as teacher, principal, and mentor to students at the "colored" schools. After he founded the Brevard County chapter of the National Association for the Advancement of Colored People (NAACP) and lobbied to equalize teacher salaries and integrate the schools, Harry and his wife, Harriette—also a teacher—were fired from their jobs.

When three young black men were unjustly convicted of raping a white woman in nearby Groveland, the activist couple teamed with the NAACP and pursued the case all the way to the U.S. Supreme Court. The justices overturned the convictions and death sentences, but the victory was short-lived. The boys were shot and killed by Sheriff Willis McCall while "trying to escape" when being transported to a new hearing. An outraged Moore called for McCall's arrest.

A few months later, on Christmas night 1951, a bomb exploded under the Moore's small wood home and shattered the peace of a quiet neighborhood surrounded by orange groves. Harry died that night, Harriette nine days later. More than 55 years passed before now-deceased Klansmen were publicly identified as the assailants.

The first assassination of a civil rights leader spurred outrage throughout the country and the world. Harry Moore once said, "Freedom never descends upon a people. It is always bought with a price." Eventually justice came home. Today, Brevard County citizens receive equal treatment under the law at the Harry T. and Harriette V. Moore Justice Center.

christened the "smooth wide beach stretching for miles" Cocoa Beach. Day-trippers streamed across the 3-mile-long wooden toll bridge built across the shallow Banana River, and then followed a short road to an oceanside boardwalk and casino. On the Fourth of July in 1922, more than 2,000 folks picnicked on the shore while enjoying car races and fireworks. Though hurricanes, the Depression years, and World War II stalled growth for a while, the barrier island was on the map.

In 1935, the U.S. Navy established the Banana River Naval Air Station on a long strip of land south of Cocoa Beach. It was a good thing they did. Ten weeks after the Pearl Harbor bombings in 1941, a German submarine fired upon and sank a U.S. tanker just 20 miles off the coast of Cape Canaveral. During World War II, German subs armed with torpedoes routinely cruised offshore, sometimes sinking as many as three freighters a night. The more than 200 families living along the coast went beachcombing for shipwreck treasures during the day and hid behind blacked-out windows at night. One ship, the *La Paz*, was towed to shore after being disabled by the Germans. Residents pitched in to aid with the salvage operation. Local lore says that the cargo, cases of Johnny Walker Scotch whisky, quickly and mysteriously disappeared.

Following the war, the United States selected the east coast of Florida as home for the business of rockets and missiles, commandeering the north end of Merritt Island and the Canaveral seashore. A large piece of land, preserved as the Merritt Island National Wildlife Refuge, continues to provide the military

"WE GO NOT BECAUSE IT'S EASY, BUT BECAUSE IT'S HARD," SAID PRESIDENT JOHN F. KENNEDY IN MAY 1961 ABOUT AMERICA'S RACE TO THE MOON. LESS THAN A YEAR LATER, JOHN GLENN BECAME THE FIRST AMERICAN TO ORBIT EARTH AND WAS HONORED IN A LOCAL PARADE.

Courtesy NASA

operations with a secure and impenetrable barrier of thick palmetto trees, snake-filled bogs, and alligators. On July 24, 1950, *Bumper 8*, the first rocket launched from the Air Force Station at Cape Canaveral, broke through gravity's hold and successfully soared 15 miles up and out. Crowds lined the beaches and cheered for the first small step on an endless path through the cosmos.

Almost overnight, two beach communities sandwiched between Cape Canaveral Air Force Station to the north and Patrick Air Force Base to the south, rose like sand castles along the water's edge. Engineers and rocket scientists thronged to the tiny island, and Brevard County had a new moniker—Florida's Space Coast. As America raced to the moon, Cocoa Beach raced to keep up with the growth, quickly building dozens of motels, restaurants, and bars—and gaining a reputation as a space-age party town. Cape Canaveral evolved into a more domestic community for space workers and their families. News media aired stories about rocket launches that were seen around the world, and then came the market exposure that tourism-development money can't buy: a hit TV show. In it, astronaut Tony Nelson found a genie-named-Jeannie in a bottle and brought her home to Cocoa Beach.

Discussions of a canal joining the ocean to the Intracoastal Waterway through central Brevard County took on a new urgency. The U.S. Army Corps of Engineers carved out a channel just south of the protruding cape. When it opened in 1951, the new inlet not only facilitated essential shipping of goods to the space center but also laid the foundation for Port Canaveral, a busy marine community and economic anchor for the area.

By 1971, when Walt Disney World opened its gates in nearby Orlando, a multi-lane, high-speed expressway called the Beeline (recently renamed the Beachline) carried visitors directly to the coast. For a while, it was the road-seldom-taken. When NASA canceled the Apollo program the local economy crashed, and the stream of visitors to the area slowed to a trickle. There was a resurgence during the 1980s and '90s, as shuttles replaced rockets and more theme parks opened in central Florida. Word began to spread about the "smooth, wide beaches" (as promoted 50 years earlier by Gus Edwards), and the area was back in business.

One longtime resident put the area on the map in a different way. In *The Book Lover's Guide to Florida,* author Kevin McCarthy writes of a gathering at the Cocoa Beach home of journalist Al Neuharth in February 1980. The group designed a national newspaper, *USA Today,* and McCarthy describes its impact on the world of print media as "a moon shot in its own right." The prototype, *Florida Today,* is still the Space Coast newspaper.

On a clear, cool January day, more than half a century after *Bumper 8* soared 15 miles into the sky, residents and visitors again gathered along the beach and scanned the heavens. The hammers of workers constructing new hotels paused as *Atlas 5* rose from the launch pad. With a blaze of fire and a roar of thunder, the powerful spacecraft broke through the clouds and set a course for Pluto, 3 billion miles away. Brevard County is still a community immersed in real estate and rocket science.

THE DREAM CONTINUES Dreamers and doers settled Brevard County, helping themselves to the abundant offerings of the land—first for survival, later for sport. Today mature communities appreciate the need to balance development with conservation and protect the environment while pursuing economic growth. Eco-tourism demonstrates that economic profit and environmental protection can work in tandem.

Port Canaveral is now the second busiest cruise port in the world. Towering liners navigate alongside cargo ships, military vessels, and small pleasure craft; restaurants and recreation facilities host millions of visitors each year. At the same time, the Port has made sure that more than 50 acres of protected parks, beachfront, and marshes remain an environmental playground.

During the 1960s rush of development, land along the Banana River was dredged to help control the mosquito population. In hindsight, the solution wasn't the best, but one positive outcome was enhancement of nearby islands from the dumping of the dredged mud. Mangroves claimed the new ground, and today the Thousand Islands are one of the jewels of the area, a vibrant habitat for fish and wildlife. They don't number a thousand, but several create narrow and winding paths for explorers in kayaks, canoes, and slow-moving boats.

Dreams continue to be written in the sands of Florida's Space Coast. The space shuttle fleet will soon be retired to make way for a new wave of exploration, its decade-long mission to ferry astronauts and materials up to assemble

THE CULTURAL LANDSCAPE

Warm, rejuvenating waters nourish the cultural landscape of Brevard County. Acclaimed and prolific writer Nora Zeale Hurston lived on the Indian River in Eau Gallie for several years. When friends asked her why she spent so much time by herself in a boat, just reading, she mused, "I enjoy it out here. I can concentrate. I can think."

Water was the highway of choice for the county's 19th-century pioneers, a colorful and entrepreneurial lot sailing south, charting a new course in the wet and rustic wilderness. Col. Henry Titus spent years skirting the law and outrunning failed business ventures before landing in Sand Point in north Brevard, where he prospered. True to his risk-taking roots, he won the right to name the town Titusville in a bet on a game of dominoes.

By the turn of the 20th century, enterprising adventurers were transformed into successful and stable town leaders. They built impressive, new-age mansions, like the two-story Queen Anne–style home of John and Nannie Lee in Melbourne, and funded ornate playhouses like the Italian Renaissance Aladdin in Cocoa.

The advent of the automobile made the beaches more accessible and reinforced a collective sunny optimism that every opportunity lost would be followed by a wave of new possibility. The space program landed on the

PORT CANAVERAL IS HOME FOR MANY OF THE LARGEST AND MOST POPULAR CRUISE SHIPS.

the International Space Station now complete. Powerful craft designed for the next adventure, travel to the moon and beyond to test the ability of humans to live in space, will move from the drawing board to the launch pads at Kennedy Space Center—poised for ignition at the edge of the universe.

shores of Brevard County around mid-century. During the race-to-the-moon 1960s, this narrow strip of land was the fastest growing area in America due to an influx of energetic, creative, and well-educated newcomers. Museums and galleries opened, and groups like the Brevard Symphony Orchestra were formed.

Today's cultural community retains the daring spirit of early settlers and the creative collaboration of space program pioneers. Artists convert small storefronts into vibrant, colorful studios, and musicians perform in coffee shops and beachside bars. Until recently, preserving the heritage of the area has been a grassroots effort. Now several cities, along with the Brevard Historical Commission, are scrambling to save old properties, collect photographs and memorabilia, and record personal stories.

Half a millennium after the ships of European explorers landed on the sandy coast of Brevard County, astronauts—star sailors—continue the journey, this time across the vast ocean of space. This book is your guide to the past and the future, a snapshot of America's space adventures, and a peek into the galleries, museums, and entertainment of Florida's Space Coast—a place where engineers, artisans, musicians, and performers dare to dream, dare to reach for the stars.

WILDLIFE PROFILE: SEA TURTLE

Sea turtles have been around for more than 100 million years and certainly qualify as the earliest visitors to Florida's Atlantic beaches. Three species of the ancient marine creatures return to this coast each year, making this the busiest turtle-nesting site in the world. The most common of the three is the 300-pound loggerhead, whose strong jaws crunch shellfish and crustaceans. Full-grown greens are about the same size but are vegetarians. The leatherback is a 1-ton giant who dines on jellyfish. Sea turtles are similar to their land-locked cousins except their limbs are flippers and their heads no longer retract. With one exception, they never leave the water.

In the dark of night a female turtle lumbers from the surf, crawls to the sandy dune line, and digs a deep hole with her flippers. After depositing more than 100 Ping-Pong-ball-sized eggs into the nest, the exhausted mom refills the opening—almost dancing as she sways and turns, creating a sandy swirl that makes the nest invisible to predators and beachgoers. Finished with her task, the turtle returns to the ocean, leaving telltale flipper tracks that are usually erased by waves and wind before sunrise.

Hatchlings incubate for about eight weeks and then pop to the surface en masse, usually at night. Following prehistoric programming, the babies, about the size of a toddler's hand, scramble toward water aglow with shimmering whitecaps. The trip is treacherous. Some never make it to water's edge—pulled off course by artificial light or eaten by predators such as raccoons or ghost crabs. Those that get to the water face a 15-mile swim through a sea teeming with hungry marine life. The lucky ones make it to the security of the weedy Sargasso Sea and remain there until grown. Adult female turtles mate and instinctively return home to familiar beaches to carry on the cycle of life.

Space Coast Sightings: Sea turtles are an endangered species, and it's illegal to interfere with nesting mothers or hatchlings. The "Recreation" chapter has information on approved organizations that conduct nightly turtle walks during the active nesting season.

LOGGERHEAD SEA TURTLE *(CARETTA CARETTA).*

Jim Angy

TRANSPORTATION

Brevard County stretches along the eastern edge of Florida like a long, lean, lazy cat napping in the sun. The Indian River, running north to south the length of the county, was the earliest transportation thoroughfare. Communities formed along its banks, and docks protruding from the shore were as common as driveways are today. People, supplies, and mail arrived by boat. At St. Michaels in Cocoa, families attending Sunday services arrived by water and tied up at the pier near the back of the church. By the beginning of the 20th century, railroads were gaining in popularity. Trains chugged through the area on tracks built parallel to the river, and stations were set up near the already established towns.

While steamers and luxurious rail cars transported America's wealthy to the wilds of Florida, automobiles carried the working class to the Sunshine State. Roads crisscrossing America connected first to the Dixie Highway and then to modern US 1, extending down the peninsula from Jacksonville to Miami. In his book *Land of Sunshine, State of Dreams,* history professor Gary Mormino gives easy directions. "Every tourist knows the way to Florida: when you hit the East coast, turn south."

Development spread eastward as bridges and causeways opened up the barrier island. All roads led to folk-loric Highway A1A, a scenic coastal alternative to US 1. During boom times, land developers promoted A1A as a yellow brick road, leading straight to the home of your dreams. Connie Francis and her girlfriends hit the strip in the 1960 movie *Where the Boys Are,* and began an annual parade of spring breakers in search of crowded beaches and Coppertone

THE MULE TRAIN TO TITUSVILLE, CIRCA 1880.
Courtesy Brevard County Historical Commission

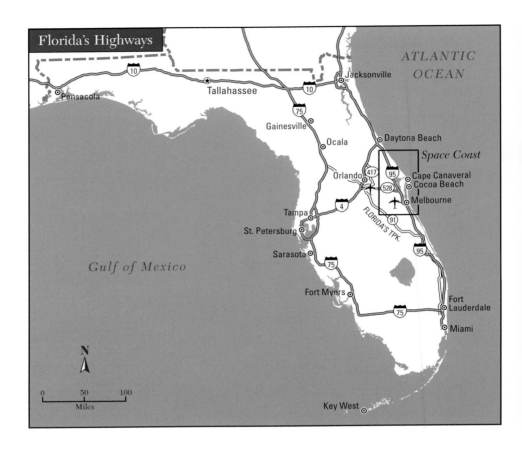

Florida's Highways

ATLANTIC OCEAN

Pensacola
Tallahassee
Jacksonville
Gainesville
Ocala
Daytona Beach
Space Coast
Orlando
Cape Canaveral
Cocoa Beach
Melbourne
Tampa
St. Petersburg
FLORIDA'S TPK.
Sarasota
Gulf of Mexico
Fort Myers
Fort Lauderdale
Miami
N
0   50   100
Miles
Key West

tans—convertibles cruising, radios blaring, ponytails blowing in the breeze, and surfboards propped in the backseat. Astronaut John Glenn celebrated his space milestones—in 1962 as the first American astronaut to orbit the earth, and 36 years later in 1998 as the oldest man in space—with parades down the Cocoa Beach stretch of A1A. A drive along this colorful highway still leads directly to fun in the sun.

GETTING THERE *By plane:* **Melbourne International Airport** (MLB), located off US 1, 26 miles south of Port Canaveral, may be a convenient arrival and departure point for some travelers. Delta Air Lines and US Airways each offer flights connecting through their major hubs. Direct Air has service to select locations. While you wait for your flight, visit the Air Museum and learn about the history of Cape Canaveral Air Station during World War II. Many Melbourne and Melbourne Beach hotels offer complimentary shuttle service to and from the airport. For more information log on to the airport's Web site, www .mlbair.com.

Most travelers elect to fly into **Orlando International Airport** (MCO), consistently noted as one of the best airports in the world. More than 50 airlines fly to Orlando, so there are usually plenty of options for schedules and fares. The airport décor and landscaping create a tropical ambience from the moment passengers deplane. Shuttle trains connect outlying gates to a central terminal; so walking is kept to a minimum (relative to other major airports). Signs direct arriving passengers to baggage claim and ground transportation, both on the ground level. Unless an airline has several planes arriving at the same time, luggage arrives promptly at the claim turntables. Departing passengers should allow extra time to check in and pass through security. The large number of families juggling small children, strollers, and other paraphernalia slows the lines. An array of restaurants and shops offers great food, and a chance to purchase some last-minute souvenirs before heading home. Information and facility maps are on the airport's Web site, www.orlandoairports.net.

BY RENTAL CAR Unless a trip is very limited, visitors to Florida's Space Coast need a car. Almost all car rental companies serve travelers to Orlando International Airport. Avoid last-minute surprises by asking beforehand about extra charges for insurance, taxes, a second driver, a young driver, or child safety seats. Families will find plenty of minivans available to rent.

Florida law requires that car drivers, front-seat passengers, and all riders under 18 years of age wear a seat belt. Children age three and under must be secured in an approved safety seat; children age four and five should be in an approved safety seat or wear a seat belt. Five car rental companies maintain lots at Cape Canaveral or Cocoa Beach, which might be helpful to visitors who encounter problems with their car rental while in the area. These firms also have locations at Melbourne International Airport.

Avis: 1-800-831-2847; www.avis.com.

Budget: 1-800-527-0700; www.budget.com.

Hertz: 1-800-654-3131; www.hertz.com.

National: 1-877-222-9058; www.nationalcar.com.

Thrifty: 1-800-367-2277; www.thrifty.com.

ONE OF 12 BRIDGES THAT CROSS THE WATERWAYS OF BREVARD COUNTY.

WILDLIFE PROFILE: BOTTLENOSE DOLPHIN

Dolphins capture our imagination: There is ample evidence they are intelligent, and without a doubt, they are curious and social. There are several hundred bottlenose dolphins that make their home in the Indian River Lagoon, and because they breathe from a blowhole every couple of minutes, they're easy to spot. Just keep an eye out for their long, sleek bodies gracefully breaking the surface of the water.

The bottlenose dolphin takes its name from the distinctive shape of its snout. The lagoon dolphins are a non-migratory coastal ecotype that has adapted to life in the shallow, warm waters of the lagoon. Their bodies are a little smaller than the average of 10 feet long and 500 pounds. They gather in smaller pods than their ocean-swimming cousins, perhaps because the enclosed setting is better protected. Their tastes have adapted to include mullet, a prevalent fish in the lagoon waters. While dolphin usually swim about 5 miles per hour, sometimes they seem to come from nowhere in a burst of speed and circle around as they feed on prey.

Female dolphins gestate for about 12 months. Calves are born in the water with an umbilical cord that snaps during or shortly after birth. Newborns are about 4 feet long and weigh around 44 pounds. They'll nurse for at least a year but will begin eating fish after six months. In the Indian River Lagoon, most births occur in April and August.

Boaters and anglers tell tales of playful interludes with dolphins that seem to be showing off for a captive human audience. They jump, dive, and catch rides in the waves around a boat. Like people, dolphins sleep about one-third of each day—but it is still unclear to scientists how they do this. One thing is certain; children of all ages will have sweet dreams after an encounter with these fascinating creatures.

Space Coast Sightings: Throughout the length of the Indian River Lagoon; on most boat and kayak tours; near the Port Canaveral locks; Haulover Canal.

BOTTLENOSE DOLPHIN *(TURSIOPS TRUNCATUS).*

Jim Angy

BY GROUND TRANSPORTATION Several businesses specialize in transportation from the airports to locations in Brevard County, including the cruise terminals at Port Canaveral. Reservations should be made at least 48 hours in advance. If you need special equipment like a wheelchair or car seat, be sure to let them know. Prices vary but generally run about $80 each way for a party of four traveling from Orlando International Airport to hotels in the Cape Canaveral and Cocoa Beach area.

A1A Ocean Drive Transportation & Limo: 386-226-1111, 1-866-356-2326; www.oceandrivetransandlimo.com.

Beachline Transportation: 321-453-9660, 1-877-382-3224; www.beachline transportation.net.

Busy Traveler Transport: 321-453-5278, 1-800-496-7433; www.abusytraveler .com (provides service to and from Melbourne International Airport).

Central Florida Shuttle: 321-749-1794, 1-888-860-4677; www.centralflorida shuttle.com

Travelynx: 321-783-2112, 1-800-226-5969; www.travelynx.net.

BY CAR Most major roadways in the state intersect in central Florida and connect to Florida Highway 528 (FL 528), the Beachline. Previous visitors might remember this road as the Beeline, an apt name for a highway that makes a straight path from Orlando to the coast. Florida's interstate highways have gas, food, and rest rooms at frequent and multiple exits; the Florida Turnpike has service plazas about every 45 miles. Some highways, including the Beachline, are toll roads. It's always good to have a map, but these are the most-traveled routes for reaching Cape Canaveral and Cocoa Beach. (Travelers to other parts of the county will usually exit to the east or west on US 1 or I-95.)

From Orlando International Airport: Exit the airport heading east on FL 528, and follow signs to Cocoa and the Kennedy Space Center. Travel time from the airport is about 35 minutes.

From Orlando-area attractions: Follow signs to FL 417 and the airport, and then continue past the airport to FL 528 eastbound. Travel time from Walt Disney World is just over an hour.

From I-95: Travelers from the north or south take exit number 205, FL 528. Travel distance is about 150 miles from Jacksonville, 200 miles from Miami.

From the north on I-75: Switch to the Florida Turnpike at exit 328 (Wildwood), and then just past Orlando pick up FL 528 eastbound.

From the southwest on I-75: Take I-4 east from Tampa. Exit at FL 417. FL 528 eastbound is just beyond the airport. Travel time from the I-4/I-75 intersection to the beach is about two hours.

BY BUS Greyhound Bus Lines (1-800-231-2222; www.greyhound.com) operates a terminal at Melbourne International Airport.

BY TRAIN The closest AMTRAK (1-800-872-7245; www.amtrak.com) station is in Orlando. Busy Traveler Transportation (1-800-496-7433) provides service from the station to Brevard County.

BY BOAT Arriving by water is an alternative way to travel to Brevard County. Enter from offshore, or via the Intracoastal Waterway (ICW). The Canaveral Barge Canal crosses the Indian River/ICW just north of FL 528 and is a direct eastbound route to Port Canaveral. This entire section is designated as a no-wake zone for protection of manatees, so you'll need to maintain a low speed. Full-service marinas at Port Canaveral provide dockage facilities on a short- or long-term basis, but space is limited, so be sure to secure reservations, especially during the busy season. All the marinas monitor channel 16 on VHF. (See *To Do* in the regional chapters for detail on services provided by each marina.)

Bluepoints Marina: 321-799-2860; www.bluepointsmarina.com.

Cape Marina: 321-783-8410; www.capemarina.com.

Sunrise Marina: 321-783-9535; www.sunrisemarina.com.

GETTING AROUND Brevard County is 72 miles long but less than 20 miles wide in most spots. Three major roadways run north and south: A1A along the beaches, US 1 on the mainland and paralleling the shore of the Indian River, and I-95 close to the western border of the county. Seven bridges and causeways run east and west across the water-rich landscape: FL 406 in Titusville, FL 405 near Kennedy Space Center, FL 528—the Beachline—leading from Orlando to Cape Canaveral, FL 520 at Cocoa, FL 404 near Patrick Air Force Base, FL 518 at Eau Gallie, and FL 192 in Melbourne. Throughout this guide, most directional references use these major thoroughfares and intersections as a point of reference. Beach parks with easy access and amenities run the length of the county.

By car: After crossing the Banana River, the speed limit slows from expressway to browsing speed. Port Canaveral has two exits just after FL 528 crosses the Banana River, and signs mark the appropriate exit for the cruise terminals. Now FL 528 curves to the right and exits onto FL A1A (commonly just called A1A), the primary axis road running north and south through the communities. Almost every road crossing A1A goes east to the ocean, but parking may sometimes be limited or unavailable. Day visitors will find free or low-cost spots at several beach parks. (See the listings under *Green Space and Beaches* in each chapter.) Overnight guests will discover that most hotels are within easy walking distance of the beach or provide a shuttle service.

By Space Coast Area Transit: The beach trolley operated by Space Coast Area Transit (www.ridescat.com) offers an affordable ride along A1A and through Port Canaveral. Every trolley has a wheelchair lift and accommodates surfboards and bicycles. Standard fare is $1.25, but seniors, veterans, the disabled, and students pay just 60 cents. Children five and under are free. In general, trolleys run from 7 in the morning until 10 at night. Pick up a brochure at your hotel or stop by the central stop on the northeast side of the intersection of Atlantic Avenue and E. Cocoa Beach Causeway. Note that trolley service does not extend to the restaurants and bars at Port Canaveral at this time, so nighttime visitors may want to go by taxi.

By taxicab or shuttle: Taxis are almost always available on short notice, and they line up outside venues at busy times, such as when guests are disembarking from cruise ships or ending an evening at the more popular nightspots.

AAT Taxi Service: 321-453-8294.

Cocoa Beach Taxi Service: 321-783-1299.

Yellow Cab: 321-636-1234.

By local car rental: Several rental firms have local lots and rent cars by the day. Many allow a one-way rental to the Orlando and Melbourne airports without an additional drop-off fee, so renting a car may be more convenient and economical than taking a shuttle when there are just one or two passengers.

Avis Rent A Car: 321-783-3643; 6650 N. Atlantic Avenue, Cape Canaveral.

Budget Car Rental: 321-784-0634; 8401 Astronaut Boulevard, Cape Canaveral.

Hertz: 321-783-7771; 8963 Astronaut Boulevard, Cape Canaveral.

National Car Rental: 321-783-7575; 1675 N. Atlantic Avenue, Cocoa Beach.

Thrifty Rent A Car: 321-783-2600; 6799 N. Atlantic Avenue, Cape Canaveral.

RECREATION

BEACHES Morning arrives as a small golden bud swiftly blossoms into a vibrant sunflower against the backdrop of the velvety blue horizon. White-tipped waves crash against the sand in rhythmic tones. Early birds arrive with bold-colored towels, canvas chairs, coolers, and toys. Music and conversation mingles with seagull laughter. Surfers tug their boards against the tide, and then stand and entertain onlookers as they catch a wave and ride it to shore. Before the sun sets, beachgoers will broaden their horizons, go with the flow, and watch time slip away like sand through the hourglass.

Wide honey-colored beaches stretch out along the eastern coast of Brevard County like an endless Southern veranda. Settle in your chair and sip a cool

drink while the sun warms your back and a soft breeze massages your skin. This is the original oceanfront property.

To find the beach, just head east on almost any street veering off A1A. In Florida the state constitution holds life, liberty, the pursuit of happiness, *and* access to the beach as self-evident rights. All land below the high-water mark is public property. Florida Supreme Court rulings have upheld the tradition. "The lure of the ocean is universal; to battle with its refreshing breakers a delight . . . the people of Florida—a State blessed with probably the finest bathing beaches in the world—are no exception to the rule . . . we, and our visitors too, enjoy bathing in their refreshing waters."

Today is your day to make a splash.

BEACH ENVIRONMENT AND SAFETY The beach begins far above water's edge at the dunes, a protective, sandy stretch of thick greenery such as saw palmetto palms and bushy sea grapes. Sea oats, the tall, wispy grasses with deep roots that trap the sand, strengthen the dunes. Tread lightly, however. While these sturdy reeds resist wind, drought, and salt water, they are often done in by the footsteps of beachgoers. The waters of Brevard County are ranked among the cleanest in the state, but it is an ongoing effort to balance between public access and habitat preservation. Waves and erosion also place a constant natural strain on sandy shores. The coastline south of Port Canaveral is replenished with sand dredged from miles out to sea so those beaches stay wide and flat.

The ocean is teeming with life. Many marine creatures, including sea turtles, sharks, and the northern right whales, migrate to the warm Atlantic waters off Brevard. Dolphins and small rays are present year-round. Less-popular sea residents are the jellyfish and Portuguese man-of-war. Stings are not common, but they happen. The usual reaction is a rash in the contact area. Get medical attention if it gets worse. These creatures sometimes wash up on shore as clear or blue-tinted bubbles that attract curiosity and probing, but stay away because the venom can still be released. Coastal birds such as gulls and pelicans are common at the beach. The tiny sanderling is a favorite with children, who love to watch them play catch-me-if-you-can with the waves. The gray and white birds dine on marine morsels left behind as the ocean ebbs and flows. Low fence posts sometimes mark off upper sections of the beach, protecting nests made during the night by giant sea turtles.

Wildlife has adapted to living in populated beach locales, but visitors not familiar with the hot Florida sun may not adapt so easily. Use sunscreen, drink plenty of water, and wear sunglasses with protective lenses. Alcohol is permitted on Brevard County beaches, but be aware that drinking and *diving* can be as disastrous as drinking and driving.

Respect the power of nature. Get indoors if there's even a hint of lightning. Swim with others and stay close to shore when the waves are strong. If you find yourself caught in a rip current, swim parallel to the coast until free from the outbound current. Review the beach park listings in each regional chapter for

THE LANDMARK COCOA BEACH PIER IS THE ANCHOR LOCATION FOR MANY BEACH AND SURFING EVENTS

BE SAFE AND CHECK FOR A LIFEGUARD BEFORE SETTLING IN FOR A DAY AT THE BEACH.

information on lifeguard coverage; pay attention to their warnings about current conditions.

BEACH FUN AND GAMES Activities at the beach range from doing absolutely nothing to doing a great deal, and then following it up with doing absolutely nothing for dessert. You might have your own favorite distraction, but here are some suggestions.

- **Beachcombing.** When the high tide recedes, it leaves behind seashells, sea beans, and other ocean remnants. Because of the strong wave action and the way the ocean floor breaks, Space Coast beaches are not ideal for collecting seashells, but there are some perfect finds. Go slowly and look closely. The best time is early morning or low tide. Several shops, including Ana Lia Gift Shop and Exotic Shells & Gifts by Eleanor, both near the Minutemen Causeway, sell an assortment of shells, along with books to help identify each type.

- **Games.** Beach shops carry an assortment of games and equipment, such as Frisbees, kites, and Velcro Ping-Pong sets.

- **Photography.** A photo at the beach is the picture postcard everyone wants. Family groupings are always fun, or take a series of pictures to tell a story. Use a landmark to distinguish the setting, maybe a departing cruise ship in the background or in front of the Cocoa Beach Pier.

- **Reading.** Settle your beach chair just beyond the incoming surf. Grab a cold drink and a crunchy snack. Close your eyes and listen to the lapping waves, squawking sea birds, and laughing children. Now reach into your beach bag, pull out a book, and drift into the pages. (For a list of Florida-themed books, see the bibliography at the end of the book.)

- **Sand Art.** With the simplest of equipment—a bucket, small shovel, and some plastic cups—the youngest member of your party will be designing sand castles held together by the grout of imagination. Seashells become giant pencils for sketching in the sand at low tide. Sculpt flowers, trees, or large fish.

- **Volleyball.** Joining a fast-paced game of volleyball is the beach version of pick-up basketball at the neighborhood court. Nets are always up and games frequently in process at Jetty Park, Cocoa Beach Pier, and the Minutemen Causeway. Bring your own ball, and chances are you'll find others ready to jump into the fun.

FAMILIES WILL LIKE THE GENERALLY MILD WAVES OFF CHERIE DOWN PARK IN CAPE CANAVERAL.

- **Walking.** The long, uninterrupted stretch of sand along Cape Canaveral and Cocoa Beach makes it the perfect path for walking, running, or biking. At low tide, the hard sand close to the water is a smooth, easy surface. Go barefoot at your own risk and keep an eye cast downward to avoid broken shells. Find a landmark to track your starting point.

- **Water Sports.** You don't have to be a world-class athlete to boogie board or bob in the waves on an inflatable dolphin or inner tube. Bring some water-

TURTLE WALKS

From May to August, in the dark of night, giant sea turtles lumber onto the beaches of Brevard County and create a nest to deposit their eggs. The sight is overwhelming. Sea turtles are protected, but designated organizations have been authorized to escort small groups onto the beaches during the late evening hours.

Each three- to four-hour session begins with a briefing on the history of these ancient creatures and instructions on observing the turtles without scaring them back to the ocean before they lay their eggs and bury the nest. Walks are not recommended for disabled people or small children. Bring bug repellent. Check booking dates and make a reservation as early as possible, although sometimes there are cancellations, and last-minute spots may be available.

To make a reservation: Canaveral National Seashore (386-428-3384, ext. 18); Merritt Island National Wildlife Refuge (321-861-0667); Barrier Island Sanctuary (321-723-3556); the Sea Turtle Preservation Society (321-676-1701); Sebastian Inlet State Park (321-984-4852).

ready gear with you and dive right in. Try skimming—jumping on a small thin board and coasting along the shallow water. Extreme water athletes might want to take a lesson in kiteboarding or stand-up paddleboarding.

NATURE PRESERVES AND PARKS "A true conservationist is a man who knows that the world is not given by his fathers but borrowed from his children." John Audubon said this, and he would have liked Brevard County, where an abundance of green space and natural habitat is preserved as a safe, secure playground for birds and wildlife. Fortunately, this also creates a myriad of great recreational opportunities for two-legged creatures to enjoy. Take a nature tour, paddle a kayak, or rent a boat and explore the waterways. Head to the ocean on a fishing charter or cruise. Pick up some binoculars and do a bit of bird-watching. Grab the family for a day at the zoo or the springtime thrill of baseball. Golfers will discover that courses are often in harmony with natural habitats.

This natural "theme park" has thrills and surprises, such as a playful dolphin scooting around a kayak, a magical snowy egret posing regally at river's edge, and stoic alligators lying in wait at Merritt Island National Wildlife Refuge. The cast of characters is unpredictable and spontaneous, and your adventure is sure to be memorable.

ATLAS OF NATURE PRESERVES AND PARKS The map depicts just a few of the brightest jewels on an exquisite chain of emerald green parcels dotting the Brevard County landscape. They are easily accessible to visitors and are popular sites for most recreational activities. Wildlife is present at all of these natural environments. For your protection and theirs, keep your distance. If the birds and animals become too accustomed to human intervention, they lose the ability to survive in the wild. Depending on the activity, consider whether you need to take along water, binoculars, bug repellent, comfortable shoes, a hat, and sunscreen.

More details on each park can be found under *Green Space and Beaches* in the regional chapters.

BIRDING Home to more than 30 Great Florida Birding Trail sites, Brevard County is definitely for the birds. Some settle here in great numbers and diversity; others rest while migrating south or stay just for the winter. With the success of the Space Coast Birding & Wildlife Festival (see the "Special Events" chapter) over the last decade, the area has earned a

SAIL DOWN THE INDIAN RIVER WITH
INDIAN RIVER CRUISES.

Courtesy Joe Carbone

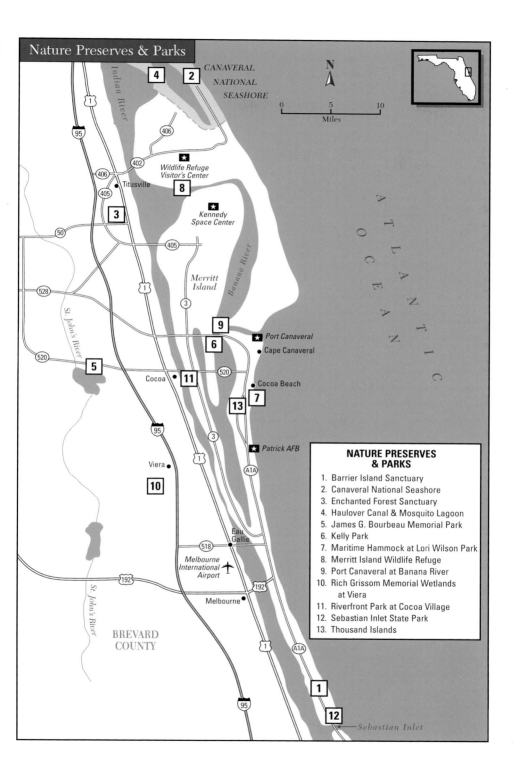

Nature Preserves & Parks

CANAVERAL
NATIONAL
SEASHORE

N

0   5   10
Miles

Indian River

① 1
95

406

402

★ Wildlife Refuge
Visitor's Center

● Titusville

405

3

4 2

8

★ Kennedy
Space Center

Banana River

50

405

528

Merritt
Island

1

3

9

520

6

★ Port Canaveral
● Cape Canaveral

● Cocoa   **11**   520

5

● Cocoa Beach

13   **7**

95

3

1

★ Patrick AFB

Viera ●

A1A

10

Eau
Gallie

518

Melbourne
International
Airport ✈

192

192

St. John's River

Melbourne ●

BREVARD
COUNTY

1   A1A

1

12 ← Sebastian Inlet

NATURE PRESERVES
& PARKS

1. Barrier Island Sanctuary
2. Canaveral National Seashore
3. Enchanted Forest Sanctuary
4. Haulover Canal & Mosquito Lagoon
5. James G. Bourbeau Memorial Park
6. Kelly Park
7. Maritime Hammock at Lori Wilson Park
8. Merritt Island Wildlife Refuge
9. Port Canaveral at Banana River
10. Rich Grissom Memorial Wetlands
    at Viera
11. Riverfront Park at Cocoa Village
12. Sebastian Inlet State Park
13. Thousand Islands

ATLANTIC OCEAN

reputation as one of the premier birding spots in the country. Individuals, families, and groups enjoy the outdoors, and the cost is minimal—just binoculars and a field guide gets you started. Experts may want to track favorites from among more than 300 species in this area, and novices will enjoy making new feathered friends. All of the following sites are part of the Great Florida Birding Trail.

MOST COMMON BIRDS Gulls frequent the shore in large numbers but are also seen inland, especially on cold or stormy days. Young birds are brownish; when mature, they all have gray backs and white bellies. To identify them, check their size and leg color. Look for three varieties of this common bird: the herring gull, the ringed-billed gull, and the laughing gull. Largest is the herring gull, with flesh-colored legs. The medium-sized ringed-billed gull has yellow legs and a black ring around its bill. The appropriately named laughing gull has a song call that sounds like a laugh. This small, red-legged gull has a handsome black head in summer.

Brown pelicans are found wherever there are fish and fishermen, but especially at the beaches and piers. Many are accustomed to beachgoers and won't fly away unless you get very close, and sometimes if you wait a few minutes, they'll preen and stretch their wings, making for some great photos. Their larger, attractive cousin, the **white pelican**, spends the winter in this area.

Along the water's edge, look for the **ruddy turnstone**, brown with a white stomach and orange legs, often turning over stones and shells looking for food. The beige and cream **willet** almost fades into the sand, while the **royal tern** steps out in a snow-white suit with a top hat of coal black feathers, black legs, and an orange beak. Children love chasing **sanderlings**, flocks of tiny birds that are constantly playing catch-me-if-you-can with incoming waves.

Elegant wading birds parade along the shallow ocean surf and the fringes of the

THE RICH GRISSOM MEMORIAL WETLANDS AT VIERA IS A HAVEN FOR BIRDERS AND PHOTOGRAPHERS.

interior waterways, using long, narrow beaks to poke for food in the moist ground. The majestic **great blue heron** is blue gray, with slightly darker plumes on the head, and stands 4 feet tall. Two smaller varieties are the **little blue heron** and the **tricolored heron**. Like a bride at the altar, the **great egret** is a stately vision in white, with a veil of long wispy feathers that cover its back like a lace cape during breeding season. The **snowy egret** is a little shorter, with a black bill and legs, and feet resembling tiny golden slippers. The **reddish egret** (very rare in North America) has a burgundy head and neck.

Often seen in residents' yards, one of the most recognizable wading birds is the **white ibis**, with black-tipped feathers and a bright orange bill and legs. The **roseate spoonbill** has pink feathers and a beak in the shape of a paddle. The endangered **wood stork** has white feathers, black wing tips, and a bare-skinned, wrinkled black head and neck.

In the lagoon, look for the **double-crested cormorant**, muddy brown or black with a pale orange sharply curved bill, and the **anhinga**, or snakebird, so nicknamed because in water the body is submerged, and only the small head and long, slender neck are visible. The **American coot** is often mistaken for a duck, but it's all black with a white triangular beak.

Two birds of prey, recognizable by their strong hooked beaks, stand guard along the Space Coast. **Bald eagles**, dark brown with a smooth white head and tail, and a 6- to 7-foot wingspan, are seen mostly in northern Brevard. The **osprey** is a little smaller than the eagle, with dark brown and white feathers on the back and head, white on the belly.

BIRDING RESOURCES **Great Florida Birding Trail** (www.floridabirding trail.com) A collection of nearly 500 sites throughout the state selected for their excellent bird-watching or bird-education opportunities, the Great Florida Birding Trail is a 2,000-mile, self-guided highway trail. Trail maps, guides, and pamphlets are available for download from the Web site.

Space Coast Audubon Society (www.spacecoastaudubon.org) Brevard County's largest all-volunteer environmental organization, the Space Coast Audubon Society maintains a checklist of local birds and hosts frequent field trips open to the public.

Space Coast Birding (www.spacecoastbirding.com) This Web site is a portal to vast amounts of birding information, both general and specific to this area.

BOATING AND PADDLING Getting out on the water is the perfect way to explore the area's natural elements, and there are marinas, ramps, and water access points all over the county (see the listings under *To Do* in each regional chapter). All boats must have safety vests available, and boat renters should expect a thorough briefing on safety and regulations before they head out on the water. Be aware that it's against the law to drink and drive a boat. Anytime you head out on the water, it's a good idea to bring a jacket to offset the cooling combination of water spray and wind.

Paddling is another way to enjoy Florida's natural beauty. Quietly gliding through the calm lagoon waters is one of the most personal ways to experience its flora

JIM ANGY'S TIPS FOR PHOTOGRAPHING BIRDS AND WILDLIFE

- Before your trip, study professional wildlife photos for setup and framing ideas.
- Visit fishing piers and parks where wildlife is more accustomed to humans.
- Shoot early in the morning when the light is good and will improve over time.
- Be patient and observe the environment.
- Get as close as possible without disturbing the bird or animal. Sit or crouch down, and avoid noises, eye contact, and quick moves. On driving paths, use your car as a blind.
- Find a natural element to add contrast and perspective to the picture, like a spiderweb, tree branch, or flower.
- Set your digital camera to continuous shooting mode to try to capture an action shot.
- Use a macro lens for close-ups of small wildlife.
- Turn off your cell phone.
- Keep your distance when photographing alligators. They can quickly turn aggressive, especially around nests or during mating season.

Area wildlife information, along with Jim's photographs, and DVD photograph collections are available at www.floridabeachbasics.com.

and fauna, and everyone from grade-school children to grandparents can learn in just a few minutes. Recreation kayaks have open seating like a canoe, and beginners may want to go with a partner in a two-seater the first time. Turning over is unusual, but it happens, and even if you stay in the boat, plan on you and your belongings getting wet. Consider taking a disposable camera; most outfitters will lock your car keys in their van so you don't risk dropping them in the water.

Space Coast Paddlers (spacecoastpaddlers.org) is a partner with Florida Paddling Trails Association and leads group paddles for beginners with experts.

CRUISING Port Canaveral is one of the world's most popular cruise ports, offering smooth sailing with straightforward directions, convenient and secure parking, and terminals that are almost as impressive as the cruise ships. Be prepared to show your cruise ticket when entering the parking area and at the terminal. Drivers can pull up to the ship to drop off passengers, but no one is allowed in the terminals without a cruise ticket. Parking is $15 per day for cars up to 20 feet in length and $26 for longer vehicles.

Security at the port is as tight or more so than at the airport. Having the right paperwork will get you quickly through check-in. Keep your ticket in hand, along with your passport, which is required now in most cases. Anyone 16 or older needs a photo ID. U.S. Customs and Border Patrol controls entry to cruise terminals and often will not begin clearing passengers until 30 minutes before embarkation time. Check with each cruise company as to required identification or documentation and restrictions on what's allowed on the ship.

If you're dropping off travelers and want to wave good-bye as they head to sea, wear a bright shirt and let them know where you'll be. Many spots are close enough to provide a great shot of guests waving from the ship. Even if you don't know anyone on the ship, watching these mega-liners head to sea is exciting. Waterside restaurants and bars along Glen Cheek Drive at the Cove all provide a front-row seat. Freddie Patrick Park at the eastern end of the Cove, and the Jetty Park pier are perfect spots and also have plenty of space to let the children burn off some energy before dinner.

COMBO VACATIONS Couple a trip to the beach with a cruise from Port Canaveral for twice the vacation and twice the fun. Staying at the beach before your cruise is a relaxing way to start your trip. Many hotels offer a Snooze and Cruise package that lets you leave your car at the hotel, take a shuttle to the cruise terminal, and save money on port parking fees.

MULTI-DAY CRUISES Carnival Cruise Lines (1-800-327-9501; www .carnival.com) Embark from Port Canaveral aboard one of the "fun" ships proudly sailing beneath the company's trademark red, white, and blue funnel. The newest and one of the largest in the Carnival fleet is the *Canaveral Dream,* which offers seven-night trips to the eastern and western Caribbean. The *Sensation* makes short jaunts to the Bahamas. Every ship features entertainment, a spa, and casinos.

Disney Cruise Line (1-800-939-2784; www.disneycruise.com) From the moment you enter the terminal, you're treated to first-class accommodations, entertainment, and guest service aboard the *Disney Magic* and *Disney Wonder.* Families will enjoy the no-gambling, no-smoking atmosphere. Separate areas and activities ensure a relaxing and romantic experience for adults. Everyone smiles as the departing horn blasts the opening bars of "When You Wish Upon a Star." Ships leave port for three- and four-night trips to the Bahamas and Castaway Cay (Disney's private island), or seven-night sails to the eastern and western Caribbean. In early 2011 the brand new *Disney Dream* will replace the *Disney Wonder* at Port Canaveral. The ship features a cruise innovation, an acrylic tube "water coaster" that takes guests on a thrill ride up, down, around, and off the side of the ship.

Royal Caribbean International (1-800-327-6700; www.royalcaribbean.com) The majestic *Freedom of the Seas* sails to the eastern and western Caribbean. Passengers can keep busy at sea conquering a rock-climbing wall or escaping into whirlpools and water parks. Climb aboard the smaller *Monarch of the Seas* for a three- or four-day cruise to the Bahamas, including great entertainment, casinos, and a fitness center.

Norwegian Cruise Line (1-866-234-7350; www.ncl.com) Here comes the sun, *Norwegian Sun*—the newest arrival at Port Canaveral. From October to April this bright liner will take passengers on 7- and 14-day excursions to the eastern and western Caribbean. They offer freestyle cruising with no fixed schedule for when or where guests dine, letting guests choose when to relax in the spa or have fun in the casino.

FISHING Water, water everywhere makes Brevard County the perfect place to get hooked on the idea of reeling in the perfect catch. Experienced fishermen and curious newcomers can mix a day in the sun with a great adventure. Port Canaveral is the starting point for deep-sea charters, which head about 20 miles out in the Atlantic to the Gulf Stream, where there are wahoo, sailfish, marlin, and dolphinfish. Closer in, captains may troll for kingfish, blackfin tuna, cobia, and barracuda. Larger fish, such as 40–100 pound yellowfin tuna, are found much farther out on "the other side" of the Gulf Stream. Bottom fishing is also productive offshore of Port Canaveral, with many species of snapper and grouper found in abundant wrecks and reefs.

Fish like sea trout, tarpon, snook, and redfish are plentiful on the quieter inland waters, such as the flats of the Banana River the Indian River, and the pristine, shallow Mosquito Lagoon. Protected by the umbrella of the Merritt Island National Wildlife Refuge, the 21,000-acre Mosquito Lagoon has been spared development and agricultural runoff, and has gained a reputation as the fly-fishing capital of the world.

Because there are so many fishing spots in Brevard County, the following list concentrates on guides who are full-time, experienced, reputable, licensed captains working in the waters off Port Canaveral, the Banana River, northern Indian River Lagoon, and southern Mosquito Lagoon. Resources are included to help you locate guides in other areas, however. Stated fares usually include license, bait, and gear; refreshments and cleaning may be extra. The Canaveral Charter Captains' Association has these suggestions: Make your reservation as early as possible to get your desired date, confirm the time and meeting place with your captain a few days ahead, and remember that a tip of 10–20 percent is customary. Always bring a jacket and sunscreen; polarized sunglasses are suggested. A guided charter may be a little expensive, but it's worth the convenience and expertise you get for your money.

CHARTERS: INLAND FLATS Backcountry Fly Fishing (321-267-9818; www.backcountryonfly.com) Mosquito and Indian River Lagoons. Captain John Turcot is passionate about the sport of fly-fishing, and he guides in north Brevard County with wisdom handed down through five generations. He has been featured in several fishing and sport television shows and publications. Captain John specializes in sight fishing and uses a skiff and quiet push-pole approach.

Captain Doug Blanton (321-432-9470; www.sightfishing.com) Cocoa Beach and Banana River Lagoon. Captain Doug is a full-time guide specializing in light tackle sight fishing. Beginners and experts will enjoy a relaxing and productive fishing trip while learning about the area from this lifelong Cocoa Beach resident and avid environmentalist. Book a partial or full day and plan to leave just before sunrise. Maximum capacity is three adults, or two adults and two children.

Lagooner Charters & Expeditions (321-868-4953; www.lagooner.com) Cocoa Beach, Port Canaveral. Captains Richard and Gina Bradley both grew up alongside the waters of Brevard County and have built a family business centered on exploring and enjoying the inshore lagoons. Guests get a package deal—an inshore or nearshore fishing adventure along with a nature tour. Outings are planned and customized for groups of three or less, for a day or portion of a day. The couple has a passion for helping parents and young anglers improve skills and bond through fishing. Have fun, catch fish, and don't forget the camera.

Mosquito Lagoon Fishing Charters (1-866-790-8081; www.irl-fishing.com) Mosquito Lagoon and Indian River Lagoon, Banana River Lagoon, Port Canaveral, Sebastian Inlet. Captain Tom Van Horn specializes in near-shore coastal fishing at Port Canaveral and Sebastian Inlet and flats fishing in the lagoons. The former firefighter and writer for *Coastal Angler* magazine is a Florida native with a lifetime of fishing experience in the area.

Mosquito Lagoon Fly-Fishing Unlimited (321-795-9259 for Captain Scott; 386-479-3429 for Captain Nick; www.mosquitolagoonflyfishing.com) Mosquito Lagoon and Indian River. Captain Scott MacCalla and Captain Nick Sassic are experienced sight guides who work together to provide local knowledge and state-of-the-art equipment and gear for fly-fishing or light tackle outings. Each boat has a one- to three-person capacity; two boats can be combined for families or larger groups.

CHARTERS: OFFSHORE Bottom Dollar Charter Fishing (321-536-0802; www.bottomdollarcharterfishing.com) Sunrise Marina, 505 Glen Cheek Drive, Port Canaveral 32920. Captain Brock Anderson has been operating fishing tours out of Port Canaveral since 1974, and his 38-foot boat accommodates one to six guests. He supplies tackle, bait, ice, rod and reel, and an icebox for your food and drinks; no hard liquor is allowed. Fish are cleaned at the dock. Children are welcome and will have a *reel* good time.

DOUG BLANTON GUIDES A SIGHT FISHING TOUR IN THE BANANA RIVER.

Cool Beans Fishing Charters (321-432-5875; www.coolbeanscharters.com) Sunrise Marina, 505 Glen Cheek Drive, Port Canaveral 32920. Book a private charter for up to four people. Captain Tim Fletcher is a frequent tournament winner, holds fishing clinics for kids, and is a proponent of marine conservation and tagging programs.

Gettin There II Charters (321-631-5055; www.gettinthere.com) Cape Marina, 800 Scallop Drive, Port

CATCH OF THE DAY AT PORT CANAVERAL.

Canaveral 32920. Captain Joe Fetro guides parties of six or fewer aboard a 28-foot Bertram, with two fighting chairs. Beginners are welcome. Fish are bagged and cleaned, and guests receive photos and a video of their trip.

Miss Cape Canaveral (321-783-5274; www.misscape.com) 670 Glen Cheek Drive, Cape Canaveral 32920. The *Miss Cape Canaveral* sails each morning at 8 for a full-day outing; half-day outings aboard *Explorer* depart at 10:45. A hot meal and refreshments are provided. Captain, crew, and galley chef are all experienced and dedicated to delivering a pleasurable fishing experience. Seafarers of all ages are welcome on this party boat. The ships have 100-person capacity; guests can relax in the air-conditioned lounge, galley, bar, and upper sundeck. Evening and overnight trips are available.

Obsession Charters (321-453-3474; www.fishobsession.com) Sunrise Marina, 505 Glen Cheek Drive, Port Canaveral 32920. Pursue serious fishing, enjoy a party, or combine the two. The 33-foot *Obsession I* has room for six and offers half- and full-day packages. The 65-foot party boat *Ocean Obsession II* accommodates up to 70 passengers for an all-day outing. Fare includes bait, fishing gear, and licenses.

Odyssey Charters (321-258-7093; www.fishingodyssey.com) Sunrise Marina, 505 Glen Cheek Drive, Port Canaveral 32920. The *Odyssey* is a 34-foot boat making full- and half-day trips offshore, as well as blue-water excursions 60–100 miles out for big game sport fishing. Families and children are welcome; they have a capacity for six. Captains Ross Lowers and Eric Kropp have experience, expertise, and a love of ocean fishing.

Orlando Princess and Canaveral Star (321-784-6300; www.orlandoprincess .com) 650 Glen Cheek Drive, Port Canaveral 32920. This fleet, family owned and operated, offers half- and full-day trips, and nighttime shark and snapper fishing excursions. The *Orlando Princess* is a stable 80-foot catamaran with 1,900 feet of deck space. The *Canaveral Star* is a 65-foot fishing boat. Both boats have a comfortable, air-conditioned cabin. Every fishing trip includes lunch (plus breakfast on all-day outings), beer and soda, rod, reel, bait, tackle, and fishing license.

Sea Legs (321-452-5315; www.atlanticdeepseafishing.com) Sunrise Marina, 505 Glen Cheek Drive, Port Canaveral 32920. Morning, afternoon, and full-day outings can be booked for one to six passengers on this charter with Captain Floyd Curington, an experienced offshore fisherman. The 32-foot sport fishing boat has all the latest electronic and safety gear. Bring gallon-sized Ziploc bags and a cooler to store your catch.

PIER FISHING Cocoa Beach Pier (321-783-7549; www.cocoabeachpier.com) 401 Meade Avenue, Cocoa Beach 32931. No license is needed to fish from this popular pier. Rod and reel rentals are available; bait is for sale. Newcomers can get a brief lesson from the pier master.

Malcolm E. McLouth Fishing Pier Jetty Park, 400 E. Jetty Road, Port Canaveral 32920. Fish 24 hours a day for snook, Spanish mackerel, drums, and other sport fish off this lighted pier. Fish-cleaning tables with running water are provided, and the pier is ADA accessible. Sunrise Marina in Port Canaveral sells fishing licenses.

Rodney S. Ketcham Park (www.portcanaveral.com) West end of Port Canaveral. Fish from the bulkheads at this 4-acre park, which also has picnic tables and rest room facilities.

Ramp Road Park Ramp Road, Cocoa Beach. The dock at Ramp Road in Cocoa Beach has been voted the best fishing spot in the area by *Florida Sportsman* magazine.

Titusville Bridge and Causeway In addition to being one of Florida's best locations for nighttime shrimping in the winter and spring, this is a popular spot to catch redfish, sea trout, black drum, and other fish. There are four bait and tackle shops within 2 blocks of the causeway to service anglers.

SURF FISHING Captain Doug Blanton (321-432-9470; www.sightfishing .com) Cocoa Beach. Catch fish the old-fashioned way: Follow the birds and cast into the ocean for whiting, pompano, snook, and other seasonal fish. Captain Doug brings everything needed for a surf-fishing expedition.

Fishing & Diving Center (321-783-3477) 6300 N. Atlantic Avenue, Cape Canaveral 32920. Try surf fishing on your own with advice and gear from owner Rob. Open daily 7–6.

FISHING RESOURCES Florida Fish & Wildlife Conservation Commission (www.myfwc.com). This state organization provides information on fish and wildlife resources along with rules and regulations regarding fishing in this area. Fishing licenses can be obtained online.

WILDLIFE PROFILE: BALD EAGLE AND OSPREY

Looking skyward, the bald eagle resembles an airplane—wide wings, out-stretched and flat, soaring effortlessly on currents of air. Like many area visitors, they fly into Brevard County in the fall and stay until spring. The eagle is an opportunistic feeder, and during this period the area teems with migratory birds and waterfowl that make for easy prey. Eagles mate for life and will return together to upgrade an old nest and roost. They prefer to settle in live trees. One nest along a Kennedy Space Center tour route has been there for at least 45 years and is the size of a queen-sized bed. The eagle has piercing yellow eyes and, like most raptors, can see much farther than humans.

The osprey is smaller than the eagle but has the same yellow eyes, curved talons to grab prey, and a strong, hooked bill. The brown and white birds fly with their wings bent at the ends. This fish hawk also has a few handy features that ensure it catches a regular diet of fish. Reversible toes let the osprey grab a fish and turn it the same direction as the body for improved aerodynamics. Also, the talons have spiny pads that make it easier to hold on to slippery marine life. Ospreys are year-round residents. They nest in the spring and prefer to use dead trees, platforms, or navigational buoys.

Spend any time at all on the water, and you're likely to spot an osprey flying about with a fish in tow. Occasionally an eagle will happen by and make the same observation, then fly below the osprey until it pushes the bird so high that it drops the fish—right into the grasp of the waiting eagle. Both birds are memorable to see.

Space Coast Sightings: Black Point Wildlife Drive at the Merritt Island National Wildlife Refuge, Cocoa Beach Thousand Islands, Wild Florida exhibit at Brevard Zoo.

OSPREY *(PANDION HALIAETUS).*

Jim Angy

Coastal Angler Magazine (www.coastalanglermagazine.com) A resource for information on fishing, boating, and conservation along Florida's east coast waterways, including links to current fishing forecasts and an events calendar.

The Fly Fisherman (321-267-0348) 1114 S. Washington Avenue (US 1), Titusville 32780. In addition to being a first-rate outfitter, this store is a clearing-house for checking on local conditions, finding a reputable guide, and picking up lessons or tips on fly-fishing, casting, and tying.

HIKING, BICYCLING, AND RUNNING Outdoor exercise will never be more enjoyable than it is in Florida. The terrain is flat, the temperature is pleasant, and the scenery is captivating, so enjoy making a jaunt on foot or bike a part of your vacation experience. Lots of walkers hit the beach at sunrise and sunset. The sand at low tide is a perfect surface for a run or bike ride. A bike path/side-walk is built on the east side of A1A, but because of all the intersecting drive-ways, pedestrians and bikers have to really be alert. Other paths might be more appealing. See *To Do* in each geographic chapter for ideas on where to go.

ATHLETIC EVENTS In recent years, the Space Coast has taken off as a popular spot with casual and serious athletes. Events are staged year round and attract fun runners, first-timers, and world-class competitors. In addition to the events listed here, the Running Zone (321-751-8890; www.runningzone.com; 3680 N. Wickham Road, Melbourne 32935) provides a comprehensive schedule of races and triathlons on their Web site.

Health First Triathlon (www.healthfirsttri.com) 1521 Pineapple Avenue, Eau Gallie. Two courses are offered for this scenic race held the first weekend in October—Olympic distance and sprint distance. Olympic competitors swim for 1.5K, bike 40K, and run 10K. The race begins and ends at Pineapple Park, at the intersection of the Indian River and FL 518 in Eau Gallie, and all routes are set in that vicinity, including a breathtaking and challenging bike route across both the Pineda and Eau Gallie Causeways.

🎿 **Reindeer Run** (www.cityofcapecanaveral.gov) 8492 Ridgewood Avenue, Cape Canaveral. HO-HO-HO! Start the holiday season off with a 5K family run from oceanside Cherie Down Park. Refreshments are served, Santa joins the race, and many participants dress in seasonal colors. The race starts at 8 AM on the second Saturday in December and finishes early enough that you can still put in a few miles at the mall.

Space Coast Runners Marathon and Half-Marathon (www.spacecoast marathon.org) Cocoa Riverfront Park. Held the last Sunday in November, Florida's oldest marathon follows a USAFT-certified course along the beautiful Indian River. Perks and prizes all capture the space theme, highlighted by a 3-2-1 launch countdown to start the race.

Surf the Sand 8K Beach Run (www.brevardparks.com) Lori Wilson Park, Cocoa Beach. On the second Saturday in May, Brevard County Parks & Recreation invites athletes of all ages to gather at 8 AM for a fun run in the sun, sand, and surf. Cool off with a dip in the ocean after completing the race.

Cape Canaveral,
Cocoa Beach, and
Port Canaveral

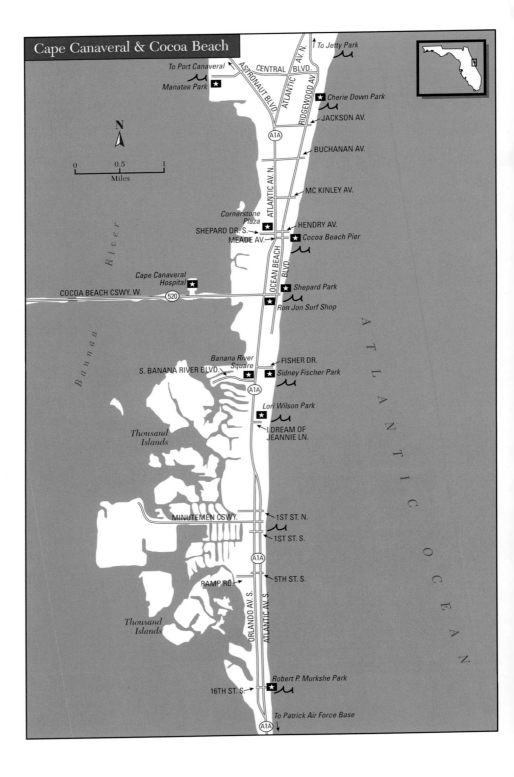

Cape Canaveral & Cocoa Beach

To Jetty Park

To Port Canaveral

Manatee Park

CENTRAL BLVD.

ASTRONAUT BLVD.

ATLANTIC AV. N.

RIDGEWOOD AV.

Cherie Down Park

JACKSON AV.

A1A

BUCHANAN AV.

ATLANTIC AV. N.

MC KINLEY AV.

Cornerstone Plaza

SHEPARD DR. S.

HENDRY AV.

MEADE AV.

Cocoa Beach Pier

OCEAN BEACH BLVD.

River

Cape Canaveral Hospital

COCOA BEACH CSWY. W.

520

Shepard Park

Ron Jon Surf Shop

Banana

Banana River Square

FISHER DR.

S. BANANA RIVER BLVD.

Sidney Fischer Park

A1A

Lori Wilson Park

Thousand Islands

I DREAM OF JEANNIE LN.

MINUTEMEN CSWY.

1ST ST. N.

1ST ST. S.

A1A

5TH ST. S.

RAMP RD.

ORLANDO AV. S.

ATLANTIC AV. S.

Thousand Islands

N

0   0.5   1
Miles

A T L A N T I C   O C E A N

Robert P. Murkshe Park

16TH ST. S.

To Patrick Air Force Base

A1A

CAPE CANAVERAL, COCOA BEACH, AND PORT CANAVERAL

M any Space Coast visitors base their stay in the shoreside communities of Cocoa Beach and Cape Canaveral, which are centrally located for easy access to the airport and theme parks in Orlando, all major Florida highways, and other areas of Brevard County. The towns offer wide beaches and a variety of lodging and dining choices. Most hotels are directly on the coast or just a short walk away. Wood crossovers lead down to the beach at almost every block. A buffer of sand dunes, sea grapes, and palms creates a natural and pretty look.

Port Canaveral, the second busiest cruise port in the world, is a working seaport bustling with marinas, parks, a 1,200-foot fishing pier, and waterside restaurants and bars. Guided fishing boats head offshore each morning and return to the docks in the afternoon with their catch. Mega-sized cruise ships passing through the channel on their way to sea are almost close enough to touch.

✷ To See

HISTORIC PLACES The footprints of ancient Indians who fished in these ocean waters and gazed out toward the same endless horizon have long since washed away. Only a frayed Spanish map from 1565, now in a museum archive, attests that Canaveral is the oldest continuous place-name in the continental United States. Nature swept away the remnants of a community of freed slaves who settled south of the geographic cape at the start of the 20th century, then moved inland to escape a hurricane. Perhaps the history of a place planted so softly in the sea is meant to be elusive. So with apologies to the Beatles—a magical history tour is waiting to take you away, take you away.

The trip begins at **Jetty Park,** where a monument just across from the playground identifies the Canaveral coast as the site of the last naval battle of the American Revolution, occurring on March 10, 1783. The *Duc de Lauzun,* heavy with gold and silver, was about a mile offshore on its way from Havana to Philadelphia. The treasure was to be used by Congress to fund the new country's first bank and reduce the war debt. Three British ships spotted the vessel and gave chase. Captain John Barry, commander of the Continental Navy's *Alliance,* came to the defense and fired on the British ships, which then turned and fled. The precious cargo was saved, and the rest, as we know, is history.

In the distance, to the northeast, stands the **Cape Canaveral Lighthouse.** The original brick tower was built in 1848 and replaced in 1868. Launch pads are near the tower, and from a distance the lighthouse is often mistaken for a rocket. The story has been told that Dr. Wernher von Braun, renowned scientist and a leader of the U.S. space program, climbed up to the railed balcony at the top to watch the early launches. The lighthouse is located on Canaveral Air Force Base property and is accessible to the public on a limited basis. See Cape Canaveral Air Force Space and Missile Museum entry in this section.

Some things never change. Relax under the gazebo at small **Center Street Park** located at the edge of the Banana River at the end of Center Street

SAMS HOUSE.

SAMS HOUSE AT PINE ISLAND

(321-255-4466;www.eelbrevard.com) Open: TBD. Admission: Free. A spot of land along the Indian River on north Merritt Island echoes with memories of a long and varied history. The abundance of vegetation and fresh water on the elevated pine flatlands once attracted ancient mastodons, giant land tortoises, and giant armadillos. About 4,000 years ago Native American tribes found food and shelter in the cabbage palm and hardwood hammocks. In 1878 John Sams settled here with his wife Sarah and their five children.

Sams, from South Carolina, went first to Eau Gallie where he built a small

(Buchanan Street heading east). Archaeologists have found numerous Indian mounds on the barrier island, echoes of a settlement from over 2,000 years ago, and it is likely that artifacts are buried deep below the silt of the quiet Banana River. Then and now, manatees congregate here to graze on sea grasses, and the sun offers a spectacular show at day's end.

In the heyday of the space program, more than 2,000 members of the media descended on the area to watch a rocket launch. Walter Cronkite was often among them, and he might have been talking about the **Mousetrap** when he dubbed Cocoa Beach "sin city." The restaurant and bar was a favorite with astronauts and space workers unwinding at the end of a long and stressful day. The building remains but is reincarnated now as Durango Steakhouse, at 5602 N. Atlantic Avenue in Cocoa Beach. Many of the original furnishings are there,

home. Three years later, he decided to move to Merritt Island. The house was dismantled, brought up the Indian River by barge, and reconstructed on this site. Descendants of John Sams lived on the homestead for nearly 120 years.

In 1996 the Brevard County EEL (Environmentally Endangered Lands) program acquired an 879-acre parcel, including the Sams land, in order to preserve and protect the house and surrounding diverse and undeveloped habitats. An interpretive center leads visitors on a journey through the natural and social history of the area.

Sams House 1 is a small, single-room pine cabin built in 1875—the oldest home in Brevard County. Square nails are visible and many windows retain the original glass panes. The restored house serves as a **Visitor and Education Center** and features fossils, artifacts, and domestic tools from the long history of life on this property.

Sams House 2 was built in the 1880s next to the cabin. The two-story wood house is an example of Florida vernacular architecture with a long front porch, multi-pitched roof, and other features to keep the house cool on hot Florida days. The interior is not open at this time.

Trails wind from the back of the house and through the yard, and will eventually connect to a network of paths already on the site and along the Indian River. Outdoor exhibits will feature re-creations of the fossil dig and the Native American settlement, along with gardens and information about early agriculture in Brevard.

Directions: From SR 528 take SR 3 (Exit 49) north for 4.6 miles and turn left on N. Tropical Trail; the property is 0.5 mile on the right. House, trails, and rest rooms are ADA accessible. Call or check Web site for hours of operation.

including the top of the grand piano, which is now mounted on the wall. Imagine everyone gathered around for a late-night songfest: "Fly me to the moon, and let me play among the stars . . ."

The entrance to the south lot of Lori Wilson Park at 1500 N. Atlantic Avenue has been designated **I Dream of Jeannie Lane** to honor the virtual heritage of Cocoa Beach captured in the 1960s television show. Thank former Cocoa Beach mayor Joe Morgan for creating a great photo opportunity.

Our magical tour ends with a genuine historic landmark, the **Cocoa Beach Community Church,** at 350 S. Orlando Avenue. In 1927, mayor Gus Edwards built the small wooden structure at the request of his mother. A large cast-iron bell, once on top of the building and now housed inside, was dedicated to her. Eighty years later, in a twist that real estate developer Edwards would appreciate, the privately owned building is available for rent.

LIBRARIES Learn more about Brevard County and Florida, or enrich your life with a workshop or lecture, at several libraries with a wealth of resources. Public libraries offer free access to the Internet and WiFi hookup. For a complete list of Brevard County Public Libraries and the most recent information on operating hours visit their Web site at www.brev.org.

Cape Canaveral Public Library (321-868-1101) 201 Polk Avenue, Cape Canaveral 32920. Open: Monday noon–8, Tuesday through Friday 9–5, Saturday 10–2, closed Sunday. This cozy library located just off A1A offers a really great assortment of movies on tape and DVD, including choices for children and families. Visitors can get a temporary library card by showing a driver's license and copy of a local rental agreement. Two adjoining parks are perfect for outdoor relaxation or reading. Veteran's Memorial Park has picnic tables, benches, and a yard full of mature live oak trees that even adults may be tempted to climb. Xeriscape Park on Taylor Avenue models ideas for conserving water through the use of natural vegetation for landscaping.

Cocoa Beach Public Library (321-868-1104) 550 N. Brevard Avenue, Cocoa Beach 32931. Open: Sunday 1–5, Monday 10–6, Tuesday and Wednesday 9–8, Thursday through Friday 10–6, Saturday 9–5. Centrally located, the Cocoa Beach library is ideal for visitors and residents looking for a quiet reading room. A newsletter located just inside the front door provides a calendar of presentations, classes, and group meetings covering just about every interest. There's an extensive collection of aerospace books. Stop by the reference desk for guidance in learning more about the local environment and history.

MUSEUMS Brevard County's cultural landscape is preserved in several entertaining, informative, and reasonably priced museums that are as enjoyable for children as they are for adults.

Cape Canaveral and Cocoa Beach

Cape Canaveral Air Force Space and Missile Museum (321-730-0055; www.capemuseum.org) State Road 401, Port Canaveral 32920. Open: Tuesday through Friday 9–2, Saturday 9–5, Sunday 12–4. Admission: Free. Exhibits illustrate the history of America's space exploration and missile systems. The gift shop carries a unique selection of space memorabilia. A complementary three-hour tour of the Air Force Station, launch pads, and Cape Canaveral Lighthouse is offered on the second Wednesday of each month. Participants must be U.S. citizens with two forms of identification. Call 321-494-5945 for reservations. Much of the tour is not handicap accessible; children must be 12 or older.

✑ **Cocoa Beach Surf Museum** (321-258-8217; www.cocoabeachsurfmuseum .org) 4275 N. Atlantic Avenue, Cocoa Beach 32931. Open: Daily 9–6. Admission: Free; donations accepted. Surfing has been the cornerstone of Cocoa Beach culture for more than 50 years, and this bright museum is dedicated to conserving and preserving the culture of the sport through stories, photographs, and artifacts. One recent event, The Big Board, showcased a collection of over 70 unusual boards, like a rare long and heavy 1957 Hobie, and a lighter, shorter board used by world champion Kelly Slater when he was a young amateur learning his craft on the waves of Cocoa Beach. The museum features lectures, movies, and other entertainment, with details posted on their Web site. The atmosphere is casual, the karma is good, and the waves are rolling. Stop by and be inspired. Located inside Ron Jon Watersports.

East Coast Surfing Hall of Fame (321-799-9930; www.ecsurfinghalloffame .com) 4001 N. Atlantic Avenue, Cocoa Beach 32931. Open: Daily 8 AM–11 PM. Admission: Free; donations accepted. For over a decade the East Coast Surfing Hall of Fame has been recognizing the extraordinary athletes of this sport, along with the men and women responsible for the development and growth of surfing, especially along Florida's east coast. Boards, photographs, and memorabilia are featured in a small exhibit on the top floor of the Cocoa Beach Surf Company.

✑ **Museum of Dinosaurs & Ancient Cultures** (321-783-7300; www.dinosaur store.com) 250 W. Cocoa Beach Causeway, Cocoa Beach 32931. Open: Monday through Saturday 11–5, Sunday 12–5. Local residents Steve and Donna Cayer began collecting fossils as a hobby, and after decades of collecting and digging now have a premier collection of authentic, ancient artifacts, many featured in traveling exhibits at world-class museums around the country. Their Cocoa Beach retail store blends themed merchandise with shells and marine fossils, meteorites, and dinosaur bones. They have a large collection of eggs, from the baseball-sized egg of the Segnosaur to the egg of an elephant bird that is as large as an elongated basketball. By early 2011, the second level of the store will be converted to a full-scale museum that encompasses all things dinosaur, as well as artifacts and information about ancient cultures like the Egyptians, Chinese, and Mesoamerican Maya and Aztec. Admission price has not yet been determined.

✳ To Do

BICYCLE RENTALS Bilt Surf and Skate (321-868-8820) 210 N. Orlando Avenue, Cocoa Beach 32931. Choose from a wide selection of bicycles for every age, including an adult tandem bike. Shop is right in the middle of downtown Cocoa Beach. $10 for two hours; $55 a week.

Cocoa Beach Surf Company Beachside (321-799-9921) 199 E. Cocoa Beach Causeway, Cocoa Beach 32931. Conveniently located right across the street from Shepard Park at the end of Minutemen Causeway. $5 for two hours; $50 a week.

Ron Jon Watersports (321-799-8840) 4275 N. Atlantic Avenue, Cocoa Beach 32931. Located on A1A, just across the parking lot from Ron Jon Surf Shop and an easy bike ride to Cocoa Beach hotels and beaches. $10 a day.

BIRDING Avocet Lagoon (www.portcanaveral.com) Port Canaveral locks. Audubon member Jason Frederick calls Avocet Lagoon a hidden jewel for birders. Follow Mullet Drive around to Rodney S. Ketcham Park and stop to enjoy a view of the harbor from the observation tower. Continue on the same road to the locks at Port Canaveral, where flocks of white pelicans settle in the winter months. Plans are in the works for an observation tower to the east of the locks that will overlook the lagoon. Keep an eye out for manatees and dolphins swimming inside the locks.

Jetty Park (321-783-7111) 400 E. Jetty Road, Port Canaveral 32920. In the early morning, hundreds of gulls, terns, and shorebirds roost on the beach, especially in fall and winter. The birds come and go throughout the day and settle back on the beach before sunset. Check offshore for rare seabirds.

Maritime Hammock at Lori Wilson Park (321-455-1385) Lori Wilson Park, 1500 N. Atlantic Avenue, Cocoa Beach 32931. The best time to visit here is between October and March, when migratory songbirds and shorebirds are present. Look for painted buntings and numerous warbler species.

BOATING: MARINAS AND RAMPS Banana River Marine (321-452-8622) 1360 S. Banana River Drive, Merritt Island 32952. Located on the Banana River about 2 miles south of FL 520, this boatyard and storage facility provides storage and maintenance, specializing in boats 20 feet and longer. Slips for transient travelers are available. Boat ramp $5.

Bluepoints Marina (321-799-2860; www.bluepointsmarina.com) 726 Scallop Drive, Port Canaveral 32920. Boaters sailing through the Barge Canal toward the Atlantic Ocean will easily spot this sunny yellow facility alongside the deep blue waters of Port Canaveral. Day cruisers will find fueling stations, pump-out services, a full-service center, a fully stocked ships store, and clean rest rooms and bathhouse. There are limited slips for transient vessels, but they do not have accommodations for live-aboard.

Cape Marina (321-783-8410; www.capemarina.com) 800 Scallop Drive, Port Canaveral 32920. For over 30 years boaters have considered this family-owned and certified-clean marina and boatyard their home away from home. Dock your boat for a day, a week, a month, or a season. The ships store carries groceries, souvenirs, and fishing supplies. Other amenities include bath and showers, laundry facilities, a do-it-yourself and full-service yard, cleaning and storage, and an easy-access, fast fuel dock.

Harbortown Marina Boatyard (321-453-0160; www.harbortownmarina.com) 2700 Harbortown Drive, Merritt Island 32952. This full-service facility is located on the Barge Canal, 2.5 miles directly west of the deepwater Cape Canaveral inlet. Boats are stored inside and outside, and launched once each day. Day boaters can stop for maintenance, fuel, and a meal at the Nautical Spirits Bar &

Grille. Slips are available for monthly rentals, which include the use of laundry facilities and a pool.

Kelly Park FL 528 and Banana River Drive, Merritt Island. Kelly Park has a natural shoreline, from which canoes and kayaks can be launched, and a four-lane lighted boat ramp and dock. The launch provides easy access to the north Banana River, where the entire area is a no-wake zone, and Port Canaveral through the locks. The lockmaster will not open for paddlers; you must wait until a motorized boat approaches. Amenities include parking and rest rooms. No fee.

Ocean Club Marina (321-783-9001; www.oceanclub-pc.com) 930 Mullet Road, Port Canaveral 32920. Transient and live-aboard boaters will discover comfort and convenience at this full-service, public access marina located just minutes from the Atlantic Ocean. Every slip has hookups for cable TV, high-speed WiFi, telephone, water, and electric. During the day, guests also have access to the private clubhouse with a lounge, business center, and entertainment room. Transient rates are set for day, week, and month stays.

Port Canaveral
Port Canaveral provides public boat ramps at two parks along the canal. **Rodney S. Ketcham Park** is just east of the Barge Canal and the closest access to the Banana River. Both parks have rest rooms and plenty of car and trailer parking. **Freddie Patrick Park** is farther east at the end of the Cove strip of restaurants. A fish-cleaning table is available. There are no fees for use of these ramps or facilities.

Ramp Road Park Ramp Road, Cocoa Beach. This relaxing green space, a picturesque place to spend an afternoon enjoying a scenic view of the Thousand Islands, is located at the west end of Ramp Road. It has two boat ramps, a fishing dock, and picnic facilities.

Sunrise Marina (321-783-9535; www.sunrisemarina.com) 505 Glen Cheek Drive, Port Canaveral 32920. Boaters will find quick service, fuel (diesel, unleaded, and ethanol-free), along with transient or long-term storage for 15- to 40-foot boats at Sunrise Marina. They are home to many of the area's most reputable fishing charters, with a check-in stand across from the marina and next door to Grill's Restaurant, where walk-ups may be able to book a same-day outing. Fishing licenses are sold in the well-stocked bait and tackle shop.

BOATING: TOURS AND RENTALS ✅ **Brevard County Parks** (321-455-1385) Ramp Road, Cocoa Beach. An interpretive canoe tour of the Thousand Islands leaves at 9:30 AM on the fourth Friday of each month. Children must be at least four years old and accompanied by an adult. $10 per person for two hours.

Calema Kayak Rentals (321-453-3223; www.calema.com) 2550 N. Banana River Drive, Merritt Island 32952. Single and tandem kayaks are available to rent at Calema Windsurfing & Watersports. Park and launch easily from their location at Kelly Park on the west side of the Banana River at SR 528. Head north or south for access to canals where manatees and dolphins usually make an

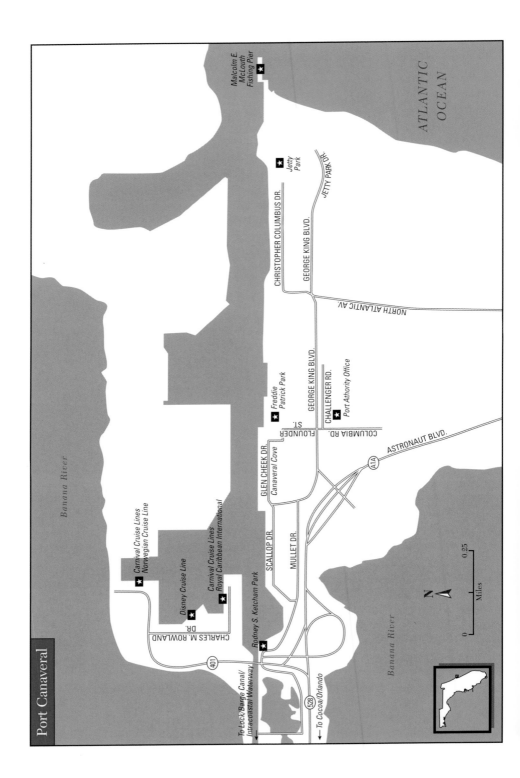

Port Canaveral

Malcolm E. McLouth Fishing Pier

Jetty Park

ATLANTIC OCEAN

CHRISTOPHER COLUMBUS DR.

GEORGE KING BLVD.

JETTY PARK DR.

NORTH ATLANTIC AV.

Freddie Patrick Park

GEORGE KING BLVD.

CHALLENGER RD.

Port Athority Office

COLUMBIA RD.

FLOUNDER ST.

GLEN CHEEK DR.

Canaveral Cove

ASTRONAUT BLVD.

A1A

SCALLOP DR.

MULLET DR.

Banana River

Carnival Cruise Lines Norwegian Cruise Line

Disney Cruise Line

Carnival Cruise Lines Royal Caribbean International

CHARLES M. ROWLAND DR.

Rodney S. Ketcham Park

Banana River

To Lock/Barge Canal/ Intracoastal Waterway

401

528

To Cocoa/Orlando

N

0   0.25
Miles

appearance. Rates for a single/tandem kayak are $30/40 for three hours or $45/55 for the day.

Cocoa Beach Kayaking (321-784-4545; www.cocoabeachkayaking.com) Ramp Road, Cocoa Beach. For a decade Kathleen Bennett has been leading nature tours out of Cocoa Beach with a focus on fun and education. She and her guides share years of experience paddling the Indian River Lagoon, and have extensive knowledge about the manatees, bottlenose dolphins, and marine wildlife found in the area. Settle in a comfortable, stable two-seat touring kayak for an unforgettable trek through the mangroves. They supply hats, towels, polarized sunglasses, sun block, and water. You bring your camera and curiosity. It's $30 per person for an estimated two-hour weekday tour. At the end of the tour guests receive a card good for a discount at selected local restaurants.

Fin Expeditions (321-698-7233; www.finexpeditions.com) Ramp Road, Cocoa Beach. Sign on for a fun paddling adventure through the mangrove emerald forests dotting the Thousand Islands off Cocoa Beach. Tim is a fifth-generation Floridian who has been exploring the lagoon since he was young. He welcomes introducing children six and older to this magical habitat, home to manatees, dolphins, river otters, and birds. Tim has one- and two-person kayaks, and every tour starts with a briefing to make sure each participant is comfortable in their boat. $30 per person. Call ahead for reservations.

Island Boat Lines (321-454-7414; www.islandboatlines.com) Climb aboard a comfortable, covered pontoon boat for the *In Search of Wildlife* tour of the beautiful Thousand Islands. Along the way the captain and narrator share entertaining local stories and information about area wildlife and birds. This cruise departs from Banana River Marine, 1357 Banana River Drive on Merritt Island. To get there, turn left at the first light west of the FL 520 Causeway. The two-hour cruises depart daily at 10 AM and 1 PM; Sundays at 2 PM. Call ahead for reservations. There are usually spots available for the same day. On-boat rest rooms are available. $28 per person, with discounts for seniors, children, and military; children under two are free.

SPACE COAST KAYAKING GUIDE LEADS A GROUP THROUGH THE THOUSAND ISLANDS OFF COCOA BEACH.

Island Watercraft Rentals (321-454-7661; www.islandwatercraftrentals.com) 1872 E. FL 520 Causeway, Merritt Island 32952. Deck boats, center consoles, and pontoons are available to rent and are a fun option for water-experienced families and groups wanting to explore the Banana River on their own, or to go waterskiing or tubing. An instructional briefing, life vests, fuel, and safety gear are provided. You bring personal gear and refreshments. Rates start at $205 for a half day. Call ahead for reservations. Boats dock at north side of FL 520 at the western intersection of the Banana River.

Ron Jon Watersports (321-799-8840; www.ronjons.com) 4275 N. Atlantic Avenue, Cocoa Beach 32931. Paddlers can rent kayaks or stand up paddleboard; $40 for 24 hours. Must be 18 or older to rent; a cash or credit card deposit is required.

⚓ **Space Coast Kayaking** (321-784-2452; www.spacecoastkayaking.net) Ramp Road, Cocoa Beach. Experienced kayakers Jim Durocher and Jaro Palma begin each tour with a brief demonstration, and then guide groups out to explore the history, environment, and ecology of the Thousand Islands. Guests will easily learn to navigate the calm and shallow Banana River, a playground for manatees and dolphins, and lined with thick, lush mangroves that are home to a variety of birds. Take a daytime tour or a relaxing sunset paddle. In the summertime they offer an after-dark bioluminescence tour, when the warm water comes alive with sparkling microscopic animals. Groups are kept small to ensure personalized service and safety. Call for reservations; tour times may be flexible. Adults $30, children (under 13) $15 when accompanied by paying adult. Children five years and younger are not encouraged to kayak. Price includes life jacket, sunscreen, and water. Custom tours can be arranged.

⚓ **Space Coast River Tours, Inc.** (321-652-1052; www.spacecoastrivertours .com) Kelly Park, FL 528 and Banana River Drive, Merritt Island. Boating has been a lifelong passion for Captains Mark and Michelle Anderson, who met on a sailing vacation and married two years later on a catamaran. Today they run the 44-foot *Blue Dolphin*, a comfortable pontoon boat with a retractable roof. Tours depart from Kelly Park on Merritt Island and sail on the beautiful, calm Banana River, venturing into the Barge Canal and through the locks into Port Canaveral, past restaurants and cruise ships in port. Passengers are treated to tropical music and lots of stories about the nature, history, and culture of this area. Bring your camera because birds, manatees, and dolphins almost always make an appearance. Special sails are arranged around space launches; private sunset and party tours can be arranged. $29 per person for adults, $25 for seniors 65 and over, $20 for children 12 and younger, free under age 3. Rate includes one free drink (beer, wine, soda, water) and snacks. Rest rooms are available and boat is handicap accessible.

Wild Side Tours (321-799-5495; www.wildsidetours.com) Ramp Road, Cocoa Beach. Captain Ben Evans, a Master Naturalist and science teacher, casts off each day for two-hour eco- and nature treks through the Cocoa Beach Thousand Islands. His pontoon-style boat, with a retractable roof and a rest room, accommodates up to 22 guests. You bring the camera. Captain Evans provides soft drinks or water, binoculars, and a wealth of information. Cruises depart Tuesday

GUESTS OF SPACE COAST RIVER TOURS EMBARK FROM KELLY PARK FOR AN ECOTOUR ALONG THE NORTH BANANA RIVER AND PORT CANAVERAL INLET.

through Saturday 10 AM; Sunday through Monday 2 PM; Tuesday and Friday two hours before sunset; Adults $29; children under 17 $18, plus $1 launch fee and tax. Seats are often available for same-day bookings, but call ahead to reserve a spot. Private tours and fishing trips can be arranged.

CAMPING AND RVING ☀ **Jetty Park Campground** (321-783-7111; www .portcanaveral.com) 400 E. Jetty Road, Cape Canaveral 32920. Thirty-five-acre Jetty Park, located alongside the Port Canaveral Inlet and the Atlantic Ocean, is one of the premier public campgrounds in Florida. Many vacationers have been repeat visitors for decades. Guests have access to beaches, rest rooms, showers, a 1,200-foot fishing pier, refreshment stand, bait shop and convenience store, grills, picnic pavilions, a playground, volleyball courts, and a wooded bicycle path. Choose from rustic tent sites, RV sites with water and electric, and RV sites with water, electric, and sewer. Campers have a front-row seat to watch cruise ships head to sea and space launches soar skyward. Reservations may be made 90 days in advance for a 2-night minimum to 21-night maximum stay. Dogs and cats under 35 pounds are permitted for RV campers, but they're not allowed in most public areas.

FAMILY FUN AND FITNESS ♪ **Adventure Zone** (321-783-7300; www .dinosaurstore.com) 250 W. Cocoa Beach Causeway, Cocoa Beach 32931. Children will cool off and have fun with fascinating hands-on exhibits at this interactive science and game place inside the Dinosaur Store. The momentum machine replicates centrifugal force in a way that even the smallest children will enjoy, while the Wild Nile Raft takes the idea up a notch with a spinning ride for older kids. Prehistoric stories are told in the Movie Cave, decorated with replications of ancient cave paintings. In the Reptile Room, discover a small zoo of snakes, tortoises, and alligators. Open Monday through Saturday 11–5, Sundays 12–5; open only on weekends and holidays from September through February. Children $8; adults $5, with a separate $2 ticket for the Wild Nile Raft ride.

✂ Calema Windsurfing & Watersports (321-453-3223; www.calema.com) 2550 N. Banana River Drive, Merritt Island 32952. The protected cove at Kelly Park is the perfect spot to try windsurfing. Everyone from the age of 8 to 80 can learn, according to the folks at Calema. Surfers venturing into the windy channel follow in the tracks of professionals and Olympic competitors from around the world, who vie here each year in windsurfing championship races. Calema has recently added lessons and rentals for sailing and stand up paddleboarding, a hybrid of canoeing and surfing that has become incredibly popular. Windsurfing: private lessons are $65 per hour and include equipment; rentals are $55 for three hours or $75 for the day. Stand Up Paddleboarding: flat-water lessons on the Banana River are $50 per person, per hour; surf lessons are $130 per person for two hours. Rent a board for $55 for three hours or $75 for the day. Sailing: private lessons $200 for up to two people for two hours; rentals are $55–75 for three hours; $70–125 for the day. Kids' camps are held throughout the summer.

Cape Canaveral Recreation Complex (321-868-1226) 7300 N. Atlantic Avenue, Cape Canaveral 32920. Reserve tennis, racquetball, and shuffleboard courts, all lighted for evening play, up to a day in advance. Racquets are available for rent, and you can join drop-in classes such as yoga and Jazzercise. Open Monday through Thursday 8 AM–9 PM, Friday through Sunday 8–8. Court fee is 75 cents per hour.

✂ Cocoa Beach Aquatic Center (321-868-3314) 5000 Tom Warriner Boulevard, Cocoa Beach 32931. This outdoor, heated Olympic-sized swimming pool, open year-round to the public, features adult swim laps, 1-meter diving board, jumbo waterslide, water sprays, and children's pool with shower umbrella and spray. Open Monday through Friday 10–3, Saturday 10–4, Sunday 12–4. Fee: $2–3 for the day.

WINDSURFING ON THE BANANA RIVER.

Cocoa Beach Health & Fitness (321-613-2969) 1355 N. Atlantic Avenue,
Cocoa Beach 32931. Short-term visitor passes provide access to fitness equipment, a weight room, dance and exercise classes, and a wet and dry sauna. Childcare is available. They also offer massages and facials. Many hotels have a relationship with the center through which their guests receive complimentary or discounted passes.

Cocoa Beach Parasail (321-212-8277) 628 Glen Cheek Drive, Port Canaveral 32920. Get a bird's-eye view of the beach on a parasailing excursion. Single and tandem options are available, and you take off and land from the back of a boat. Photo packages capture the memory. Continuous flights are offered throughout the day from March through September; reservations are required. It's $70 for an 800-foot flight and $65 for a 500-foot flight. Boat docks at Rusty's Seafood & Oyster Bar.

Cocoa Beach Skatepark (321-868-3238) 1450 Minutemen Causeway, Cocoa Beach 32931. Visitors are welcome at this park, which features more than 32,000 square feet of smooth concrete in a mix of traditional and new configurations, such as bowls, pools, handrails, ledges, and stairs. The park opens at 4 PM Tuesday through Friday, 1 PM Saturday and Sunday, and skating continues under the lights until 9 each evening. Closed Mondays. Helmets are required and are available to rent or purchase. Admission is $4 per day.

Funntasia Fantasy Golf (321-783-4653) 6355 N. Atlantic Avenue, Cape Canaveral 32920. Two 18-hole miniature-golf courses wind through caves, streams, tropical foliage, and waterfalls. Refreshments and an arcade are located inside. Open mornings at 10; closes Sunday through Thursday at 10 PM, Friday and Saturday at 11. For 18 holes: adults $6.75, children and seniors $5.75, children four and under free; play another 18 holes the same day for $3.

Manatee Sanctuary Park (321-868-1226) Thurm Boulevard, Cape Canaveral 32920. A 380-foot boardwalk connects three decks along the edge of the Banana River. A large picnic pavilion, walking path, 0.5-mile fitness trail with 10 exercise stations, and rest rooms are available. This is a popular spot for spotting manatees, especially in the morning. In the evening this quiet park offers a front-row seat for the sunset. Located on Thurm Boulevard, at the west end of Central Boulevard.

✍ **Port Canaveral Navigation Lock** Lock Park, at the end of Mullet Drive, Port Canaveral. In 1965 the U.S. Army Corps of Engineers built the Port Canaveral navigation lock to minimize the effect of tides and saltwater intrusion at this connection between the Atlantic Ocean and the Banana River. The size was larger than planned, to accommodate passage of the Saturn rocket stages on the way to Kennedy Space Center. Shuttle booster rockets followed the same path home after being dropped during launches and recovered from the ocean. A small park has been built alongside the lock, where you can watch boats make the transition between the waterways. The lock is equipped with a system to protect the manatees, dolphins, and pelicans that play in the contained area.

The Racquet Club of Cocoa Beach (321-868-3224) 5000 Tom Warriner Boulevard, Cocoa Beach 32931. This professional complex has 2 clay courts and 10 hard courts, including 4 lighted. Professionals are on staff, and lessons are available. The pro shop sells and rents equipment. Open daily from 8 AM; reservations are suggested. The fee for visitors is $4–8 for one-and-a-half-hour singles or two-hour doubles.

Surf & Ski Jet Ski Rentals (321-984-9986) 1872 E. Merritt Island Causeway, Merritt Island 32952. The gentle Banana River is a great place for novices and experts to take a spin on a Jet Ski. Leave from the northwest intersection of the Banana River and FL 520. No reservations are necessary, but it's a good idea to call ahead and check on availability. Jet Skis seat up to three. You must be at least 21 to rent, but children can ride with an adult. Rates are $55 for a half hour and $85 for an hour, with a discount if you have a local hotel key. Life vests and instructions are included. Open daily 10:30 AM.

Xtreme Fun at Jungle Village (321-783-0595) 8801 Astronaut Boulevard, Cape Canaveral 32920. A pink elephant outfitted in giant sunglasses stands guard over this small amusement park, with bumper cars, go-karts, laser tag, a rock-climbing wall, arcade, and miniature golf course. Open daily 10 AM. Golf $5, children three and under are free; play a second round of 18 holes the same day for $3.

FISHING See the "Recreation" chapter.

GOLF Because of Florida's wide-open spaces and great weather year-round, golf is a favorite passion for residents and visitors. The course environments are a sanctuary for wildlife and particularly popular with sandhill cranes—tall, red-headed birds that are harmless and move slowly enough that you can get a great picture. Courses are usually open daily from sunrise to early evening, and most require guests to dress in appropriate golf attire: collared shirts, no denim or tank tops, and no metal spikes. Pricing is based on 18 holes and a cart, in peak season, which usually runs December through April. Expect discounts for off hours, seniors, or residents.

Cocoa Beach Country Club (321-868-3351; www.golfcocoabeach.com) 5000 Tom Warriner Boulevard, Cocoa Beach 32931. Price: Moderate. Dotted with 17 lakes and surrounded by the Banana River, three 9-hole courses are played in three 18-hole combinations. Each hole is named for one of the many species of birds you're likely to see on the course. Also keep your eyes open for dolphins, turtles, and the occasional alligator. Amenities include public driving range, putting greens, pro shop, club and cart rental, snack bar, and restaurant.

The Savannahs (321-868-3351; www.golfthesavannahs.com) 5000 Tom Warriner Boulevard, Cocoa Beach 32931. Price: Moderate. Consider walking this flat course set on a natural savanna, amid a hardwood forest and several lakes. Water and wetlands are a daunting factor on 13 of the holes. Amenities include a public driving range and a snack bar.

PEDESTRIAN AND BICYCLE ROUTES The **FL 520 Causeway** has a wide, paved, safe path running

GREENS FEES
Inexpensive: Under $25
Moderate: $25–50
Expensive: More than $50

along its south side. Begin at the small Banana River Bridge, where you'll often see dolphins playing or feeding. Take a leisurely stroll part of the way, or a more challenging 10-mile workout if you go across the river and back.

A 1.5-mile loop through Port Canaveral runs from Jetty Park to Rodney S. Ketcham Park and to the Cove. Access is from N. Atlantic Avenue. If you want to watch the cruise ships head out or grab lunch at one of the Port restaurants, this is a nice bike ride.

Minutemen Causeway from A1A to the Banana River is a short and scenic 2-mile round trip.

SALONS AND SPAS After a day at the beach or before heading home or embarking on a cruise, consider some pampering.

Cocoa Beach Spa (321-613-2943; www.cocoabeachspa.com) 117 Barlow Avenue, Cocoa Beach 32931. After decades of experience in the spa industry, Mellisa Coates has brought her gift for healing and relaxation to Cocoa Beach. Licensed professionals provide massages, manicures and pedicures, facials, body treatments, and more. Their signature service is a copper-pot pedicure, which optimizes the balancing properties of copper, sea salts, rose petals, and lemon slices to soak, soften, and pamper your feet before finishing with a natural buff or polish. Appointments are recommended, but walk-ins are accepted if time permits. Closed Sundays.

SURFING Surf's up! The Space Coast beaches are perfect for weekend surfers and experts honing their skills. If surfing is something you've never experienced but always wanted to try, this is the perfect place to start. Coaches promise that with a small investment of time (one or two hours) and money, almost anyone at any age can ride a wave—a great photo for the mantel back home. The waters along the Cape Canaveral and Cocoa Beach coast are usually mild, and the ocean is rock-free. The beaches at Patrick Air Force Base and farther south are for more experienced surfers. Sebastian Inlet, with strong surf and challenging waves, is for experts. For reports on surf conditions and surf cam videos, go to www.surfguru.com.

WORLD CHAMPION AND BREVARD COUNTY FAVORITE SON KELLY SLATER MASTERS THE WAVES OF COCOA BEACH.
Roger Scruggs

🏄 **Cocoa Beach Surf Company Surf School** (321-868-8966; www.cocoabeachsurf.com) 4001 N. Atlantic Avenue, Cocoa Beach 32931. Learning to surf the gentle waves of Cocoa Beach is fun and easy. For novices, lessons begin in the school located across the breezeway from the Cocoa Beach Surf Company mega-store. Students begin with practice on a pop-up board until ready to move into the ocean at a spot just down the street near Shepard Park. Take private lessons or sign up with a group. Three-hour clinics start every Saturday and Sunday at 9 AM when there are enough folks registered. Summer camps are conducted from May through August. Lesson rates per student are $50 per hour for one student, $45 for two students, and $40 for groups of three or more; the Weekend clinic is $60. Soft and epoxy surfboards, skimboards, bikes, ocean kayaks, and wet suits are available to rent.

Mary Moon's Surf Art Camp (321-799-3432; www.marymoonarts.com) Cocoa Beach 32931. Renowned local artist Mary Moon has created an extraordinary experience that combines surf lessons, art projects using materials collected along the shore, and a kayak nature tour through the Thousand Islands. Each day begins with yoga and stretching by the beach. Certified instructors teach the basics of surfing and water safety. Children as young as four can participate in the five-day summer camp; adults of any age will have an equal amount of fun in three-day sessions.

CATCH A WAVE

Surfing was born in Hawaii, swept into California, flowed across America, and rolled up on the shores of Cocoa Beach. Dick Catri, already an accomplished surfer on the world stage, was ready and waiting, and became coach and mentor to a generation of teens who moved here with their family during the buildup of the space program. These new kids in town hit the waves and never looked back. They learned to surf when "hang 10" was a skill set, not a catch phrase—the art of balancing on a longboard with all 10 toes hooked around the front edge.

By the time Neil Armstrong stepped onto the lunar surface, Cocoa Beach was gaining recognition and respect from surfers around the world. Under the tutelage of Catri, homegrown athletes like Gary Propper, Mimi Monroe, and Joe Twombly were competing and winning world championships. In the workshop, sons and daughters of engineers were experimenting with foam, fiberglass, and resin to create boards that were shorter, lighter, and more flexible.

Cocoa Beach proved to be an ideal training ground. The distinctive cape jutting into the ocean creates swells along the coastal curve, with smaller and shorter waves. Surfers have to develop maneuverability and finesse to have a great ride. A good analogy might be parallel parking in a tight space. After mastering that, pulling into a parking lot spot is much easier. At Sebastian, in the south, the ocean floor contour rises about a third of a mile from the beach, and often has monster waves that challenge the experienced surfer.

Nex Generation Surf School (321-591-9577; www.nexgensurf.com) 3901 N. Atlantic Avenue, Cocoa Beach 32931. Brian Gale has been surfing since 1987 and competing since 1992. He and a team of experienced instructors offer private and group lessons, parties, and summer camps. Every session begins with a 15-minute ocean water safety and marine life awareness discussion. Participants range from as young as age four to well past retirement years. Competitive training sessions are available. Lessons are given at the Comfort Inn & Suites. Three-hour surf clinics begin every Saturday at 9 AM. Private lessons are $70 per hour; clinic $60 per person for three hours. A photographic memento of your outing can be provided for an additional charge.

Oceansports World (321-783-4088; www.oceansportsworld.com) 3220 S. Atlantic Avenue, Cocoa Beach 32931. Surfer Roy Scafidi and his wife, Pam, run this outpost on the narrowest part of the island, near the beaches of Patrick Air Force Base. Rent surfboards, kayaks (with life jackets), paddleboards, wave skis, and kiteboards. Used equipment is for sale. Lessons are available by the hour or through one of the weekly camps, held in the ocean or river near the shop.

Today Cocoa Beach is an international center of excellence for the sport. Young Kelly Slater grew up on these waves, guided by Catri, who by now was the acknowledged Godfather of east coast surfing. Slater has captured a record nine world titles during his professional career; his friends and twin brothers Damian and C. J. Hobgood are also winning competitors on the world surfing tour. Somewhere in Cocoa Beach, future champions dream of their turn in the sunshine. When word spreads that the waves are good, local teens grab their boards, paddle out toward the horizon, and wait to catch the wave.

SURFING TEAM CHAMPIONS COACHED BY LEGENDARY DICK CATRI IN 1967.

Courtesy Joe Twombly

Surfboard rental is $30 for a day; private lessons are $50 per hour.

Quiet Flight Surf Shop(321-783-1530; www.quietflight.com) 109 N. Orlando Avenue, Cocoa Beach 32931. Rent boards by the day from this shop, conveniently located just a few blocks from downtown Cocoa Beach. Private lessons are available for groups of one to three surfers. Check their Web site for daily reports on wind, tide, and wave conditions. A credit card deposit is required for all rentals. Surfboard rental is $20 for a day; private lessons are $40 per hour.

✎ **Ron Jon Surf School by Craig Carroll** (321-868-1980; www.ronjonsurf school.com) 150 E. Columbia Lane, Cocoa Beach 32931. Professional surfer Craig Carroll has been riding the waves of Cocoa Beach for 40 years and now runs this school for beginner and advanced students. Summer camps are held for students age eight and older. Private and group lessons are available. Safe, soft surfboards are used, and lessons include safety and marine-awareness instructions. Lessons begin at the school building and continue at nearby Shepard Park. Private lessons are $65 per hour. Take surfing to the next level with an intro kiteboarding lesson; $79 per hour.

SoBe Surf (321-926-6571; www.sobesurf.com) Cocoa Beach. Girard Middleton, lifelong surfer, experienced lifeguard, and one-time team chaplain for University of Miami sports is passionate about surfing, and for a decade has been instructing and coaching novices and experienced surfers in the Miami area. Now Middleton and his team have opened operations in Cocoa Beach. In addition to individual and group lessons and camps for surfers, they also are pros in the newest craze—stand-up paddleboarding. Middleton and his team give lessons on the calm Banana River, and hold clinics where students have a 20-minute orientation and then practice on their own in the water. Per person private lessons are $65 per hour/$100 for two hours for one student, $50 per hour/$80 for two hours for two or more students. Per person clinics are $40 per hour/$60 for two hours for one or two students, $30 per hour/$50 for two hours for three or more students. Discounted rates for Florida residents and active military. Equipment is included with instruction; surfboards and stand-up paddleboards are available to rent. Call for appointment.

Surfet (321-271-2225; www.surfet.com) Cocoa Beach. Monica Monslave specializes in teaching girls and women to hit the waves with confidence in programs for individuals and groups, beginner and advanced. Take a private or group class, or plan a special event like a mother-daughter session. Surfing camps for ages 6 through 18 run from May through July. Private lessons begin at $35 per hour.

✳ Green Space and Beaches

BEACHES ✎ **Cherie Down** 8492 Ridgewood Avenue, Cape Canaveral 32920. From A1A, turn left on Jackson Avenue. Turn left again on Ridgewood Avenue and travel for 5 blocks. Open: Daylight hours. Parking: Free, in a small lot; tickets are issued for parking on the grass. Lifeguards: Seasonal. Etchings of whimsical sea life lead to a ramped 200-foot boardwalk over the sand dunes and down to the beach. This small neighborhood beach park has been designed with children in mind. The clean, quiet beach is convenient if you're driving over from the Orlando area to spend a few hours by the surf. At low tide, the wide expanse of hard, flat sand is ideal for playing and building sand castles. The park has rest rooms, outdoor showers, drinking fountains, picnic pavilions, and grills. Call ahead to book a picnic shelter.

Cocoa Beach Pier (www.cocoabeachpier.com) 401 Meade Avenue, Cocoa Beach 32931. The pier is about 12 blocks north of FL 520. Open: 7–2 AM. Parking: Fees vary based on activity level. Lifeguards: Year-round. Built in 1962 as a family attraction and beachside entertainment complex, the 800-foot Cocoa Beach Pier is a historic landmark and a great spot to sun, swim, surf, fish, eat, drink, and dance. Waves break around the pilings, making the surrounding beaches popular with surfers and great for boogie boards and wave jumping. Follow the pier ramp that leads up to shops, restaurants, and bars and continues over the water to the Mai Tiki Bar. Spectators pay $1 to access the back section of the pier; $5 to fish, with gear available to rent. Amenities include beach chair and umbrella rentals, amusements, volleyball nets and equipment, and a photo booth. Check out the live surf cam on the Web site for a great preview of the area.

Fischer Park 2200 N. Atlantic Avenue, Cocoa Beach 32931. One mile south of FL 520 and A1A. Open: Daylight hours. Parking: $5 per car per day; gated lot for 120 cars. Lifeguards: Seasonal. Families love this less-hectic beach within walking distance of food outlets. Amenities at the park include picnic tables and pavilions, indoor and outdoor showers, rest rooms, and vending machines with snacks and cold drinks. The parking lot fills up quickly. The gate is automatic, and $1 or $5 bills are necessary to get through.

Jetty Park 400 E. Jetty Road, Port Canaveral 32920. Exit port entrance B and follow George King Boulevard east to the end. Open: Daylight hours; fishing pier open 24 hours. Parking: $10 per car to park for the day; $20 for resident's annual pass. Lifeguards: Year-round. The Jetty Park beach is wide and long, the sand light and silky, the water clean and cool. Parking is plentiful unless it's an especially busy time, like a space launch day or holiday weekend. The name comes from the jetty—a long stretch of rock piled high to separate the beach from the sea inlet. From the beach or the fishing pier, visitors are entertained by a parade of boat traffic—personal watercraft, fishing boats, massive cruise ships, and even the occasional military submarine. Amenities include nearby picnic pavilions, grills, and a playground; and rest rooms, changing rooms, and showers. Inquire at the nearby campground office for use of volleyball and horseshoe equipment, and beach-accessible

Lifeguard coverage is defined as Year-round (every day from 10 to 5) and Seasonal (weekends beginning in late March, every day from Memorial Day weekend to early August, and weekends again until late October). These dates are always subject to change. For more timely information call 321-637-5777. Dogs are not permitted on any Brevard County beaches.

wheelchairs. A ramp extends from the parking lot to the boardwalk, and the chairs have large pneumatic wheels that roll through the soft sand. Alcohol and pets are not permitted. A small bait and tackle shop sells basics such as sunscreen, hats, towels, and drinks. The snack bar offers burgers, hot dogs, fries, and other items, and features an inside air-conditioned dining room and a rooftop patio.

🐾 **Lori Wilson Park** 1500 N. Atlantic Avenue, Cocoa Beach 32931. The park is found 1.4 miles south of FL 520 and A1A. Open: Daylight hours. Parking: Free; two large lots are located on the north and south sides of the park. Lifeguards: Year-round. This is the beach that feels most like a park. Enjoy the playground, sand volleyball court, pavilions, picnic tables, and grills on the north side. More picnic tables and a recently opened dog park are near the south lot. Both sites have rest rooms, outdoor showers, drinking fountains, and vending machines. Almost all facilities are wheelchair accessible. This stretch of beach is perfect for swimming or celebrating a special occasion or family gathering. Parking is plentiful and free, and concessions are within walking distance. Have your picture taken next to the I DREAM OF JEANNIE LANE street sign at the entrance to the south parking lot. If it seems a little high, it's because when it was lower it was often mysteriously missing.

WELCOME TO THE BEACH!

Minutemen Causeway in Cocoa Beach East end of Minutemen Causeway, Cocoa Beach. The causeway is 2.7 miles south of FL 520 and A1A. Open: Daylight hours. Parking: Private lots and metered street parking. Lifeguards: Year-round. This popular beach spot has long been a giant magnet drawing carloads of day-trippers on weekends and hot summer days. Teens and young adults cruise to see and be seen in this retro beach town. This is the kind of beach where you lug a cooler full of food and cold beverages, spread out the blanket, and make yourself at home. Dueling bars at the end of the Minutemen Causeway ensure lots of laughter, music, and good times. (Both bars feature live music on the weekends and some weekday evenings.) Volleyball games are often in progress. Finding a parking place is a challenge, however; a few private lots offer paid spots. If you park at a meter, bring plenty of quarters and stay paid up, because patrols continuously monitor and issue tickets. There are no public amenities, but the nearby bars are easygoing about letting folks use the rest rooms. A wide variety of restaurants and food choices is available, and the more casual ones are fine with bathing-suit attire at lunch.

Patrick Air Force Base Seashore A1A, south of Cocoa Beach. Seven miles south of FL 520. Open: Daylight hours. Parking: Free; two lots. Lifeguards: None. Since 1940, U.S. military forces have maintained a base of operations south of Cocoa Beach, on a narrow strip of land between the Banana River and the Atlantic Ocean, and kept 4 miles of gorgeous, undeveloped beachfront open to the public. The coast curves a little here, providing a panoramic view of blue sky and cresting, white-tipped waves. Experienced surfers flock to this beach due to its highly desirable wave action. Two parking lots are at spots known locally as First Light and Second Light. As you head south, ignore the blinking light that's been added since the monikers were given, and you can easily find them. Amenities are about 3 miles away in downtown Cocoa Beach.

Robert P. Murkshe Memorial Park 1600 S. Atlantic Avenue, Cocoa Beach 32931. Five miles south of FL 520. Open: Daylight hours. Parking: Free; small lot. Lifeguards: Seasonal. Robert Murkshe was mayor of Cocoa Beach from 1963 to 1972 and an avid surfer. The crowds are usually sparse on this wide, sandy beach. Active waves make it a great spot for intermediate surfers. Amenities include rest rooms, an outdoor shower, and a picnic shelter. Parking and rest rooms are ADA accessible.

Shepard Park East end of FL 520 at Ocean Beach Boulevard. One block east of FL 520 and A1A. Open: Daylight hours. Parking: $7 per car weekdays; $10 weekends and holidays March through Labor Day; gated lot for 320 cars. Lifeguards: Year-round. Old-timers remember when this was a quiet beach at the end of FL 520, once the main road from the inland. Today this city park, named for astronaut Alan Shepard, is right in the middle of the action and a quick walk from shops, food outlets, and hotels. There are surf lessons and rentals for gear, and chairs and umbrellas are available on the beach or at nearby locations. The parking lot fills up by midday during busy times. Amenities include picnic tables and pavilions, indoor and outdoor showers, and rest rooms. A wheelchair-accessible boardwalk leads to the beach.

NATURE PRESERVES AND PARKS ✍ **Maritime Hammock at Lori Wilson Park** (321-868-1123; www.brevardparks.com/nature) 1500 N. Atlantic Avenue, Cocoa Beach 32931. At Lori Wilson Park, 1.5 miles south of FL 520. Open: Sunrise–dark. Admission: Free. Activities: Birding, wildlife. Located in the middle of Lori Wilson Park, this nature boardwalk offers a glimpse of one of the last undeveloped maritime hammocks at the beach. The short walk is ADA accessible, and signs identify plants and trees. Birds, butterflies, raccoons, snakes, and other small critters call the area home. Guided tours are available for groups.

Kelly Park (321-455-1380; www.brevardparks.com) 2550 N. Banana River Drive, Merritt Island 32952. Located at the south side of the Banana River, at the FL 528 and Banana River Drive exit. Open: 7 AM–dark; boat ramp 24 hours. Admission: Free. Activities: Birding, boating, windsurfing. This popular all-purpose park is a stop on the Great Florida Birding Trail and a launching point for private and commercial boats. The shallow, protected cove along the Banana River has a small natural beach and catamaran/sailboard launch, and the area has acquired international acclaim with windsurfers. A scenic area near the lagoon has pavilions seating up to 100, volleyball courts, and a playground. Groups are advised to book the pavilions in advance. The large parking lot has plenty of spots for cars and boat trailers, but it still fills up quickly on weekends. Most facilities are ADA accessible. No pets. Alcohol is restricted to posted areas.

Port Canaveral at Banana River (321-783-7831; www.portcanaveral.com/recreation) FL 528 at Cape Canaveral. Exit into the port at George King Boulevard off FL 528. Open: Varies by activity. Admission: Free, except for $10 day parking fee at Jetty Park. Activities: Birding, boating, camping, cruising, fishing. Port Canaveral is a man-made inlet connecting the Atlantic Ocean and the Banana River, and locks at the port minimize the impact of tides on the river's water level. Small recreational boats, deep-sea fishing ships, large cruise ships, and commercial and military barges all ply the waters of the busy port. Marinas and launches in the port offer boaters quick access to the ocean, and three public waterside parks host recreational facilities: Jetty Park, Freddie Patrick Park, and Rodney S. Ketcham Park. Observe posted security rules.

VISITING BOATERS LIKE THE EASY ACCESS PORT CANAVERAL PROVIDES TO THE ATLANTIC OCEAN AND THE LAGOON WATERWAYS.

Thousand Islands (321-868-3300; www.cityofcocoabeach.com) Ramp Road, Cocoa Beach 32931. From A1A, go west on Fifth Street S. Take a left on Brevard Avenue, and then turn right on Ramp Road. Open: Daylight hours. Admission: Free. Activities: Boating, fishing, paddling. Ramp Road Park or the Cocoa Beach Country Club are entry points to the Thousand Islands of Cocoa Beach, a group of about 50 unadorned mangrove islands located just south of FL 520 in the Banana River Aquatic Preserve. Shallow-water trails teem with manatees, dolphins, and birds, and paddlers will find this to be a very easy and enjoyable experience. The park has two ramps, picnic facilities, and a fishing dock. Boat and paddling tours leave from Ramp Road on weekdays; Cocoa Beach Country Club on the weekends.

✳ Lodging

HOTELS AND MOTELS Beach Island Resort (321-784-5720; www .beachislandresort.com) 1125 S. Atlantic Avenue, Cocoa Beach 32931. Price: Moderate. Wheelchair Access: No. This charming, older motel has 20 units that circle a courtyard and look directly out on the Atlantic Ocean. All the colorful rooms have one or two bedrooms, a living area, and fully equipped kitchen. Updated facilities like a hot tub, pool, and wireless Internet enhance the property. Families will enjoy this very affordable spot that is out of the mainstream but just blocks away from the restaurants and action of downtown Cocoa Beach.

♂ **Beach Place Guesthouses** (321-783-4045; www.beachplaceguest houses.com) 1445 S. Atlantic Avenue, Cocoa Beach 32931. Price: Very

Expensive. Wheelchair Access: Yes. If you've dreamed of living on the beach, this is your chance. Two motels from the 1960s have been combined and renovated in warm, tropical tones, and decorated throughout with original art. Each of the 16 one- and two-bedroom guesthouses has a separate living room and a full kitchen. Some have courtyard views, while others look out at the ocean, but every room is steps away from a quiet stretch of beach. Rocking and Adirondack chairs

---

LODGING PRICES
Inexpensive: Up to $100
Moderate: $100–150
Expensive: $150–200
Very Expensive: Over $200

HAPPY HOUR AT BEACH PLACE GUESTHOUSES.

are plentiful and inviting. Three beachside decks offer grills, tables, hammocks, and chairs so guests can take full advantage of the outdoors. There's no pool, but there are plenty of complimentary towels, beach chairs, and umbrellas—as well as volleyball, bocce ball, and croquet equipment. The residential neighborhood is minutes from restaurants and shops. Joseph Paulus and Hernando Posada have created a beautiful, cozy, and comfortable home-away-from-home. The lush beachside gardens make this a perfect setting for family reunions, weddings, and other gatherings.

✔ ☀ **Best Western Ocean Beach Hotel & Suites** (321-783-7621, 1-800-962-0028;www.bestwesterncocoa beach.com) 5600 N. Atlantic Avenue, Cocoa Beach 32931. Price: Moderate. Wheelchair Access: Yes; some rooms with roll-in shower. At the Best Western oceanfront hotel neighborhood, several buildings in shades of sunrise yellow and ocean blue provide accommodations to fit every price range, from standard rooms to oceanfront suites. Many rooms adjoin to accom-modate families and groups traveling together. Two pools, an upper-deck bar and grill, barbecue grills, benches, and gardens weave through the grounds. The newly remodeled lobby area has a sundry store and business center. A deluxe continental breakfast is part of each stay, or sample one of the many restaurants within walking distance. The Cocoa Beach Pier is next door, and the beach is close enough to hear the surf and feel the salt air. Meet the neighbors at a reception on Tuesday, Wednesday, and Thursday evenings, offering complimentary drinks and hors d'oeuvres. This hotel campus has successfully blended being conveniently located in the middle of everything with a quiet, peaceful ambience. A multi-lingual staff is available to provide personalized service. A limited number of smoking rooms are available.

Comfort Inn & Suites (321-783-2221, 1-800-247-2221; www.comfort inncocoabeach.com) 3901 N. Atlantic Avenue, Cocoa Beach 32931. Price: Moderate. Wheelchair Access: Yes. With a ballroom able to accommodate

RIDING THE GREEN WAVE

Visitors to the Space Coast can help maintain the quality of our environment by staying in a Florida-designated Green Lodging. A few years ago the state introduced a program of guidelines to encourage members of the lodging community to operate in a way that helps protect the environment and conserve resources. The response has been terrific with over 600 participating properties and more signing up every day. To receive a Green Lodging designation, hotels must meet specific goals around reusing and recycling, saving water, and improving air quality. So when you stay in a green hotel you might notice energy-efficient lighting and thermostats, a request to reuse linens, or green cleaning supplies in the housekeeping cart. Hotels that were part of the program at press time are identified at the end of their listing, but a current directory is available at www.dep.state.fl.us/greenlodging.

up to 450 guests, this hotel, centrally located in Cocoa Beach, is a popular spot for business events and receptions. Guests can choose from a standard room with two double beds, an efficiency that adds a full kitchen, or a suite with a living area, kitchen, bedroom, and private balcony or patio. A standard and efficiency can be adjoined to provide even more space for a family or group. The hotel is a short walk to the beach; the tower rooms have a great view. Guests gather in the tropical courtyard with a playground, shuffleboard courts, sand volleyball court, swimming pool, hot tub, and a snack bar and grill. At the end of the day, adults can relax in the Lagoon Lounge, while kids have fun in the adjoining game room. A host of restaurants and other conveniences are an easy walk. Smoking rooms are available.

☞ **Country Inns & Suites by Carlson** (321-784-8500, 1-888-201-1746; www .countryinns.com/capecanaveralfl) 9009 Astronaut Boulevard, Cape Canaveral 32920. Price: Moderate. Wheelchair Access: Yes. This member of the Carlson family, located close to Port Canaveral and the Beachline, has quickly found a niche among cruisers and business travelers. Every room comes with a refrigerator, microwave, and coffeemaker. Select from several different guest room options, including an in-room Jacuzzi or a second room that sleeps three children. One Executive Suite provides a huge living, dining, and kitchen area adjoining two other rooms and makes an ideal gathering spot for groups. The hotel is on the riverside of A1A, but the beach is just a few blocks away. On-site, take care of work in the 24-hour business center, or relax in the regular pool, a kids' pool with a mushroom waterfall, Jacuzzi, arcade, and health center. A complimentary hot breakfast buffet is served every morning; fresh-baked cookies are always available in the lobby. The facility has received a Green Lodging designation from the state of Florida.

Courtyard by Marriott Cocoa Beach (321-784-4800, 1-800-321-2211; www.courtyardcocoabeach.com) 3435 N. Atlantic Avenue, Cocoa Beach 32931. Price: Moderate–Expensive. Wheelchair Access: Yes. Step into the lobby and you know this is a hotel prepared to meet your needs. The high-tech lobby is a business center, information source, and gathering spot. This is just one example of how leisure guests at this oceanside hotel share in a long list of amenities designed to meet the needs of business travelers. Every room is planned for comfort and convenience, with a coffeemaker, mini refrigerator, microwave, high-speed Internet access, desk with ergonomic chair, and bathtub with spray jets. Families

EXPANSIVE RECEPTION AND BUSINESS ACTIVITY AREA AT COURTYARD BY MARRIOTT COCOA BEACH.

will appreciate the pullout sofa bed and self-serve laundry facilities. Stroll to the beach or grab lunch by the chlorine-free mineral pool. Beach chairs, umbrellas, and other beach paraphernalia are available to rent. All guests enjoy a private balcony. From east-facing rooms you can sip coffee and watch day break over the ocean, or savor a glass of wine and a panoramic sunset in the western skies over the Banana River. The restaurant serves three meals a day, including a choice of healthy dishes; room service is available during the dinner hours. This site is a multiple winner of the Chairman's Award, Marriott's most prestigious guest service recognition. The facility has received a Green Lodging designation from the state of Florida.

🐾 **Days Inn Cocoa Beach** (321-784-2550, 1-800-245-5225; www.days inncocoabeach.com) 5500 N. Atlantic Avenue, Cocoa Beach 32931. Price: Moderate. Wheelchair Access: Yes. The Days Inn brand promises a clean, comfortable room; great value; and "sunsational" service, and this conveniently located property delivers, having consistently been awarded the top honor of five sunbursts. Choose a standard room with a king or two queen beds, or efficiency with queen bed and sofa or two queens. There is a pool and sundeck, and the beach is 1 block away. Every room includes a complimentary breakfast. Smoking rooms are available.

Discovery Beach Resort (321-868-7777, 1-800-352-4874; www.discovery beachresort.com) 300 Barlow Avenue, Cocoa Beach 32931. Price: Very Expensive. Wheelchair Access: Yes. At this impressive complex, decorated with tropical turquoise touches, every spacious one-, two-, and three-bedroom apartment has a balcony and oceanfront view, as well as a full kitchen, laundry facilities, and a sleeper sofa. The ground floor is all common area and includes an expansive lobby, exercise room, library and computer area, arcade and poolroom, and sauna. Open the outside door to a pool, hot tub, and direct path to the beach, as well as tennis and basketball courts. The resort has a restaurant, and lounge; music, meals, and drinks are served poolside during busy times. The Cocoa Beach Pier is just 3 blocks south, chair and umbrella rentals are handy, and plenty of restaurants are nearby. If you need more, staff at the full-service activity desk can help. Advance deposit is required to hold reservations. The front desk is staffed from 7 AM to 11 PM. There is 24-hour security.

🐚 **Doubletree Oceanfront Hotel** (321-783-9222, 1-800-723-1026; www .cocoabeachdoubletree.com) 2080 N. Atlantic Avenue, Cocoa Beach 32931. Price: Expensive. Wheelchair Access: Yes. Welcome to one of the more luxurious hotels on the beach. Arriving guests are greeted by valets, treated to a fresh-baked chocolate chip cookie, and escorted to a spacious ocean-view room, perhaps with a private balcony. Stay on the Plaza Club level for more spacious accommodations, concierge service, and a private lounge with complimentary breakfast and evening receptions. Grab a thick, terry towel from the towel bar and relax by the pool and sundeck while enjoying music and refreshments at the bar. Dine in the elegant 3 Wishes Oceanfront Restaurant & Lounge or at one of the outside tables overlooking the beach. The hotel has private access to the beach; chairs, umbrellas, cabanas, and beach gear are available to rent. A small sundry shop has a few gift items and other essentials you may have forgotten to pack. The Shore Thing boutique provides hair braiding and corn row with beads. Guests have 24-hour access to the fitness room and business center. End your day tucked into an extra comfortable bed, with a plush-top mattress, jumbo down pillows, and high-count linens. Sweet dreams. The facility has received a Green Lodging designation from the state of Florida.

☙ Fawlty Towers Resort Motel (321-784-3870, 1-800-887-3870; www.fawltytowersresort.com) 100 E. Cocoa Beach Causeway, Cocoa Beach 32931. Price: Inexpensive. Wheelchair Access: Partial. This pastel pink building with a sky blue roof is a calm oasis right in the middle of a bustling seaside neighborhood. The property, one of the oldest at the beach, was acquired by anglophiles Paul and Terrie Hodge nearly 20 years ago and renamed for their favorite British television show. The theme continues with decorative touches of the home

country and European beers and ciders at the tiki bar. From the tiny lobby, enter into a lush courtyard with pool where guests gather for a pint or two each evening. Comfortable and clean rooms open onto the gardens. Choose a regular room with king or two double beds, an efficiency with a kitchen, or a mini-suite. Smoking rooms and on-site coin laundry are available.

♂ ☙ Four Points by Sheraton Cocoa Beach (321-783-8717, 1-866-225-0145; www.fourpoints.com/cocoa beach) 4001 N. Atlantic Avenue, Cocoa Beach 32931. Price: Moderate. Wheelchair access: Yes. Families with tweens and teens might consider riding a wave into this new, bright hotel located inside the multi-story Cocoa Beach Surf Company. In addition to the huge merchandise shop, surf rentals and lessons are available. The hotel is just 1 block away from wide beaches and great waves. Rooms are decorated in the colors of the ocean, and surf art hangs on the walls. In addition to a traditional room with one king- or two queen-sized beds, there are suites (with and without a

POOL DECK OF DOUBLETREE OCEANFRONT HOTEL.

whirlpool) that have a separate living area separated by a half-wall from the bedroom. Some accommodations overlook the surf shop, but the windows are soundproof, and the noise from shoppers and the piped music doesn't filter into the rooms. Dine at the Shark Pit Bar & Grill or grab a treat at Starbucks, both located inside the facility. The small pool is well suited to a quick dip after an afternoon spent at the beach. Take care of business with WiFi throughout the complex and a business center for guest use, and then unwind in the fitness center. Small, well-behaved pets are welcome. The facility has received a Green Lodging designation from the state of Florida.

Hampton Inn (321-799-4099, 1-877-492-3224; www.hamptoninncocoa beach.com) 3425 N. Atlantic Avenue, Cocoa Beach 32931. Price: Moderate. Wheelchair Access: Yes. The rooms are comfortable and the staff helpful at this attractive hotel conveniently located a few blocks south of FL 520

and Shepard Park. A 200-yard landscaped walkway leads directly to the beach. Standard rooms have one king or two queen-sized beds. Some add a sofa bed for extra capacity; others have a private balcony with a view of the ocean or the Banana River. Every room includes a refrigerator, microwave, and coffeemaker. Start your day with a complimentary hot breakfast buffet; room service is available for lunch and dinner. Smoking rooms are available. The facility has received a Green Lodging designation from the state of Florida.

♂ **Hilton Cocoa Beach Oceanfront** (321-799-0003, 1-800-526-2609; www.hiltoncocoabeach.com) 1550 N. Atlantic Avenue, Cocoa Beach 32931. Price: Moderate–Expensive. Wheelchair Access: Yes. Cocoa Beach's most prestigious hotel has welcomed world leaders, Oscar winners, and space superstars, and it promises roomy, comfortable accommodations and VIP hospitality for every guest at this full-service Hilton resort. The modern and bright hotel offers a standard room with city and coastline view at a surprisingly reasonable rate; or upgrade to a junior suite, or executive room with ocean view and concierge-level service. No matter what room you pick, all resort amenities are at your disposal. Every room is fitted with luxury bedding, coffee set-up, and pay-per-view movies and video games. Dine inside or by the pool at Atlantis Bar & Grill, open for all meals; room service is available from dawn to late night. Grab a chair on the largest oceanfront deck on the Space Coast and enjoy a refreshing swim, or step down the walkway to the beach and easy access to chairs, umbrella service, surfboard and boo-

OCEAN VIEW FROM THE HILTON COCOA BEACH PRESIDENTIAL SUITE.
Courtesy Hilton Cocoa Beach Oceanfront

gie board rentals, and a volleyball court. Private surf lessons can be arranged. Valet service and baggage storage, a business center, fitness room, and activity desk are also at your disposal, assuring a first-class vacation experience. A small number of smoking rooms are available. The facility has received a Green Lodging designation from the state of Florida.

Holiday Inn Express Hotel & Suites (321-868-2525, 1-888-465-4329; www.hiexpress.com/es-cocoa beach) 5575 N. Atlantic Avenue, Cocoa Beach 32931. Price: Moderate. Wheelchair Access: Yes. The location is convenient but not scenic at this recognizable property located just off A1A, within walking distance of the beach, restaurants, and a supermarket. The bright, attractive property is comfortable and clean. Choose from smoking and nonsmoking rooms. There's a small pool and most of the common amenities, such as a fitness center, complimentary breakfast bar, and a microwave and mini refrigerator in every room.

♂ The Inn at Cocoa Beach (321-799-3460, 1-800-343-5307; www.the innatcocoabeach.com) 4300 Ocean Beach Boulevard, Cocoa Beach 32931. Price: Expensive. Wheelchair Access: Yes. This European-style adult resort is perfect for a peaceful retreat or a romantic interlude. With 50 rooms, it's too big to qualify as a bed-and-breakfast, but it has all the same luxuries and amenities, and the staff works hard to make you feel like a guest in their home. Outside, one of the busiest strips of the beach is just steps away, with plenty of choices for recreation and concessions. Inside the inn, the mood is quiet and relaxed. Every room is decorated in a distinct

style with king, double, or twin beds, and many have an oceanfront view. Deluxe rooms have a private balcony and sofa sitting area; a few are Jacuzzi suites. Relax in common areas like the salon and library, or settle in a chair next to the pool and spa. A complimentary breakfast is served inside or on the patio; early evening wine and cheese on the breezeway porch. Coffee and an honor bar are always available. Be prepared for a wonderful experience. The most frequent comment in the guest book is a wish to stay another night.

♂ ✿ International Palms Resort (321-783-2271, 1-800-354-8332; www.internationalpalms.com) 1300 N. Atlantic Avenue, Cocoa Beach 32931. Price: Moderate. Wheelchair Access: Yes. Families have a blast at this full-service hotel, located directly on the beach. Previous visitors will recognize it as the space-era landmark Holiday Inn. Management changed as this guide went to publication and the new owners are beginning an extensive renovation that will update the look, refresh the rooms and furnishings, and add additional amenities like a flat-screen TV and a refrigerator and microwave in each room. The oceanfront Surfside Building will be all suites. The size and breadth of the hotel continue to make it an excellent choice for families. Choose from 500 rooms, including standard rooms, suites, two-level ocean lofts with a sitting room and kitchenette, three-room ocean villas, and accommodations that include a separate sleeping area for the kids with a TV and movie player. Captain's Grill restaurant serves all meals, there is a snack bar by the pool, or dine seasonally at Mambos Beachside Bar &

Grill. Room service is also available. Outside, enjoy the Olympic-sized pool and sundeck while the children play in a special pirate-ship pool. Other amenities include tennis and sand volleyball courts, shuffleboard, a fitness center, and a whirlpool spa. With so many choices, don't forget to head to the beach. Smoking rooms are available.

🐾 **La Quinta Inn** (321-783-2252, 1-800-795-2252; www.622.lq.com) 1275 N. Atlantic Avenue, Cocoa Beach 32931. Price: Inexpensive– Moderate. Wheelchair Access: Yes. Although this inn is on the west side of A1A and surrounded by concrete and city noise, it all fades away when you step into the spacious inner yard, with a large pool and garden, and a

MONUMENT AT LA QUINTA INN PAYS TRIBUTE TO THE ORIGINAL SEVEN ASTRO- NAUTS WHO FOUNDED THE MOTEL.

tiki bar that opens with drinks and snacks when things get busy. Start off the day with an upscale continental breakfast with hot and cold foods. Guests enjoy great service and comfortable, value-priced rooms. A traffic signal makes it easy to cross the street to the beach and Lori Wilson Park. Smoking rooms are available.

🐾 **La Quinta Inn & Suites Ocean-front** (321-784-3126, 1-800-874-7958; www.laquintacocoabeach.com) 1 Hendry Avenue, Cocoa Beach 32931. Price: Moderate–Expensive. Wheelchair Access: Yes. This tropical-themed beachfront property (previously the Oceanside Inn) is conveniently located right next door to the Cocoa Beach Pier. The rooms have been redone with attractive wood floors and a citrus green and orange décor, and each has one king or two queen beds, a refrigerator, microwave, flat-panel TV, and a private balcony. Some of the rooms face the ocean; others face the pier. Ground-floor views are obstructed, so ask for an upper floor if having a view is important. Suites and patio rooms that can accommodate larger groups are available. A complimentary continental breakfast is served each day, and a variety of restaurants are within walking distance. The hotel has a large pool and a private access boardwalk to the beach. The bilingual staff assures that every guest receives great service.

Luna Sea Bed & Breakfast Motel (321-783-0500, 1-800-586-2732; www .lunaseacocoabeach.com) 3185 N. Atlantic Avenue, Cocoa Beach 32931. Price: Inexpensive. Wheelchair Access: Partial. For more than 30 years this small, family-owned motel has provided guests with value and service. The beach is a short walk away after crossing A1A, but the location is very convenient to dining, fast food, and shops. Standard rooms are available with king or two double beds, and there are larger rooms that also come with a pullout sofa and small kitchen; some are designated as smoking rooms. Tropical landscaping surrounds the pool and the backyard garden, which feature lawn chairs and barbecues. Guests enjoy a complimentary full breakfast at the Sunrise Diner, a local favorite.

Mai Tiki Studio Apartments (321-783-6890; www.mytikistudioapts.com) 251 Minutemen Causeway, Cocoa Beach 32931. Price: Inexpensive–Moderate. Wheelchair Access: No. Experience the culture and heart of Cocoa Beach with a stay in one of these studio apartments above the famous Mai Tiki Studio & Gallery. The blue, green, and tangerine décor mirrors the vivid colors artist Wayne Coombs uses in his art. Each three-room unit is comfortable enough for an overnight or longer stay, with a king-sized bed, flat screen TV and DVD, and fully equipped kitchen. Guests are in the midst of historic downtown Cocoa Beach, and walking distance from the beach, restaurants and bars, and the golf, tennis, and pool amenities of the Cocoa Beach Country Club.

Radisson Resort at the Port (321-784-0000, 1-800-395-7046; www.radissonportcanaveral.com) 8701 Astronaut Boulevard, Cape Canaveral 32920. Price: Moderate–Expensive. Wheelchair Access: Yes. With color, design, and lush landscaping reminiscent of a tropical paradise, this luxury facility provides guests with first-class accommodations, an award-winning restaurant, and a helpful staff to make sure you enjoy your stay. The hotel is

TROPICAL GARDEN PATH AT RADISSON RESORT AT THE PORT.

minutes from the cruise ships, dining, and nighttime entertainment at Port Canaveral, and provides free shuttle service to Kennedy Space Center. Each spacious room includes a king bed or two doubles with sleep-number mattresses and plush bedding, ceiling fans, coffeemakers, microwaves, full-sized desks, and in-room movies and games. Two-room mini-suites with whirlpool tubs and a small dining table are also available. In addition to the free-form pool and waterfall, there's a children's pool, Jacuzzi, and tennis court. The Flamingo Restaurant, lounge, and poolside tiki bar provide meals and refreshments. The resort caters to groups for business, weddings, or reunions. One suite has an expansive living, dining, and kitchen area and adjoins to rooms on either side, making it a great spot for receptions or gatherings. The facility has received a Green Lodging designation from the state of Florida.

Residence Inn by Marriott (321-323-1100, 1-800-331-3131; www

EVERY UNIT AT THE RESORT ON COCOA BEACH IS A SPACIOUS APARTMENT.

.marriott.com) 8959 Astronaut Boulevard, Cape Canaveral 32920. Price: Expensive. Wheelchair Access: Yes. Families and travelers staying several days will appreciate having significantly more space at this all-suite hotel. Accommodations include a separate living, eating, and sleeping area and a fully equipped kitchen. Start each day with a complimentary hot breakfast, and relax with late-afternoon snacks and drinks on selected weekdays. While this property is not located on the beach, it is very convenient to the restaurants, clubs, and cruise ships at Port Canaveral. Jump into the eco-friendly mineral pool, soak in the Jacuzzi, or get some exercise on the multi-functional sports court or in the fitness center. The facility has received a Green Lodging designation from the state of Florida.

The Resort on Cocoa Beach (321-783-4000, 1-866-469-8222; www .theresortoncocoabeach.com) 1600 N. Atlantic Avenue, Cocoa Beach 32931. Price: Expensive. Wheelchair Access: Yes. A stay at the Resort on Cocoa Beach is not just a room for the night; it's a total vacation experience. Imagine a cruise ship anchored to land, and with bigger rooms. Two-bedroom, two-bath apartments have a full kitchen, laundry facilities, and a balcony—and host up to six guests. The complex is right on the water, and every room is oceanfront or ocean view. Leave your room, and you'll find: a super-sized swimming pool, water splash pad, an arcade, fitness center and sauna, indoor and outdoor play center for kids, basketball and tennis courts, a theater with 24-hour running movies, and—last but certainly not least—the beach! There are events for every age, including supervised activities for children ages 4 to 12. Azteca II restaurant is open for lunch on weekdays and dinner every evening. A large outdoor tiki bar provides meals and refreshments around the pool. Pack a small bag with a bathing suit and change of clothes, and use the locker room to extend your stay for a few hours on the day you check out.

Ron Jon Cape Caribe Resort (321-799-4900, 1-888-933-3030; www .ronjonresort.com) 1000 Shorewood Drive, Cape Canaveral 32920. Price: Very Expensive. Wheelchair Access: Yes. More than just a place to stay, this destination resort is a one-of-a-kind Caribbean vacation experience with more than 200 rooms available by the night or week. Choose a studio that sleeps 4, standard and deluxe one- and two-bedroom units, or the spacious three-bedroom villa that sleeps up to 12 and includes a living room, full kitchen, sitting room, separate kitchenette, laundry facilities, and a whirlpool tub. All rooms, except

for the studio, have a balcony. In addition to a beautiful, wide stretch of beach, guests have access to a slew of amenities, most at no cost. Enjoy the children's play center, theater, game room, fitness center, spa, miniature golf, tennis, basketball, shuffleboard, and special daily activities. Especially impressive is the water park with a huge pool, Lazy River ride, water-play features, and a four-story-high water-slide. The sundry shop has food, necessities, and, of course, merchandise and beach paraphernalia carrying the famous Ron Jon Surf Shop logo. Dine inside or out, from 11 AM to 10 PM, at the Ron Jon Surf Grill; a full bar is inside. All rooms, except for the studio, have a balcony, but only a few are oceanfront.

Sea Aire Motel (321-783-2461, 1-800-319-9637; www.l-n.com/seaaire) 181 N. Atlantic Avenue, Cocoa Beach 32931. Price: Inexpensive–Moderate. Wheelchair Access: Partial. For over 50 years this intimate, family-owned motel has been hosting Cocoa Beach

WATER PARK AT RON JON CAPE CARIBE RESORT.

visitors. Most of the 16 rooms front directly on the ocean. Located a block from downtown, the motel offers guests the advantage of low prices, a clean and comfortable place to stay, and amenities typical of a public beach, including rentals, restaurants, bars, and entertainment. Rooms circle around a well-kept lawn, and the beach really is just steps away. Every room includes two double beds, a fully equipped kitchenette, a small dining table, and cable TV. Boogie boards and beach toys are available for children, as well as lawn games like croquet, badminton, and horseshoes. The flowery landscape, wide yard, and oceanfront setting make this a popular spot for beach weddings. Housekeeping is self-service with fresh linens available daily.

🐾 **South Beach Inn** (321-784-3333, 1-877-546-6835; www.southbeachinn .com) 1701 S. Atlantic Avenue, Cocoa Beach 32931. Price: Inexpensive–Moderate. Wheelchair Access: No. This small, older motel is located right on the beach and is a good choice for travelers looking for less-expensive oceanfront accommodations. Each of the 18 efficiency units in this two-story building has a fully equipped kitchen and small dining area. The two-bedroom unit sleeps six. There is a sundeck and pavilion with grills, but no pool, and daily maid service is not provided. Smoking is permitted. Murkshe Park, one of the more popular surfing spots, is located right next door. Advance reservations require a minimum two-night stay.

🐾 **Surf Studio Beach Resort** (321-783-7100; www.surf-studio.com) 1801 S. Atlantic Avenue, Cocoa Beach 32931. Price: Moderate. Wheelchair

Access: Yes. Owners and siblings Greg and Gina Greenwald grew up at this small beachfront motel built by their father in 1948, and their love for the property is evident in the well-maintained and modernized facilities. Eleven ground-floor units circle around an immaculately groomed courtyard. Sundecks furnished with chairs and umbrellas sit at sand's edge and overlook the surf. Cool off with a dip in the pool or a breezy swing in a hammock. Choose an efficiency room or a one-bedroom apartment that sleeps six. Families are welcome, and many visitors have been returning for years, feeling like part of the family. This is a nonsmoking facility.

🐾 **Wakulla Suites** (321-783-2230, 1-800-992-5852; www.wakullasuites .com) 3550 N. Atlantic Avenue, Cocoa Beach 32931. Price: Expensive. Wheelchair Access: Yes. At the center of the all-suites, friendly, and comfortable hotel is a lush, lengthy courtyard landscaped with more than 100 varieties of tropical plants. Interspersed are benches, picnic tables, grills, courts for shuffleboard and sand volleyball, and pools for adults and children. A walk through the gardens is like a stroll through the neighborhood, with guests mingling, playing cards, or sharing a meal. The Polynesian motif continues in the spacious and modern units. Each includes living room, complete kitchen, and two bedrooms, one with a king bed and the other with a full and twin bed. Most accommodations circle the courtyard. A few, including those with handicap access, face the street. Others are by the ocean but without an ocean view. All guests have access to a private oceanfront deck overlooking the sand. Parking is limited, but most amenities are within walking distance, so once you find a space you may not need to move your car.

Vacation and Condo Rentals

Canaveral Towers Resort (321-783-3226, 1-877-773-2866; www.avonby thesearealty.com) 7520 Ridgewood Avenue, Cape Canaveral 32920. Price: Expensive–Very Expensive. Wheelchair Access: No. This nine-story building is the tallest on the Cape Canaveral beaches, and every unit has a direct or angled view of the ocean. The apartments are individually owned and furnished, but all are well maintained and roomy, with two or three bedrooms, two baths, a full kitchen, large living room, and sliding doors that open to a patio or balcony. A minimum stay of a week is required. No daily housekeeping service is provided, but there is a great pool and sauna, and a putting green for golf aficionados. The Cocoa Beach Country Club course is about 6 miles south. Pictures of rental units are available on the Web site.

Cape Winds Resort (321-784-4311, 1-800-248-1030; www.resortreserva tions.cc) 7400 Ridgewood Avenue, Cape Canaveral 32920. Price: Expensive–Very Expensive. Wheelchair Access: No. This upscale property, situated along the beach at the halfway point between the Cocoa Beach Pier and Port Canaveral, is an upscale condo with many hotel touches, such as daily housekeeping service and high-speed Internet access in each unit. The one- and two-bedroom units are comfortably furnished with a sleeper sofa in the living room, a bright, full-sized kitchen, and table and chairs on the oceanfront patio or balcony. Relax in the pool, hot tub, or sauna; work out on the tennis or basketball courts; or enjoy the beach right outside the door. Smoking is permitted on the balconies.

Cocoa Beach Club Condominiums (321-784-2457; www.cocoabeach club.com) 5200 Ocean Beach Boulevard #214, Cocoa Beach 32931. Price: Expensive. Wheelchair Access: Partial. The design and exterior of this 1970s property is a little dated, but

GUESTS MINGLE AT WAKULLA SUITE'S COURTYARD POOL.

the location is ideal, and Joyce Hebert, manager since opening, ensures everything is well maintained. The apartment units are roomier than newer facilities and renovated on a regular basis. The 60-foot-long pool is perfect for swimming laps. Choose from mostly two- and three-bedroom individually owned and uniquely decorated condos, some with an oceanfront setting. You can request a digital image before finalizing the booking. Credit cards are not accepted and a deposit is required to hold your reservation.

Ocean Landings Resort & Racquet Club (321-783-9430, 1-800-323-8413; www.oceanlandings.com) 900 N. Atlantic Avenue, Cocoa Beach 32931. Price: Moderate–Expensive. Wheelchair Access: Partial. This well-managed time-share resort is all about choices. Select a one- or two-bedroom unit, oceanfront or off-ocean, for a daily or weekly stay. There are two pools; four courts each for tennis and racquetball, a playground for the kids, and fitness center for adults. A daily list of social activities adds to the enjoyment. Every unit has a fully equipped kitchen and living area with a pullout couch. The off-ocean suites sleep six in the one-bedroom (two queens and the sofa) and eight in the two-bedroom (king, two queens, and the sofa). Smaller hotel-sized accommodations are available. Gregory's, a fine dining restaurant, is located at the resort, and Gregory's Comedy Club stages performances every Thursday night.

Ola Grande Condominiums (321-783-3101; www.olagrande.com) 5350 Ocean Beach Boulevard, Cocoa Beach 32931. Price: Moderate–Expensive. Wheelchair Access: No.

Ola Grande, or "big wave," is a fitting name for the cozy and surprisingly quiet property located right next door to the Cocoa Beach Pier. Two-bedroom condominiums are rented by the week or month, each with a patio or balcony overlooking the neatly trimmed lawn, like row houses in a friendly suburban locale. Individual owners furnish the units, but each is set up for a lengthy stay with a full kitchen and laundry facilities, and some permit smoking. On a warm day, head down to the beach via a private crossover, or take a refreshing dip in the pool. A deposit is required to hold your reservation; credit cards not accepted.

Royal Mansions (321-784-8484, 1-800-346-7222; www.royalmansions .com) 8600 Ridgewood Avenue, Cape Canaveral 32920. Price: Expensive. Wheelchair Access: Yes. This compound of beachside villas claims one of the best locations along the coast— a quiet strip just south of Jetty Park and an easy bike ride to the restaurants and clubs at the port. Unpack

POOLSIDE VIEW OF OCEAN AT ROYAL MANSIONS.

and settle into a one-bedroom atrium or patio unit, or splurge by treating yourself to the two-bedroom penthouse. For a premium, oceanfront units are available in each category. The condos are privately owned and individually furnished, and every one includes a fully equipped kitchen and daily housekeeping. C & W Hotel Management Company operates the property with an emphasis on hospitality and community. Join other guests around the pool, at social events, and in the clubroom for continental breakfast or a weekly wine reception. They require a minimum stay of six nights.

Seagull Beach Club (321-783-4441, 1-800-386-6732; www.seagullbeach club.com) 4440 Ocean Beach Boulevard, Cocoa Beach 32931. Price: Moderate. Wheelchair Access: Partial. This small complex, conveniently located next to Shepard Park where FL 520 meets the ocean, offers warm, homey, and affordable accommodations. The pool and deck are a little small, but they are so close to the ocean that you can almost touch the waves at high tide. Select a one- or two-bedroom unit with a separate living and dining space, and a fully equipped kitchen. The staff is friendly and works hard to make your stay enjoyable and entertaining with activities like a group lunch and bingo at the park.

✳ Where to Eat

✦ **Atlantic Ocean Grille** (321-783-7549; www.cocoabeachpier.com) 401 Meade Avenue, Cocoa Beach 32931. Price: Moderate–Expensive. Cuisine: Seafood. Meals Served: D, SB. Enjoy fine dining at the Cocoa Beach Pier. Tiered tables and glass walls ensure a panoramic view of the Atlantic Ocean in a comfortable air-conditioned environment. Dinner service begins at 5 each evening, and seafood is the star with appetizers like coconut beer shrimp and entrées such as scallops au gratin. For a more robust meal, partner seafood with chicken or steak. The Venetian chicken and shrimp with Italian herbs and spices or a grilled filet mignon with golden-fried shrimp are good selections. Their signature dessert is Pier Pleasure Bread Pudding topped with a warm buttery rum sauce. The champagne brunch begins at 10 AM on Sunday. Closed Mondays.

✦ **Atlantis Bar and Grill** (321-799-0003; www.hiltoncocoabeach.com) 1550 N. Atlantic Avenue, Cocoa Beach 32931. Price: Moderate–Expensive. Cuisine: American-Gourmet. Meals Served: B, L, D. The setting and the food are both exceptional at this oceanfront restaurant, located

Price codes are based on an appetizer, dinner entrée (or lunch if dinner is not served), and dessert, but they do not include tax, tip, or beverages.

Inexpensive: Up to $15
Moderate: $15–25
Expensive: $25–35
Very Expensive: $35 or more
The following abbreviations are used to identify what meals are served:

B: breakfast
L: lunch
D: dinner
SB: Sunday brunch

within the Hilton hotel. Dine inside, where many seats have an ocean view, or choose a table on the large outside deck and enjoy sea breezes and music with your meal. The menu is limited to the basics with steak, chicken, and seafood combined with fresh ingredients to create simple and elegant dishes. Shrimp cocktail with an orange salsa is a great appetizer to pair with a one of their dinner favorites, tenderloin filled with Boursin cheese, served with risotto, asparagus, and cherry tomatoes. Young seafood lovers can try a pint-sized grilled salmon portion with oriental vegetables. A full bar is available, and the blender is always churning out tropical fruit drinks. Reservations are recommended for groups.

Azteca Two (321-784-1188) 1600 N. Atlantic Avenue, Cocoa Beach 32931. Price: Moderate. Cuisine: Mexican. Meals Served: L (Monday through Friday), D. You don't have to be staying at the Cocoa Beach Resort to enjoy eating at their on-site Mexican restaurant, with indoor and outdoor seating. The lunch menu includes tacos and burritos, sandwiches, and the Azteca Salad, a blend of chicken, avocados, cheeses, and vegetables with a special house dressing. For dinner consider a 12-ounce steak grilled with onions and green chilies and served with a cheese enchilada, rice and beans, or the enchilada Del Mar, stuffed with crab and shrimp. The huge circular bar stocks Mexican beers and 70 varieties of tequila. Mexican décor and music add spicy flavor to a fun evening. Reservations are recommended.

Barrier Jack's (321-784-8590; www.barrierjacks.com) 410 N. Atlantic Avenue, Cocoa Beach 32931 Price: Inexpensive. Cuisine: Eclectic. Meals Served: B, L. Ahoy, matey! Look for the pirate sign near the north A1A split in Cocoa Beach and grab a table in the dining room or under the shaded breezeway of this small, casual eatery. Before coming to Cocoa Beach, Chef Jack spent time floundering off the California coast, then wandered east to the Smoky Mountains, and finally headed south. The service is friendly, the portions are large, and the food is an all-American mix of hot Tex-Mex, barbecue, seafood, and steak. For lunch try salad, soup, and a hot or cold sandwich, such as a fresh-baked hoagie topped with oysters, scallops, shrimp, fish, or catfish, along with their crispy, homemade potato chips. Youngsters can try the Pirates Planks. Closed Monday; reservations are recommended for groups.

ℱ **The Boardwalk** (321-783-7549; www.cocoabeachpier.com) 401 Meade Avenue, Cocoa Beach 32931. Price: Inexpensive–Moderate. Cuisine: American-Casual. Meals Served: L, D. Grab some lunch, take a break from the sun, and enjoy a great view. Adults and children will feel comfortable in their bathing suits at this open-air eatery and bar at the center of the Cocoa Beach Pier. Choose from burgers, fish sandwiches, wings, salads, and finger-food appetizers like crabby patties. Most weekends and some evenings, house band Dugan & Birks covers all the favorite sit-back-and-relax tunes. Complete the scene with a tropical drink like a strawberry or mango margarita.

Boston Beef and Seafood (321-784-4000; www.bostonbeefandseafood.com) 5990 N. Atlantic Avenue, Cocoa Beach 32931. Price: Inexpensive–

Moderate. Cuisine: Seafood and Beef. Meals Served: B, L, D. By land or by sea, patriot Paul Revere would have found a hearty meal at this restaurant that brings northeast flavor to the beaches of Brevard. Owner Charles Saffron is so committed to real New England seafood that several times a week he drives to the Orlando airport to pick up a new batch flown in from Boston, and then cooks it up—fresh, never frozen. Specialties are New England favorites from the sea, such as belly clams, scallops, and rich, creamy chowder thick with tender clams. Lobster rolls are a Friday night favorite with locals. For meat lovers they offer their signature slow-cooked roast beef, piled high on a bun, topped with a special barbecue sauce, and paired with crispy onion rings. This is a great stop for a hungry family. The atmosphere is casual, portions are huge, service is friendly, and the prices are reasonable. Red Sox fans will be right at home amid home-team memorabilia.

Brano's Italian Grill (321-783-6031; www.branos.net) 3680 N. Atlantic Avenue, Cocoa Beach 32931. Price: Moderate. Cuisine: Italian. Meals Served: L, D. After a day at the beach, visitors will appreciate this cool, relaxing oasis amidst the fast-food chains lining A1A near the Cocoa Beach Causeway intersection. Brano's is a family-friendly restaurant with Italian classics like antipasto salad, spaghetti and meatballs, eggplant parmigiana, and manicotti. Hearty eaters may want to try the Chef's Parade, a platter of lasagna, grilled chicken, and fettuccine Alfredo. Choose from a nice selection of Italian wines. A special room is available to accommodate large groups, but call ahead to reserve.

☃ ⸙ **Captain Ed's Tiki Bar & Grill** (321-542-6606; www.captainedstikibar andgrill.com) 1891 E. Merritt Island Causeway, Merritt Island. Price: Moderate. Cuisine: American-Casual. Meals Served: B, L, D. Captain Ed and Princess Erin invite all buccaneers in search of a good time to gather for food, music, and fun. Walking the plank at this waterside eatery will take you safely to your table on the outside deck alongside the beautiful Banana River. Watch fishermen and birds compete for the day's catch off a nearby dock. The cuisine is casual with a Caribbean twist. Start the evening with a round of tropical drinks and a table of seafood appetizers like lobster quesadillas, ahi tuna, or oysters on the half shell. They have inside dining, but outdoors is far and away the best place to be. For dessert, this family-friendly restaurant has an ice cream parlor featuring an old-fashioned banana split. Breakfast only on the weekends; closed Monday.

BRANO'S ITALIAN GRILL.

✍ **Captain J's Ocean Deck Restaurant** (321-783-1717; www.captain
js.com) 211 E. Cocoa Beach Causeway, Cocoa Beach 32931. Price: Moderate. Cuisine: Seafood and Beef.
Meals Served: L, D. The ambience,
breeze, and view are a magic combination on the upper deck of this
Cocoa Beach landmark at the corner
of the Cocoa Beach Causeway and
the Atlantic Ocean. Blue-and-white
cushioned chairs pull up to umbrella-
shaded tables, where you can enjoy a
fruity drink while deciding on your
order. For an appetizer, try oysters on
the half shell or peel-and-eat shrimp.
Pair homemade crab cakes or blackened mahi-mahi with fries for a
lunchtime sandwich, or add salad and
vegetables and enjoy as a dinner
entrée. After dark, head inside, where
a cascading fountain, plantation-style
furniture, and ceiling fans continue
the tropical effect. On the weekends,
there is live music outside on the
deck. No wheelchair access to upper
deck.

Captains Grill (321-392-1693; www
.internationalpalms.com/cocoabeach)
1300 N. Atlantic Avenue, Cocoa
Beach 32931. Price: Moderate. Cuisine: American-Gourmet. Meals
Served: B, L, D. Sun streams in
through the wide windows surrounding this bright and cheerful dining
room, which overlooks the pool at the
International Palms Resort. Tropical
green plantings landscape the deck;
tables shaded by the overhang are
perfect for outdoor dining. Enjoy a
full breakfast buffet until 11 AM.
Favorites for lunch are blackened
grouper, Buccaneer burger, and barbecue chicken salad with a marvelous
vinaigrette dressing. For dinner try
the mango mahi-mahi, sweet and sour

pork, or home-style meat loaf. Check
for daily dinner specials.

✍ **Coconuts on the Beach** (321-
784-1422; www.coconutsonthebeach
.com) 2 Minutemen Causeway, Cocoa
Beach 32931. Price: Moderate–
Expensive. Cuisine: American-Casual.
Meals Served: B (Saturday/Sunday),
L, D. Locals continually select
Coconuts as the best beach waterfront restaurant in Brevard County.
The view is phenomenal, and the
service and food are terrific. Just step
in from the beach, slip on your sandals, and head to a table on the deck.
The lunch menu has lots of sandwiches, including a Coconut's original—
blue crab on an English muffin
topped with melted cheese and Hollandaise sauce. For dinner, start with
peel-and-eat shrimp, then a tropical
entrée like a blackened mahi-mahi fillet topped with mango salsa, or the
fresh catch of the day, caught by their
own local fishing fleet and then
grilled, blackened, or jerked, and flavored with Key lime mustard sauce.
Much of the time this is a great family
restaurant where the kids enjoy the
comfortable atmosphere and watching
all the beach activity. During spring
break and summer weekends, however, the music cranks up, and a young
party crowd gathers to meet, greet,
and sample the daily drink special.

DiLorenzo's (321-784-5662; www
.dilorenzositalian.com) 8125 Canaveral Boulevard, Cape Canaveral 32920.
Price: Inexpensive–Moderate. Cuisine: Italian. Meals Served: L, D.
Luigi DiLorenzo has been the owner-
chef of this friendly, neighborhood
restaurant, the oldest in Cape
Canaveral, for over 25 years. He
learned to cook at home in Italy and
then traveled around Europe before

COCONUTS ON THE BEACH IS POPULAR FOR GREAT FOOD AND FUN SPOT TO PEOPLE-WATCH.

coming to America. Decorative murals reflect his native country. A large menu covers the familiar Italian dishes, tempting seafood, great pizza, fresh pasta, and wonderful salads suitable as entrées. The wine list includes domestic California varieties and some from Sicily and Australia. Closed Sunday. No wheelchair access in rest rooms.

Durango Steak House (321-783-9988) 5602 N. Atlantic Avenue, Cocoa Beach 32931. Price: Moderate–Expensive. Cuisine: Steakhouse. Meals Served: L, D. Named for an old mining town in Colorado, this Florida-based chain made a claim on the local dining market when it settled in a spacious, rustic facility that was the Wild West of Cocoa Beach during the space-age gold rush. Many of the interior furnishings, including the long, mahogany bar, remain from the days when astronauts, engineers, and reporters shared stories over steaks and cocktails, and photos depicting scenes from Cocoa Beach's history adorn the walls. Today, a pleasant aroma from an oak-fire grill reminds you you're hungry, and this is

the right place for a hearty meal. Entrées include chicken, fish, pork chops, and steaks in a variety of cuts and sizes. If you dare, try the 20-ounce Jesse James Porterhouse. The children's menu offers a small sirloin. The specialty of the full-service bar is a homemade mix that is the base for a rainbow of flavored margaritas. The service is exceptionally friendly; the steaks are tender and prepared just as you request. During busy times there may be a wait. Reservations are recommended for groups.

The Fat Snook (321-784-1190; www .thefatsnook.com) 2464 S. Atlantic Avenue, Cocoa Beach 32931. Price: Expensive. Cuisine: Seafood. Meals Served: D. The Fat Snook is a dining newcomer located on a narrow strip of the barrier island a little south of the beaten path. Under the guidance of owners Mona and John Foy, this intimate restaurant has quickly become the talked-about place for fresh, gourmet seafood. The décor is more flair than fancy, with bright blue and green walls and art deco furnishings. The food is exceptional and the service is attentive, so plan to linger and enjoy. Every evening they offer Catch #1 and Catch #2 specials starting with fresh, local seafood, cooked simply, blended with unexpected ingredients and spices, and presented as a work of art. Meat lovers have plenty of choices, from tender steaks to grilled breast of duck. Choose from a nice assortment of wines and ales. They make all their own desserts; the tart and tasty Key lime pie is always on the menu.

✔ Fishlips Waterfront Bar & Grill

(321-784-4533; www.fishlipswater front.com) 610 Glen Cheek Drive, Port Canaveral 32920. Price: Moderate–Expensive. Cuisine: Seafood. Meals Served: L, D, SB. Whether you dine downstairs or on the upper deck, inside or out, you can be sure of a great seat to view a parade of birds, boats, and cruise ships along the Port Canaveral waterway. Beef, chicken, pork, and vegetarian dishes are available, but the house specialty is seafood, prepared as simply as you like or presented in gourmet treats such as lobster ravioli, fettuccine Alfredo with fire crusted mahi-mahi, or sesame tuna mignon. A special menu for kids has all the traditional choices, as well as a basket of fried lobster bites. Desserts are tasty and big, especially the Brownie Overboard, which you might want to order with extra spoons to share. Stop by from 10 to 2 on Sunday for the Mimosa Brunch, which features crab cakes Benedict, an island twist on a traditional favorite. Sometimes there is live entertainment on the deck. Reservations are recommended for groups.

Flamingos at the Radisson Hotel

(321-868-6571; www.radissonport canaveral.com) 8701 Astronaut Boulevard, Cape Canaveral 32920. Price: Expensive. Cuisine: American-Gourmet. Meals Served: B, L, D, SB. The Radisson is home to an upscale restaurant that vies for the best fine-dining experience in the area. Fresh flowers on every table, and windows overlooking the pool and a garden of tropical greenery create an idyllic setting. The menu includes à la carte choices, along with specialties such as veal cutlet with sage butter and spinach, or portobello mushroom and shallots in a parmesan cream sauce. They offer seafood, steaks, and chicken simply grilled with your choice from a selection of seasonings. The extensive wine list includes domestic and imported labels. There is a gala seafood buffet every Saturday evening and a champagne brunch on Sunday. Reservations are recommended.

Florida's Seafood Bar & Grill

(321-784-0892; www.floridas-seafood.com) 480 W. Cocoa Beach Causeway, Cocoa Beach 32931. Price: Moderate–Expensive. Cuisine: Seafood. Meals Served: L, D. Crowds line up for this popular restaurant known for seasonal rock shrimp, broiled or fried, and an ocean of seafood cooked in a variety of ways. Clam chowder served in a crusty bread bowl is a meal in itself. The fish sandwich is made with a flaky whitefish and fills up the plate; the fried oyster sandwich is tasty and unusual. For dinner start with conch fritters, and then select an entrée such as the Canaveral combo, with rock shrimp, fish, scallops, medium shrimp, and a crab cake. This family-friendly restaurant offers little mates lots of seafood choices, along with fries and ice cream. Grown-ups can finish with a slice of Key lime pie. Reservations are recommended for groups.

Gregory's (321-799-2557; www
.gregorysonthebeach.com) 900 N.
Atlantic Avenue, Cocoa Beach 32931.
Price: Very Expensive. Cuisine: Steakhouse. Meals Served: D. This upscale
dining room, which shares part of the
ground floor with Ocean Landings
Resort, is the setting for an elegant
evening. Chicken and seafood are
available, but steak is the star. Gregory's serves only USDA prime beef,
hand cut and grilled to your specifica-
tions. Most of the starters are culinary
twists on seafood, such as bite-sized
portions of Maine lobster wrapped in
bacon and topped with teriyaki sauce.
For the entrée, select your favorite
cut of beef—sirloin, New York strip,
porterhouse, or filet mignon, or prime
rib served with au jus and horseradish
sauce. Pair dessert with a Gregory's
coffee flavored with Kahlúa, Baileys,
or Grand Marnier and topped with
whipped cream and a cherry. On

Thursday's, pair your dinner with a
visit upstairs to Gregory's adult-only
Comedy Club; performances at 9 PM.
Rest rooms at this facility are not
wheelchair accessible.

✦ **Grills Seafood Deck** (321-868-
2226; www.grillsseafood.com) 505
Glen Cheek Drive, Port Canaveral
32920. Price: Moderate–Expensive.
Cuisine: Seafood. Meals Served: B, L,
D. Locals and visitors mingle at this
indoor/outdoor diner anchoring the
restaurants at Port Canaveral Cove.
Start your evening watching the
cruise ships leave port and the fishing
fleets returning home. True to the
diner's name, fresh fish is marinated
and grilled (never fried) for a delicious and healthy meal, and served
with Tahiti taters, wild rice, steamed
vegetables, and crusty cheese bread.
Entrées include favorites like shrimp
scampi or the more unusual grilled
shark kabobs. Sandwiches and burg-

RELAXING AT GRILLS SEAFOOD DECK AT PORT CANAVERAL.

ers, including vegetarian versions, are available. Breakfast is served daily starting at 7. In addition to the standard fare, try a seafood omelet or lemon-seared tilapia. On weekends, there are live music and dancing on the deck. Reservations are recommended for groups.

Heidelberg Restaurant (321-783-4559; www.heidelbergcocoabeach.com) 7 N. Orlando Avenue, Cocoa Beach 32931. Price: Expensive–Very Expensive. Cuisine: European. Meals Served: L, D. More than 20 years ago, Heidi and Edmund arrived from Europe and opened a restaurant featuring classical continental dishes, including old-world favorites from Austria. This may be the only place in Brevard County where you'll find Beluga caviar, escargots bourguignonne, Wiener schnitzel, and sauerbraten on the same menu. They specialize in quality, seasoned beef fillets, served as a full-portion dinner entrée or a smaller cut in a sandwich for lunch. Breads and pastries are made from scratch each day. Meisterchef Edmund's fresh, flaky, melt-in-your-mouth apple strudel is topped with homemade vanilla ice cream. Lunch is casual and comfortable, but it's not suitable for bathing-suit attire. Dinner is served in a setting of crisp white linens, fine china, and an accompaniment of American musical standards Tuesday through Sunday evenings. This award-winning restaurant is tops in food and service. Heidi's Jazz Club is adjacent to the restaurant. Reservations are recommended for dinner.

Italian Courtyard (321-783-0413; www.italiancourtyard.com) 350 W. Cocoa Beach Causeway, Cocoa Beach 32931. Price: Moderate. Cuisine: Italian. Meals Served: L daily, D Saturday and Sunday. *La vita e bella.* Life is good at this spacious pastaria, lavishly designed to transport you to an Italian village for the evening. For two decades the DiPasquale's have prepared traditional dishes flavored with a robust blend of herbs and garlic. Families are easily accommodated, and there's a special Bambini menu with favorites like spaghetti and lasagna. For dessert try the spumoni: gelato in vanilla, strawberry, and pistachio layers. Pizza is also available, and they have a full bar. Dine indoors or on the covered outdoor patio. Reservations are recommended for groups. Wheelchair access is not available in rest rooms. *Buono appetitto!*

Izzy's Bistro (321-783-4548; www.izzysbistroflorida.com) 6615 N. Atlantic Avenue, Cape Canaveral 32920. Price: Moderate–Expensive. Cuisine: American-Gourmet. Meals Served: D. This comfortable restaurant is a good choice for a relaxing evening with friends. Izzy's escargot with Shiitake mushrooms and a garlic sauce is among several seafood appetizer choices, and their extensive selection of entrées guarantees everyone will get just what they want, like fresh herb scampi with jumbo shrimp over fettuccine, lobster pot pie, a tender filet mignon encrusted with bleu cheese, or the chili-crusted pork tenderloin. For dessert, consider sharing the rich chocolate seduction cake. On Friday and Saturday evenings they also feature a special German menu with ethnic favorites, including Wiener schnitzel with home fries and red cabbage. Beers and wines from around the world are available. Closed Sunday.

Kelsey's Pizzeria (321-783-9191) 8699 Astronaut Boulevard, Cape Canaveral 32920. Price: Moderate. Cuisine: Italian. Meals Served: L, D. A tantalizing aroma of fresh ingredients steeped in garlic and Italian spices fills the dining room. The full menu offers soups, salads, pizzas, calzone, and a variety of pastas. The Tuscan bean soup is a hearty and robust starter. Penne Gorgonzola has sautéed mushrooms, Roma tomatoes, grilled chicken strips, garlic, and penne pasta tossed in a creamy Gorgonzola sauce. Portions are generous; share a pizza and Greek salad. Families with small children will enjoy the casual environment and friendly service. Reservations are recommended for groups.

La Fiesta (321-783-7755; www.la fiestamexicanrest.com) 7802 N. Atlantic Avenue, Cape Canaveral 32920. Price: Inexpensive–Moderate. Cuisine: Mexican. Meals Served: L, D. If buildings could talk, this landmark restaurant would tell tales of astronauts and engineers lingering over a morning cup of coffee, sketching out rocket telemetry on the back of a napkin. Nearly 50 years later, the all-American Moon Hut has been transformed into a popular eatery featuring zesty Mexican cuisine, including enchiladas, tacos, and burrito combo plates, or sizzling steak, chicken, vegetable, or shrimp fajitas served with rice and refried beans. For dessert that is *muy bueno,* try the Bunuelos, a deep-fried tortilla topped with honey and cinnamon. The memories remain, captured in photos and mission badges adorning the walls.

⨍ Lobster Shanty & Wharfside (321-783-1350; www.cocoabeach lobstershanty.com) 2200 S. Orlando Avenue, Cocoa Beach 32931. Price: Moderate. Cuisine: Seafood. Meals Served: L, D. This restaurant is one of the few on the eastern shore of the Banana River, and patrons enjoy a great sunset view along with excellent seafood, good prices, and efficient service. Kids of all ages enjoy feeding the fish at the entrance pond or off the dock. Dine inside or by the river. Every table gets piping hot, crispy hush puppies dusted with powdered sugar. Daily seafood specials always include several seasonal fish entrées cooked almost any way you like— grilled, barbecued, blackened, or Jamaican jerked. The long, impressive salad bar can be the main course or accompany your meal. Save room for dessert; maybe the turtle cheesecake. Reservations are recommended.

⨍ Marlins Good Times Bar and Grill (321-783-7549; www.cocoa beachpier.com) 401 Meade Avenue, Cocoa Beach 32931. Price: Moderate–Expensive. Cuisine: American-Casual. Meals Served: L, D. Surfing memorabilia and marine décor line the walls and hang from the ceiling of this restaurant anchored about halfway down the Cocoa Beach Pier. Photographs on the wall and videos on the televisions are topped only by the continuous surfing action on the waves just outside your table window. Enjoy the casual setting and a relaxed meal featuring burgers, sandwiches, and wings. Main Sail dinners include grilled salmon and lemon pepper grouper, and are served with a salad, rice, and rolls. Children can select from the Minnow's Menu. For a sweet treat, try the Pier Pleasure bread pudding, topped with a buttery rum sauce and whipped cream. A full bar can serve up a beer or a frozen and fruity beach drink.

✦ **Milliken's Reef** (321-783-0100; www.millikensreef.com) 683 Dave Nisbet Drive, Port Canaveral 32920. Price: Expensive–Very Expensive. Cuisine: Seafood. Meals Served: L, D. The sunset yellow building along the Port Canaveral canal is a beacon inviting diners, partiers, and families to stop by for fun and food. Milliken's Reef is an eating, drinking, and entertainment complex, with a large, comfortable indoor restaurant, a wrap-around deck, and a sandy, man-made beach. Inside, dinner patrons can chat while listening to familiar tunes played on the piano. Outside, the party rocks with bikini fashion shows, sports contests in the sand, and music from the tiki bar. Everybody is treated to great seafood cooked to order. For an appetizer, dig into fresh,

ENJOY DINNER AND DRINKS AT MILLIKEN'S AT PORT CANAVERAL.

steamed littleneck clams, or try the clams casino, baked with garlic butter, bacon, bread crumbs, and topped with cheese. Order the fresh catch of the day broiled, blackened, or grilled, or choose the snapper Hemingway, Parmesan crusted, sautéed, and topped with jumbo lump crabmeat and shallots. Children's meals are available, along with smaller-sized portions of their best entrées offered at a reduced price for seniors. Most evenings, those arriving by 4 PM will start the evening watching a parade of departing cruise ships. Granddaddy Asburn Milliken, who long ago opened a small oyster house in North Carolina, would be proud to see his legacy continued in such grand style.

Oh Shucks Seafood Bar (321-783-7549; www.cocoabeachpier.com) 401 Meade Avenue, Cocoa Beach 32931. Price: Inexpensive–Moderate. Cuisine: Seafood. Meals Served: L, D. Relax in this open-air, bathing-suit-casual restaurant and bar situated right at sea and sand level at the Cocoa Beach Pier. Grab a stool and order your favorite beach drink, maybe a tropical breeze blend of banana, strawberry, and Midori, or gather the family at a table and choose from a full menu of sandwiches and seafood. As you might guess, the specialty of the house is oysters, raw or steamed. Kids will enjoy the outdoor atmosphere during the day, but their menu choices are limited.

Pig & Whistle English Pub & Restaurant (321-799-0724) 240 N. Orlando Avenue, Cocoa Beach 32931. Price: Inexpensive. Cuisine: European. Meals Served: L, D. Visitors may feel a little disoriented when they pass a quaint wood cottage along beachside A1A. This little bit of England in Cocoa Beach has been a favorite of locals for years. Hearty food like fish and chips, Shepherd's pie, and all-American burgers is served up along with sport broadcasts on TV screens everywhere you look. Doors open at 8 AM on weekdays and 10 AM on Saturday for fans in search of a good seat for the game, or wanting to catch a soccer match on Europe-time. They have a full liquor bar with lots of brew on tap or bottled, and an outside smoking patio with more televisions.

Roberto's Little Havana (321-784-1868; www.robertoslittlehavana.com) 26 N. Orlando Avenue, Cocoa Beach 32931. Price: Moderate. Cuisine: Caribbean/Cuban. Meals Served: B, L, D. When Cuban native Roberto came to Cocoa Beach decades ago, he brought the taste of the island with him. All his recipes are original and prepared using traditional methods. A large painting of the beautiful Havana harbor, called *The Malecon*, hangs in the dining room, and copies of a local Spanish paper, *La Voz Latina en la Florida*, are available in a stand near the front door. Breakfast favorites, along with eggs, include the *plantanos muduros* (sweet plantains) and chorizo (Cuban sausage). Lunch patrons like *sandwiche de ropa vieja*, loosely translated as "old clothes" but actually spicy shredded beef on Cuban bread. The dinner menu offers *camarones enchilados*, shrimp Creole-seasoned with garlic, onions, green peppers, and spices. Other dishes feature *pollo, carnes*, and *pescados y mariscos* (chicken, beef, and seafood). Locals agree with *The New York Times*, which cited Roberto's as one of Florida's best local spots. Closed for dinner on Monday.

Ron Jon Surf Grill (321-328-2830; www.ronjonresort.com) 1000 Shorewood Drive, Cape Canaveral 32920. Price: Expensive. Cuisine: Seafood and Beef. Meals Served: L, D. Rattan chairs with warm coral-striped cushions make for an inviting setting at this tropical restaurant inside the lively Ron Jon Cape Caribe Resort. Dine inside or out on the pool deck, landscaped with lush greenery and overlooking the water park, where music is often playing. Menu selections are limited but varied. A bowl of the exceptional Atlantic Coast seafood chowder is a good start, followed by a large salad with chicken or shrimp, a pizza and house salad, or The Burger, 8 ounces of sirloin topped with just about everything and served with fries or onion rings, slaw or salad. Dinner entrées include pasta dishes such as citrus shrimp fettuccine, filet mignon, baked Florida haddock, and baby back ribs smoked in a special cola barbecue sauce. This is a family resort, and there are several choices on the children's menu, although most are the usual fare. Adventurous youngsters might prefer splitting an adult entrée. A large indoor bar is a great spot to chat or watch a game while waiting for others in your party. No bathing suits, please. Reservations are recommended.

ⴼ Rusty's Seafood & Oyster Bar (321-783-2033; www.rustysseafood.com) 628 Glen Cheek Drive, Port Canaveral 32920. Price: Moderate. Cuisine: Seafood. Meals Served: L, D. Rusty's is a fun and pleasantly crowded family restaurant at Port Canaveral Cove. Every chair has a great view of the water, whether it's a stool at the oyster bar, a table in the dining room, or outside on the waterfront patio.

Fishing captains and crew stop here, so you might hear some entertaining fish tales. The menu offers plenty of options for landlubbers, but the main course is seafood. From the oyster bar, get buried treasures of clams, mussels, or oysters by the bucket (raw or steamed). Baskets come with a generous portion of fish, shrimp, clam strips, fried oysters, or chicken tenders, along with sides of fries and slaw. Pair an appetizer of yummy, gooey Gorgonzola bread with a salad that includes shrimp, scallops, grouper, or tuna. At the end of the menu, X marks the spot for great treasure, a baked fudge brownie à la mode. Or finish the meal with Mississippi Mud Pie. Music is usually playing, and the drinks are always cold and refreshing after a hot day on the boat or at the beach. Reservations are recommended for groups.

Shark Pit Bar and Grill (321-868-8952; www.cocoabeachsurf.com) 4001 N. Atlantic Avenue, Cocoa Beach 32931. Price: Moderate–Expensive. Cuisine: Eclectic. Meals Served: B (Saturday and Sunday), L, D. Guests at this restaurant located inside the Cocoa Beach Surf Company complex are surrounded by a wall of falling water along one wall and the centerpiece 5,600-gallon aquarium stocked with tropical fish and small sharks on the other. The restaurant name comes from a rumored secret wave break along the east coast—popular with surfers and sharks. The menu offers a variety of tasty and well-prepared items. Crusty and flavorful pizza is cooked in the open brick oven in the corner. Salads, sandwiches, burgers, fish tacos, and entrées such as bourbon-glazed pork chops and baby back ribs complete the choices. Serving

sizes are large, and the staff easily accommodates patrons who choose to share an entrée. The junior surfer menu has all the usual options; vegetarians will enjoy the grilled vegetable salad with a balsamic glaze dressing. While you're finishing a slice of Key lime pie or tropical guava cheesecake, check out the daily surf report on your cell at 321-868-8967. Open until midnight on weekends with a limited "Late Night Feeding Frenzy" menu. Reservations are recommended for groups.

Siam Orchid (321-783-4545; www.siamorchidmelbourne.net) 1275 N. Atlantic Avenue, Cocoa Beach 32931. Price: Moderate. Cuisine: Thai/Japanese. Meals Served: L, D. Siam Orchid is the restaurant that locals recom-

THE AQUARIUM AT SHARK PIT IS A GREAT PLACE TO POSE FOR A PHOTO.

mend for great Thai and Japanese cuisine, served in an authentic setting where diners choose from a seat at the sushi bar, traditional low tables and pillows, or full-sized table and chairs. The six-page menu is almost overwhelming and offers everything you might imagine, à la carte or in a variety of recommended combinations. Dishes are as beautiful as they are tasty, presented as delicate works of art, and decorated with a small flower. The bar carries a full line of imported beers and sake-based mixtures by the glass or bottle. The staff is happy to answer questions and help you make a good choice. Closed Sunday for lunch.

Silvestro's (321-783-4853; www.silvestros.com) 2039 N. Atlantic Avenue, Cocoa Beach 32931. Price: Very Expensive. Cuisine: Italian. Meals Served: D. A native of Rome, Chef Silvestro Antonioli learned the joy of cooking from his mother, and later he developed his craft at the legendary Il Pasticcio in Savannah, Georgia. The elegant, simple dining room is set with fresh flowers, crisp linens, sparkling glassware, and gleaming silverware. Romantics might start with the antipasti Italiani, a meat, cheese, and vegetable appetizer-built-for-two. Main courses always include a specially prepared fresh catch of the day, along with menu standards like grilled rack of lamb, veal scaloppini, or the abundant Zuppa di Pesce, a combination of mussels, shrimp, clams, scallops, and the fresh catch served in a savory seafood broth. *Florida Today* gave this authentic Italian restaurant its highest rating. Their location in the Banana River Square strip center is unimpressive, but the gourmet creations and exceptional service make

AWARD-WINNING CHEF SILVESTRO IS PASSIONATE ABOUT COOKING!

this a good choice for an extra-special occasion. Reservations are recommended.

Simply Delicious Café and Bakery (321-783-2012) 125 N. Orlando Avenue, Cocoa Beach 32931. Price: Inexpensive. Cuisine: American-Casual. Meals Served: B, L, SB. In 2001, Chie and Larry Wahl converted a cozy Cocoa Beach cottage into a whimsical gathering spot with citrus-colored walls and glass bottles on a mantle atop a blue-and-white fireplace. Chie, originally from Japan, greets the guests; Larry is an experienced chef. For breakfast try thick slabs of French toast topped with strawberries, bananas, chocolate chips, or a pecan-apple glaze. Quiche and soup are standard menu items, but the selections change each day. Either goes well with a raspberry or peach iced tea. Light eaters can mix a flavorful soup, salad, or half sandwich stuffed with fresh fixings piled high on fresh-baked bread. An abundant assortment of pastries from the front display makes for a difficult dessert decision. Consider having one on the spot and taking another home for later. Children are welcome, but because the tables are close together, they might disturb other diners if they get restless. Closed Monday; reservations are recommended for groups.

Slow and Low Barbeque Bar & Grill (321-783-6199; www.slowand lowbarbeque.com) 306 N. Orlando Avenue, Cocoa Beach 32931. Price: Moderate. Cuisine: Barbecue. Meals Served: L, D. Dine indoors or outside on the covered patio while you enjoy slow-cooked, hickory-smoked pork, chicken, beef, and turkey. Ribs cooked St. Louis style nearly fall off the bone. The specialty sandwiches are delicious, and messy, especially the Low Down and Dirty, with pork, onions, and green peppers drenched in a sweet sauce. Select from a list of sides, the best of which may be the sweet potato fries. If there's room left for dessert, the peanut butter pie in an Oreo cookie crust is Southern sweetness on a plate. Take note of a small plaque near the front door: This building was the site of the first doctor's office in Cocoa Beach. Weekend partiers can choose from a limited menu served on the patio until 2 AM. Reservations are recommended for groups.

The Sunrise Diner (321-783-5647) 365 W. Cocoa Beach Causeway, Cocoa Beach 32931. Price: Inexpensive. Cuisine: American/Greek. Meals Served: B, L, D. This landmark diner, previously called the Ranch House, has endured through the decades with good cooking, fast service, and

fair prices. Slip into a 1950s-style vinyl-upholstered booth or onto a counter barstool, listen to oldies on the jukebox, and sip a cup of coffee while you check out the menu. The décor is minimal, and the food, served from sunrise to sunset daily, is simple and hearty. The dinner menu features Greek entrées, salads, Italian dishes, and seafood. No wheelchair access in rest rooms.

⨍ Sunset Café Waterfront Bar & Grill (321-783-8485; www.sunset waterfrontcafeandbar.com) 500 W. Cocoa Beach Causeway, Cocoa Beach 32931. Price: Moderate. Cuisine: American-Casual. Meals Served: L, D. This aptly named eatery is right at the Cocoa Beach side of the Banana River at the start of the Cocoa Beach Causeway. From the spacious waterside deck or down on the docks, diners can watch boaters and dolphins pass through the channel. Pelicans dive for dinner as you savor yours, delivered right to your table. As the day ends, crowds gather at this ideal spot to share a drink and enjoy musical entertainment. The ringing of a bell calls attention to the prime time attraction in the western sky, and guests bid farewell to the sun in homage to an ancient Roman ritual. For dinner try a cornucopia of seafood, including Florida grouper, mahi-mahi, shrimp, scallops, flounder, or snow crab legs. Chicken and beef are other menu choices, as well as sandwiches, salads, and burgers.

The Surf Bar and Grill (321-783-2401; www.thesurfbarandgrill.com) 2 S. Atlantic Avenue, Cocoa Beach 32931. Price: Expensive. Cuisine: Seafood and Beef. Meals Served: L, D. Pull open the large oak door and step into a time capsule of Cocoa

WATERFRONT DINING AT SUNSET CAFÉ.

Beach history. Since 1948, the Surf Bar and Grill (formerly Bernard's Surf) has been a favorite spot for locals and the fine-dining place recommended to visitors. In the heyday of the Apollo program, astronauts, media, and visiting celebrities gathered here to savor steaks that were large and rare, and linger over brandy and a cigar. Favorites still include appetizers such as shrimp cocktail and oysters on the half shell. Caesar salad is prepared with great flourish right at your table. Fresh seafood and tender cuts of meat are presented in entrées that include bleu-cheese-crusted filet mignon and Adriatic pasta with scallops, mussels, jumbo shrimp, and artichoke hearts in a basil and garlic sauce. Complement your meal with a selection from the extensive wine list. Save room for Bananas Foster Flambé, a specialty of the house. For more casual dining, order sandwiches and salads, or grab a spot at Shuckleberry Fin's Oyster Bar. The large mahogany bar in the lounge has a history all its own: Before there was a bank in town, space workers stopped here to cash their paychecks. That's no longer the case, but one tradition remains. ANYONE HAVING A DRINK IN THE LOUNGE DURING THE TIME OF A LAUNCH FROM THE CAPE WILL RECEIVE A FREE DRINK, promises the now-fading sign on the wall. Reservations are recommended for dinner. Closed Sunday.

Three Wishes (321-783-9222; www.cocoabeachdoubletree.com) 2080 N. Atlantic Avenue, Cocoa Beach 32931. Price: Expensive–Very Expensive. Cuisine: American-Gourmet. Meals Served: B, L, D. Enjoy a skillet breakfast such as the garden frittata, a light salad or sandwich for lunch, and fine dining in the evening at this beachside restaurant at the Doubletree Hotel. It has a panoramic view of the Atlantic whitecaps just beyond the dunes. Start dinner with toasted ravioli and fried calamari, and then choose from among gourmet seafood entrées or the daily market catch, broiled, blackened, or grilled. For a meat selection, consider the Caribbean glazed pork chops or sautéed chicken with spiced rum and a tropical fruit salsa. They have an extensive wine list and an assortment of themed beach drinks, including the infamous Florida Hurricane. A trademark dessert is bananas Foster, served in a chocolate-chip cookie bowl. A breakfast buffet is served on the weekend. Reservations are recommended.

Yen-Yen (321-783-9512; www.yenyen chinesecuisine.com) 2 N. Atlantic Avenue, Cocoa Beach 32931. Price: Moderate–Expensive. Cuisine: Asian. Meals Served: L, D. Original Asian artwork surrounds tables draped in crisp white linens at this upscale restaurant that serves gourmet Chinese cuisine. Snow-white prawns, fresh seafood, and sides, like pineapple-fried rice, are among their signature dishes. Crispy egg rolls are stuffed with tasty meat and vegetables, and are much larger than the typical Chinese take-out version. In addition to expected choices like Moo goo gai pan and chicken with broccoli and cashews, they will also prepare Peking or Beijing duck for those who call in advance. Service is sometimes a little slow, but each order is handled with care. A well-stocked bar can handle your drink order. Closed Monday; reservations are recommended for dinner.

Zachary's Family Restaurant (321-784-9007; www.zacharysrestaurant .com) 8799 Astronaut Boulevard, Cape Canaveral 32920. Price: Moderate. Cuisine: American/Greek. Meals Served: B, L, D. A picture of the Acropolis on the cover of the menu sets the tone for the Greek recipes. Breakfast, served until 3 in the afternoon for late risers, features traditional dishes, as well as ethnic touches like a feta cheese, spinach, and tomato omelet. For lunch, they have sandwiches, salads, and pork, beef, and chicken gyros. Traditional Greek dishes dominate the dinner menu. If they all sound good, try the Mezedakie, a combination of lamb chops, souvlaki, stuffed grape leaves, spinach pie, cheese pie, and tzatziki (cucumber) sauce. The beer and wine list includes Greek varieties when available.

CAFÉS AND COFFEE SHOPS

While leisurely dining is part of the vacation experience, sometimes you want something quick and easy. Local venues provide more variety and healthier alternatives than the fast-food chains, and are great choices for coffee and a light breakfast, a quick meal, or fixings packed to go for a picnic or to take back to your hotel while the little ones wind down from a day in the sun and surf.

The Art of Coffee (321-783-0626) 2053 N. Atlantic Avenue, Banana River Square Plaza, Cocoa Beach 32931. Paintings and pottery from local artists provide a colorful canvas for this welcome corner café. Sip a cappuccino or espresso, along with

ENJOY A LATTE AND NEWSPAPER AT THE ART OF COFFEE.

light breakfast or lunch. The doors may close early on weekends if the surf's up.

The Bald Strawberry Coffee Shop & Bakery (321-208-0559) 6811 N. Atlantic Avenue, Cape Canaveral 32920. Linda Lopez and her family prepare decorative and delicious pastries, cookies, breads, and other delicacies, including offerings with an international flair, like Irish soda bread in March. Everything is fresh-baked with no preservatives, and many selections, including the doggie treats, are gluten-free. Grab-and-go or relax in the Florida Room, Zen Room, or Record Room where guests pick what they want to hear from an assortment of vinyl oldies. Works of local artists are on display; open mike nights held for budding musicians. Open at 6 AM, closed Mondays.

BunJava Coffee Shop (321-473-4352) 811 N. Atlantic Avenue, Cocoa Beach 32931. Owner Janie Lowing invites you to catch up on email, read the morning paper, visit with friends, or grab a book off the shelf and relax while enjoying coffees, smoothies, bagels and baked goods, sandwiches, and wraps in this community café.

The Green Room Café (321-868-0203) 222 N. 1st Street, Cocoa Beach 32931. The Acai berry is the star at this organic café dedicated to tasty and healthy food. Along with sandwiches, salads, and wraps, the specialty of the house is the high-nutrient Acai Bowl, blended into a soft fruit mixture and topped with granola and honey. Many of the sandwiches, wraps, and salads are vegetarian, vegan, wheat, and gluten-free. Pause for a Bowl of Soul, Mexican coffee served in a heavy, handle-free bowl to

encourage the drinker to slow down and savor the experience.

Juice N Java (321-784-4044) 75 N. Orlando Avenue, Cocoa Beach 32931. Sit at a table or take your newspaper to a comfortable chair or sofa, and savor a really good cup of fresh roasted coffee with a pastry, bagel, or egg burrito. They open at 6 AM weekdays; 7:30 AM on the weekends.

The New Habit (321-784-6646) 3 N. Atlantic Avenue, Cocoa Beach 32931. Before healthy eating was so popular, Connie, the owner, was mixing natural ingredients into salads, sandwiches, smoothies, and specialties such as spinach pie or a black bean enchilada. Flavored fat-free and sugar-free frozen yogurt is a specialty of this small shop located just steps from the beach ramp at the end of the Minutemen Causeway. Eat in or grab to-go for a picnic on the beach.

Oceanside Cafe (321-868-0088) 6710 N. Atlantic Avenue, Cape Canaveral 32920. This casual diner

INDULGE IN A TASTY AND HEALTHY TREAT AT NEW HABIT.

located along A1A is a convenient stop for a quick meal. They open at 6 for breakfast and carry one of the best assortments of bagels on the beach. Lunch includes sandwiches and salads; Thai cuisine for dinner.

Starbucks (321-868-8950) 811 N. Atlantic Avenue, Cocoa Beach 32931. Feed your passion for your favorite flavored latte–skinny, no whip; you know the drill, and so do the baristas, who will have you quickly on your way, coffee in hand. It's part of the Four Points by Sheraton and is open daily from 6 AM until late evening. You can use short-term parking at the rear and enter through the lobby, or walk in via the separate front door.

ICE CREAM AND SWEET TREATS

Dairy Queen (321-784-8787) 3690 N. Atlantic Avenue, Cocoa Beach 32931. Smooth, cold soft ice cream is just the thing on a hot beach day. Walk over to this longtime favorite for a cone or shake, a specialty such as the Peanut Buster Parfait, or a banana split.

Harvey's Indian River Groves (321-783-8640) 3811 N. Atlantic Avenue, Cocoa Beach 32931. The Indian River Lagoon area has produced world-famous sweet and juicy citrus for more than 150 years. Take some fresh oranges, grapefruits, or other selections home during the season. Open late October through late April/early May.

Ice Cream Junction & Oriental Food Mart (321-799-2714) 214 W. Cocoa Beach Causeway, Cocoa Beach 32931. This colorful, friendly shop has an unusual name, but the ice cream is just what you're looking for, rich and creamy with a wide assortment of flavors and toppings. Take it to go, or sit and enjoy Karaoke and browse the array of oriental food products.

The New Habit Frozen Yogurt Bar (321-784-6646) 3 N. Atlantic Avenue, Cocoa Beach 32931. On busy days a line forms inside this landmark near the corner of A1A and Minutemen Causeway where locals know you'll find cones and cups of tasty, refreshing, and healthy fat-free, sugar-free frozen yogurt blended with fruit and other flavors.

Petite Bakery (321-473-4352) 4001 N. Atlantic Avenue, Cocoa Beach 32931. This small bakery located inside BunJava Café is big on rich and flavorful brownies, cookies, cupcakes, and baked goods.

LATE-NIGHT FOOD AND FUEL

The beach communities get quiet late in the evening, especially on weekdays. Many bars remain open until 2 AM and will serve some food. Here are some other locations where food, snacks, and gas are available 24 hours a day.

Cape Canaveral

Circle K (gas and groceries) 7700 N. Atlantic Avenue; 321-799-2173.

McDonald's Restaurant (fast food, 24-hour drive-through), 8780 Astronaut Boulevard; 321-784-5520.

Race Trac (gas and groceries) 8899 Astronaut Boulevard; 321-784-3444.

Cocoa Beach

Denny's Restaurant (food) 1245 N. Atlantic Avenue; 321-783-4005.

Dunkin Donuts (fast food) 5810 N. Atlantic Avenue; 321-784-0426.

McDonald's Restaurant (fast food/drive-through) 3920 N. Atlantic Avenue; 321-783-3450.

7-11 Food Stores (groceries) 190 E. Cocoa Beach Causeway; 321-784-3267.

PIZZERIAS AND QUICK STOPS

A N.Y. Pizza House (321-868-7177) 281 W. Cocoa Beach Causeway, Cocoa Beach 32931. The ovens are always busy and the food moves fast at this big-city option for pizza, calzone, and subs. Order from the menu and then eat in or take to go. They always have some pre-prepared, single-serving options ready to heat and pack up in a hurry.

Anacapri Pizzeria (321-868-2266) 605 N. Atlantic Avenue, Cocoa Beach 32931. This charming restaurant offers crispy thin-crust pizza, baked to perfection and loaded with cheese, along with sandwiches, pasta dishes, and warm-from-the-oven yeast rolls dripping in butter.

Cazoni's Pizza (321-783-1112) 6290 N. Atlantic Avenue, Cape Canaveral 32920. Choose from pizza, 23 subs on fresh-baked bread, or their specialty— a Calzoni, a baked pizza sandwich that is part calzone and part stromboli.

The Cape Codder (321-868-2500) 2690 S. Atlantic Avenue, Cocoa Beach 32931. Once upon a time, a transplanted Boston businessman grew very hungry for fresh seafood from home, so he opened a restaurant. Enjoy fresh, imported Ipswich clams; full-bellied steamers, oysters, shrimp, and chowder; and Maine "lobstah" in rolls or salad.

Juice N Java (321-784-4044) 75 N. Orlando Avenue, Cocoa Beach 32931. Drop in at this neighborhood eatery for coffee drinks and healthful smoothies. Grilled sandwiches and deli wraps are made to order. Fresh bagels are served with cream cheese and salmon, or egg and cheese, plus meats, peppers, and onion. They stay open until 10 PM on Friday serving appetizers, desserts, wine, and beer. Pets are welcome at outdoor seating.

Kim Bo (321-868-0188) 5675 N. Atlantic Avenue, Cornerstone Plaza, Cocoa Beach 32931. Wide selections of Chinese foods are prepared at this small storefront, geared mostly for take-out. No MSG.

Papa Vito's (321-784-0050) 6200 N. Atlantic Avenue, Cocoa Beach 32931. This family-run restaurant is where locals stop for pizza. The dining rooms are casual, comfortable, and nicely decorated. Pizza is the star and can be ordered by the slice as well as a whole pie. A pasta dish paired with antipasto salad and Papa's zesty bread makes a delicious dinner that is easy on the pocketbook.

Sonny's Real Pit Bar-B-Que (321-868-1000) 2005 N. Atlantic Avenue, Cocoa Beach 32931. This chain began decades ago in a small shack just a few blocks from the University of Florida campus in Gainesville and quickly spread across the state. This Banana River Square location serves ribs, pork, beef, and chicken with a great selection of sides.

Taco City (321-784-1475) 2955 S. Atlantic Avenue, Cocoa Beach 32931. This roadside diner with a casual western décor has been part of the southern Cocoa Beach landscape for years. Order at the counter and take your enchiladas, tostadas, or quesadillas to go or eat in. Wine and beer are available. Closed Sunday.

Thai Basil Takeout Cuisine (321-868-8262) 675 N. Atlantic Avenue, Cocoa Beach 32931. Appetizers, soups, salads, curry, noodles, fried rice, and dinner entrées are all available for take-out.

Thai Thai Restaurant & Sushi Bar (321-784-1561) 8660 Astronaut Boulevard, Cape Canaveral 32920. The smiling fish sign invites guests to dine in or take out at this convenient spot featuring Thai and Japanese food. The menu is extensive and includes options for children.

SPECIALTY MARKETS Canaveral Meats and Deli (321-799-2875) 8109 Canaveral Boulevard, Cape Canaveral 32920. This small store off N. Atlantic Avenue is a one-stop shop for prepared salads, soups, and sandwiches; cold cuts and cheeses; and a sampling of grocery and produce products. The location is ideal for visitors staying in a Cape Canaveral vacation rental.

Deli at Publix Supermarket (321-783-1014) 5645 N. Atlantic Avenue, Cornerstone Plaza, Cocoa Beach 32931; (321-784-0667) 2067 N. Atlantic Avenue, Banana River Square, Cocoa Beach 32931. This Florida-based chain has two convenient area locations—one north of FL 520 and the other a few miles south. The deli features Boar's Head meats and cheeses, sandwiches made to order, and roasted and fried chicken with sides. In the produce section you'll find prepared salads and fruit bowls.

Seafood Atlantic (321-784-0333) 520 Glen Cheek Drive, Port Canaveral 32920. Order fresh fish by the fillet, or pick from crabs, mussels, clams, scallops, and shrimp. Some choices, such as the crab cakes, are ready to pop in the oven.

Smokehouse Foods (321-784-9300) 525 Glen Cheek Drive, Port Canaveral 32920. For more than a decade, locals have enjoyed Smokehouse's smoked meats and seafood in sandwiches, salads, or packaged to go in six kinds of fish dip.

Sunseed Food Co-op (321-784-0930) 6615 N. Atlantic Avenue, Cape Canaveral 32920. For more than 30 years, Sunseed has carried a complete supply of natural foods, including bread and dairy products, produce, cereals, frozen meals, and baby food.

Wild Ocean Seafood Market (321-783-2300) 710 Scallop Drive, Port Canaveral 32920. Ocean-grown seafood is the specialty of this portside market. Purchase shrimp with or without the shell, whole lobsters or lobster tails, crab legs, and fish in season. Seasonings and sauces are extra; cooking advice is on the house.

✳ Entertainment

MOVIES Merritt Square 16 (321-459-3737; www.cobbtheatres.com/merritt.htm) Merritt Square Mall, 777 E. Merritt Island Causeway, Merritt Island 32952. Merritt Square Mall is located on the north side of FL 520, 4.7 miles west of A1A.

MUSIC AND NIGHTLIFE "And they danced by the light of the moon, the moon. They danced by the light of the moon," said the owl to the pussycat in the poem by Edward Lear. Soft lights, bright lights, and moonlight mix with music throughout Brevard County, especially at the beach, where you'll find almost every musical genre. At many restaurants, live entertainment accompanies dinner, but at several locations music is the main course. Some areas have evolved into centers for dancing; club hopping; imbibing, if you like; and savoring a feast for the ears. Web sites often post upcoming talents and events. Unless otherwise noted, smoking is permitted, and there is no cover charge.

Cape Canaveral and Cocoa Beach

Gregory's Comedy Club (900 N. Atlantic Avenue, Cocoa Beach; 321-799-2557; www.gregoryscomedyclub .com) opens its doors every Thursday night for live performances. Just down the street at Commander's Club (1300 N. Atlantic Avenue, Cocoa Beach; 321-866-0222) **Groucho's Comedy Show** stages performances on Friday evenings. The format is similar, with a different mix of comedians and audience. Bring an open mind and sense of humor, and you'll have a great time. The topics and language are for adults; both are non-smoking facilities. Reservations are suggested, but in the off-season tickets are usually available at the door.

The Cove at Port Canaveral is a waterside entertainment center blending melodies and sea breezes until the wee hours of the morning. Convenient taxi service is available between beach hotels and the port clubs. Locals and visitors meet and mingle at the outdoor **Tiki Bar at Grills** (505 Glen Cheek Drive), where bands perform Friday night, Saturday afternoon and evening, and Sunday afternoon. Dress is casual, the mood is fun, and classic rock music keeps the dance floor hopping. Relax on the upper deck at **Fishlips Waterfront Bar & Grill** (610 Glen Cheek Drive), a gathering spot for young and old. Dance to live entertainment on Friday and Saturday, or a DJ most other evenings. Sports fans can catch the game on one of the big-screen

TVs. Come as you are and enjoy live entertainment Thursday through Sunday on the outside deck at **Rusty's Seafood & Oyster Bar** (628 Glen Cheek Drive). Boaters returning from excursions and fishing trips mix with landlubbers cooling off after a day at the beach. Kick off your shoes for the beach party at **Milliken's Sand Bar** (683 Dave Nisbet Drive). This outdoor playground alongside the Port Canaveral canal provides music, drinks, contests, and fun until the wee hours of the morning.

Bars dot A1A in Cocoa Beach like seashells scattered along the shoreline. Ocean waves fill in the backbeat for live music at the **Cocoa Beach Pier** (401 Meade; 321-783-7549). Stop by the open-air **Oh Shucks Seafood Bar** for Sing-Out-Loud Karaoke on Tuesday or Cool Runnin' Reggae on Wednesday. On the weekends, music blends with the sound of surf on the **Boardwalk**, where local house band Birks & Dugan has perfected the art of beach entertainment.

The **Beach Shack Blues Bar** (1 Minutemen Causeway), located where the road meets the sand at the end of Minutemen Causeway, is the premier spot for blues in central Florida. Each week six bands from all over the world stage shows: inside on Thursday, Friday, Saturday, and Sunday nights; on the beachfront deck on Saturday and Sunday afternoons. Manager Bill, who hails from Detroit, has created a juke-joint atmosphere that attracts blues lovers of every age. Directly across the street, join the party at the **Coconuts on the Beach** deck (2 Minutemen Causeway). Cover bands entertain after-dinner and late-night partiers and dancers from Wednesday through Sunday.

During spring break and summer, expect a young, hip, and sometimes rowdy crowd. Relax and enjoy soft music and the art of conversation at the family-owned **Cocoa Beach Brewing Company** (150 N. Atlantic Avenue). They offer a variety of hand-crafted beers, all brewed in small batches from their own recipes. Wine is also available.

Heidi's Jazz Club (7 N. Orlando Avenue, 321-783-4559; www.heidis jazzclub.com) has been a cozy retreat for jazz lovers on the Space Coast since the 1990s. The club is open Tuesday through Sunday from 5 PM to 1 AM and features world-class live entertainment. Sunday night is an open-mike jam session. The dress code, atmosphere, drinks, and prices are a little more upscale than the typical beach bar, but this is a first-class showroom decorated in warm reds and soft lights, and dotted with small tables covered with white linen cloths. Food may be ordered off the lighter bar menu or from the full dinner

HEIDI'S JAZZ CLUB IN DOWNTOWN COCOA BEACH.

NOLAN'S IRISH PUB

A thousand welcomes await visitors to this authentic Irish pub on the shores of Cocoa Beach. Irishman John Nolan has created a friendly neighborhood bar where locals and visitors gather to chat and sing along to traditional Celtic tunes. Come early on Tuesday for the popular and always crowded trivia night; Irish music on Friday, Saturday, and Sunday. Guinness and Harp are just a sample of the beers are on tap. Try a house specialty like Black Velvet, a blend of Guinness and champagne. This is a great place to have a wee bit of fun—and that's no blarney (321-783-8499; www.nolansirishpub.net; 5675 N. Atlantic Avenue at the Cornerstone Plaza).

menu of the adjoining Heidelberg's restaurant. Special shows require a ticket purchase, and reservations are recommended.

PERFORMING ARTS Surfside Playhouse (321-783-3127; www .surfsideplayers.com) 300 Ramp Road, Cocoa Beach 32931. For more than 25 years, the Surfside Players have staged high-quality theatrical productions in Brevard's only beachside venue, the Surfside Playhouse. Every seat in the house is a good one in this small, comfortable facility that features traditional works, like *Fiddler on the Roof,* as well as shows targeted to families and children. Productions appealing to more contemporary audiences are presented under the

A SCENE FROM *FIDDLER ON THE ROOF* PERFORMED BY THE SURFSIDE PLAYERS.

Second Stage brand. Summer programs provide theatrical arts education and experience to young people.

✳ Selective Shopping

BOOKS **Barnes & Noble Booksellers** (321-453-8202; www.barnesandnoble.com) 780 E. Merritt Island Causeway, Merritt Island 32952. This bookstore and café, located across the street from the Merritt Square Mall, is a convenient and cool retreat after a day in the sun. They carry an extensive collection of Florida- and space-related publications. Head to a room in the back filled with selections for infants through young adult, with interactive toys and small-sized tables and chairs. Browsers will find it hard to resist the aroma of just-baked pastries from the café, perfect when paired with coffee, tea, and conversation.

Books-A-Million (321-453-5177; www.booksamillion.com) 777 E. Merritt Island Causeway, Merritt Island 32952. Books, small gifts, cards, and a huge selection of magazines fill this store. They also have a children's section with movies for sale. The Jo Muggs Café offers a variety of drinks and snacks. Enter from parking lot or from inside the Merritt Island Mall.Most of the stores at the beach are on or near A1A and are easy to find and have a breezy seaside ambience. If you're in the mood for some mall shopping or just want to get out of the sun for a few hours, head to the Merritt Square Mall (321-452-3270; www.merrittsquaremall.com; 777 E. Merritt Island Causeway, Merritt Island 32952), located on FL 520 just 5 miles from Cocoa Beach. It features Macy's, JCPenney, Dillard's, and Sears; specialty shops; a fast-food court; an arcade; and the Cobb Merritt Square 16 Cinema.

MAKE A STATEMENT AT THE BEACH WITH A HAT THAT'S FUNCTIONAL *AND* STYLISH.

CLOTHING, SHOES, AND ACCESSORIES

Flirt (321-783-2626) 4265 N. Atlantic Avenue, Cocoa Beach 32931. The young and daring will find brief and glitzy swimsuits, casual clothes, club outfits, short shorts, and high heels.

Mar Chiquita Swimwear (321-868-0868) 1 N. Atlantic Avenue, Cocoa Beach 32931. Fit and stylish young women will find a great selection of bathing suits, beachwear, and accessories at this tiny, hip storefront, located just 1 block from the beach at the Minutemen Causeway. They carry comfortable T-shirts and baggy shorts for guys.

Shady Characters Sunglass Emporium (321-783-4244) 25 S. Atlantic Avenue, Cocoa Beach 32931. Capture a cool look with a selection from the newest and best assortment of surf, skate, and casual sunglasses on the beach, including popular brands like Spy, Electric, and Vonzipper.

Shobha's Boutique (321-784-4441) 2031 N. Atlantic Avenue, Cocoa Beach 32931. Shobha's, which offers brand-name casual wear and more than 2,000 bathing suits (including tan-through, long-torso, and mix-and-match separates), is the perfect stop for stylish women beyond the bikini years. Mastectomy apparel including swimsuits, bras, and prosthetics are available. Accessorize with cover-ups, beach bags, hats, and jewelry.

Susan's Birkenstock Shoes (321-799-9858) 227 W. Cocoa Beach Causeway, Cocoa Beach 32931. Life at the beach is all about comfort. Susan helps you take care of your feet with shoes that look good and feel good. Slide into a comfortable pair of shoes or sandals from respected names such as Birkenstock, Mephisto, Ecco, Teva, and La Plume.

GALLERIES The casual and carefree tone of downtown Cocoa Beach is reflected in the eclectic collection of galleries. The seaside location inspires local artists and influences their work—and sometimes their work ethic. When the waves are good, don't be surprised to discover a GONE SURFING sign on the door. In addition to storefront galleries, many of the area restaurants are decorated with original works of art that are available for purchase.

Beachside Gallery (321-799-9336) 133 N. Orlando Avenue, Cocoa Beach 32931. Open: Tuesday through Saturday 10–5:30. The style and heritage of the 1939 house on Cottage Row in downtown Cocoa Beach is the perfect setting for this fine-arts gallery. The original works of more than 40 talented artists are on display. In addition, owner and resident artist Kate LaDuke specializes in applying natural, gentle methods to restore damaged, aged, and weathered pieces. Full-service custom framing is also available.

Courage Belle Art Studio and Gallery (321-783-5033) 38 N. Brevard Avenue, Cocoa Beach 32931. Open: By appointment. In 2002, painters and friends Carolyn Cherry and Susan Tully combined their talent and passion for creating tropical watercolors. Vibrant works credited to each woman are on display; as well as joint paintings signed TouCan (because they believe two can work together to create beautiful pieces). Often you'll see a work in progress on the center table as you browse through originals and prints. *Neptune's Party*, a TouCan watercolor of life under the sea, was selected to appear on posters and T-shirts for the 2006 Space Coast Art Festival.

Rick Pipers' Big Art Studio (321-604-0817; www.piperart.com) 18 N. Brevard Avenue, Cocoa Beach 32931. Visitors to downtown Cocoa Beach often experience the work of artist Rick Piper, even if they don't visit his studio. Piper's art is big and beautiful and his murals have transformed the town, like the rolling wave and beach scene at Juice N Java on the corner of North Orlando Avenue and Minutemen Causeway. His paintings and prints are available to view and buy inside the cafe. Piper is in his studio most afternoons, but if not, call him and he'll meet you there. His work has developed a national following among collectors.

Mai Tiki Studio & Gallery (321-783-6890; www.maitiki.com) 251 Minutemen Causeway, Cocoa Beach 32931. The tropical gallery and studio of internationally renowned artist Wayne Coombs is a rainbow of colorful carvings, masks, and paintings. The distinctive tiki carved from palm wood is his trademark. Coombs was in high school when he carved his first tiki from a piece of sabal palm wood. Thirty years later, art inspired by nature remains his passion. In the studio, he and other artists sculpt the now world-famous and instantly identifiable statues, available from 18 inches to an imposing 6 feet tall. Any size can be shipped.

Yet this is just the edge of a spectrum of imaginative art Coombs creates. Many works begin with natural materials that are transformed into images or creatures fitting with the shape and size of the recycled wood, like a bright-eyed palm frond owl or a graceful driftwood dolphin. This is a gallery that children will enjoy as much as adults.

RJK Studio (321-252-2588) 6200 N. Atlantic Avenue, Cape Canaveral 32920. Like the morning sun rising above the waves, Rachel Kercher's tiny storefront is a bright, glittering spot on the A1A horizon. The designer fuses layers of glass and creates sparkling works in vivid, deep tones. Commission large window or door pieces, or select from smaller items such as bowls, platters, wind chimes, and a stunning collection of jewelry. Surfboard-shaped incense holders reflect the studio's beach environment. Rachel also carries incense and all-natural bath products.

GIFTS AND SOUVENIRS **Ann Lia Gift Shop** (321-783-2323) 38 S. Atlantic Avenue, Cocoa Beach 32931. For more than 50 years, this small emporium has been a favorite of Cocoa Beach residents and visitors,

WHIMSICAL GIFTS ABOUND AT ENCHANTED SPIRIT.

who stop for its souvenirs, space memorabilia, beachwear, sundries, and ornaments, along with the selection of books and toys for children. Paintings and photographs of the area, wildlife sculptures, and hand-crafted Ironwood pieces are also featured. A nostalgic choice would be a vintage toy or decoration from the *I Dream of Jeannie* days.

The Dinosaur Store (321-783-7300) 250 W. Cocoa Beach Causeway, Cocoa Beach 32931. Children absolutely love visiting this one-of-a-kind science and nature store, which has an amazing collection of dinosaur

LOCAL SURF LEGEND JOE TWOMBLY PRESENTED UNIVERSITY OF FLORIDA FOOTBALL COACH URBAN MEYER WITH A UNIQUE GIFT FROM THE TWOMBLY'S NAUTICAL FURNITURE COLLECTION.

teeth and claws, fossil shark teeth, and dinosaur reproductions. Educational toys and books are also available. Mom will find vivid jewelry crafted from gemstones and amber specimens.

Enchanted Spirit (321-784-2213) 320 N. Atlantic Avenue, Cocoa Beach 32931. This small shop along A1A is stocked with treasures selected by owner Johanna Harris to inspire the spirit and soothe the soul. Amid the aroma of incense and tickle of wind chimes you'll find crystals, candles, dream catchers, and Japanese tea sets. Pick a card linked to your birthday and find guidance for balancing your life.

Exotic Shells and Gifts by Eleanor (321-783-0848) 1 S. Atlantic Avenue, Cocoa Beach 32931. This small shop at the corner of A1A and Minutemen Causeway is a Cocoa Beach landmark. Eleanor carries a huge selection of shells and ornaments made from shells, as well as costume jewelry, hanging decorations, lamps, and nautical-themed art. Beachgoers will also find shirts, hats, and beach gear.

The Perfect Gift and Florist (321-799-4438) 6550 N. Atlantic Avenue, Cape Canaveral 32920. Owner Shirley Nelson Brown stocks a wonderful assortment of foliage, gifts, and edible treats. Her specialty is creating flower arrangements, as well as one-of-a-kind gift baskets for adults and children. Treat yourself or a loved one to a bon voyage basket delivered directly to the stateroom while cruise ships are in dock at Port Canaveral.

Twombly's Nautical Furniture (321-783-8610) 101 Manatee Lane, Cocoa Beach 32931. Joe Twombly, a Cocoa Beach–raised surfer and 2000 inductee into the East Coast Surfing

Hall of Fame, has gained a national following as a nautical furniture designer. Diners at local restaurants like the Shark Pit and Dixie Crossroads will see his work, an artistic and colorful mosaic of shells and beach finds protected under layers of clear epoxy resin. The combined shop and factory have a small number of items that are ready to go, but most are custom orders. Stop by for a visit. Joe or his manager and fellow surfer Mike Meyer are usually available and stock a wealth of surfing stories along with the furniture.

SPORTS, SURFING, AND BEACH GEAR

Beach $ Plus (321-613-3910) 5675 N. Atlantic Avenue, Cocoa Beach 32931. Small storefront is packed with recreation and convenience items for the beach; located in Cornerstone Plaza.

Beach Unlimited (321-784-3310) 3650 N. Atlantic Avenue, Cocoa Beach 32931. Choose from a wide assortment of reasonably priced beach towels, T-shirts and tanks, sand toys, and practical supplies.

Beach Wave & Xtreme Surfshop (321-783-0180) 5490 N. Atlantic Avenue, Cocoa Beach 32931; (321-783-8700) 3800 N. Atlantic Avenue, Cocoa Beach 32931; (321-783-3399) 1275 N. Atlantic Avenue, Cocoa Beach 32931; (321-783-1848) 185 W. Cocoa Beach Causeway, Cocoa Beach 32931. Four stores scattered along A1A supply low-cost necessities for hitting the beach and catching some rays, including towels, chairs, umbrellas, mats, bathing suits, sunscreen, and more. Customers will find a large selection of merchandise with the COCOA BEACH logo.

Bilt Surf and Skate (321-868-8820) 210 N. Orlando Avenue, Cocoa Beach 32931. Inside this small beachside convenience store located just 2 blocks from the Minutemen Cause-

SHOPPING AT COLOSSAL BEACH STORES RON JON SURF SHOP AND THE COCOA BEACH SURF COMPANY IS A MUST-DO WHEN VISITING THE AREA.

Roger Scruggs

way beaches is a surprisingly large selection of beach shirts, shorts, and shoes, along with sunglasses, hats, and other necessities for a day in the sun. Owner Craig Hiller also rents surfboards and bicycles, including a "little nipper" version for small children and a tandem bike "bilt" for two. Surfboard rental rates range from $10 to $20 for two hours, $20 to $40 for a day.

Cocoa Beach Surf Company (321-799-9930) 4001 N. Atlantic Avenue, Cocoa Beach 32931. This bright beach mega-store that claims to be the world's largest surf complex has three stories of hip, fun merchandise, such as Body Glove and Life is Good, in juniors, misses, and men's sizes, as well as a large selection of sandals, flip-flops, and water shoes for children and adults. They also carry toys, towels, and other accessories for surfing and water sports. The third floor is for hard-core players and features top-of-the-line, professional brands of surfboards and skateboards for sale and rent. The beach is just a short walk away, but drivers can park in their multi-story free parking garage. Open daily from 8 AM to 11 PM. Also see *To Do—Surfing*.

Cocoa Beach Surf Company Beachside (321-799-9921; www.cocoabeachsurf.com) 199 E. Cocoa Beach Causeway, Cocoa Beach 32931. Beachgoers near Shepard Park at the end of the Cocoa Beach Causeway are just steps away from a store stocked with beach gear to rent for a few hours or by the week. Set up for the day with beach umbrella and chairs starting at an affordable $4 for two hours and increasing to $40 for the week. Now get moving with body boards, skimboards, and surfboards

suitable for beginners or pros with rates for four hours ranging from $8 to $30. Beach bikes and kayaks are also available.

Jetty Park Bait & Tackle Shop 400 E. Jetty Road, Cape Canaveral 32920. This small general store carries basics such as sunscreen, hats, and towels. Snacks, cold drinks, beer, small coolers, ice, and souvenirs are also available. The bait side of the house supplies most fishing needs.

Matt's Bicycle Center (321-783-1196) 166 N. Atlantic Avenue, Cocoa Beach 32931. Matt Molnar is a community advocate for biking and bike safety. Buy a bicycle, purchase apparel and accessories, and get sound advice on maintaining your bike in good form.

Oceansports World (321-783-4088) 3220 S. Atlantic Avenue, Cocoa Beach 32931. This sporting gear shop in south Cocoa Beach carries equipment to get you on the waves or the river, including surfboards, kayaks, wave skis, kiteboards, and paddleboards. Watch surfboards being shaped, or order a custom board under the Island or Slater brand. Also see *To Do—Surfing*.

Quiet Flight Surf Shop Inc. (321-783-1530) 109 N. Orlando Avenue, Cocoa Beach 32931. Select a board from the showroom, or order one custom made at the Cape Canaveral factory, and find swimwear, wet suits, and beach accessories.

Ron Jon Surf Shop (321-799-8888; www.ronjons.com) 4151 N. Atlantic Avenue, Cocoa Beach 32931. Since 1963, Cocoa Beach visitors have made a stop at this flagship site of the most famous surf shop in the world. The mega-store is open 24/7 and promises

RON JON WATERSPORTS.

it has the best selection of surf, skate, swim, and beach essentials on earth. Spread over 2 acres, it has a huge selection of tropical fashions and accessories, racks of bathing suits, and Ron Jon souvenir merchandise. Surfboards, however, are still their most important product. Find them in every color and style—long, mini, egg, and fish with a notched tail at one end. For variety, look for Indo boards, skateboards, and skimboards. They carry everything you need to hit the waves, including wax, protective pads, wet suits, and leashes. Look through a collection of DVDs and books for surfing entertainment. There may be numerous Ron Jon Surf Shops around the world today, but a visit to the Cocoa Beach location is still a one-of-a-kind excursion.

Ron Jon Watersports (321-799-8840; www.ronjons.com) 4275 N. Atlantic Avenue, Cocoa Beach 32931. Located just across the road from Ron Jon Surf Shop, this store has everything you need for an active day at the beach. Surfers can rent foam and fiberglass boards, beach bikes, kayaks, and wet suits. Renters must be 18 or older, and a credit card deposit is required. Surfboard rental is $10–20 for a day; beach bike rental is $10 a day.

SUNDRIES AND EXTRAS Cocoa Beach Harley-Davidson (321-799-2221) 3688 N. Atlantic Avenue, Cocoa Beach 32931. Bikers will discover a great selection of T-shirts, accessories, and gifts themed to the Harley-Davidson style and trademark, including functional riding gear and, for the collectors, Dip Dots.

CVS (321-784-0503) **Walgreens** (321-799-9112) Located next to each other at the corner of A1A and FL 520, both are open 24 hours for convenient shopping for basic beach needs, forgotten personal products, medicines, and prescriptions. Both sell photo supplies and offer quick service on film development or downloading memory-card photos to a CD.

Fairvilla (321-799-9961) 500 Thurm

WILDLIFE PROFILE: ROSEATE SPOONBILL

If the local wildlife community had a red-carpet night, the roseate spoonbill would garner all the attention. The wading bird stands about 3 feet high and has bright red eyes, long pink legs, and a white back, neck, and chest. A feather shawl, in hues of rosy pink fringed in coral, wraps around the lower back, wings, and belly. The roseate spoonbill is named for its flat bill that is narrow at the top and spoon-shaped at the end.

Its beauty was nearly the downfall of the glamorous bird. Turn-of-the-20th-century travelers shot the roseate spoonbill to use the sought-after colorful plumage for hats and fans. Today the population has recovered. Bird lovers capture photographic images of these majestic flyers as they travel in a row with their legs and long necks extended straight out, wings stretching to a span of 4 feet.

The sociable creatures thrive in coastal flats and often live in large colonies with herons, egrets, and other roseate spoonbills. They forage by sweeping their bill from side to side. When prey is detected by touch, the bill snaps shut on a crustacean, snail, small fish, or marine insect. In the spring, a male and female will mate and roost in the mangroves. They stay together to build a nest and care for the eggs and young. Eggs incubate for about 22 days, and the babies develop and learn to fly five or six weeks later. Immature roseate spoonbills are all white with a slight pink color on the tip of their wings. They are adults by about three years of age.

Space Coast Sightings: Black Point Wildlife Drive at the Merritt Island National Wildlife Refuge, Wild Florida Exhibit at Brevard Zoo.

ROSEATE SPOONBILL (*AJAIA AJAJA*)

Jim Angy

Boulevard, Cape Canaveral 32920. Spice up a romantic weekend with an assortment of adult toys and games, sexy clothing, costumes, and paraphernalia. The mega-store is bright and designed to ensure a comfortable but adventurous shopping experience.

✳ Special Events

Monthly: ✒ **Friday Fest at Cape Canaveral** (Taylor Avenue, Cape Canaveral) On the first Friday of each month visitors are invited to join residents for a family street party overflowing with music, food, and fun. Vendors display arts, crafts, and jewelry; children enjoy special activities like the bounce house. Held near the Recreation Center, just off A1A.

January: **Cape Canaveral Fine Arts Show** (321-636-3673; www.brevard art.org; Cape Canaveral Library, 201 Polk Avenue, Cape Canaveral 32920) The Central Brevard Arts Association kicks off their year with an amazing showcase of member talent at this small community show. The organiza-

tion, committed to promoting the visual arts in this area, holds several other exhibits throughout the year. The event is held in late January.

March: **Calema Midwinters Windsurfing Festival** (321-453-3223; www.calema.com; Kelly Park, Merritt Island) World Cup professionals, Olympic-class competitors, and amateurs of all ages compete for four days. Races are held in the Banana River off Kelly Park. Participants and spectators enjoy this premier event, which is also a stunning display of color.

April: ✒ **The Art of Sand Festival** (321-690-6817; 8701 Astronaut Boulevard, Radisson Resort, Cape Canaveral) Artists participating in this extraordinary event need more than a pail and shovel to create these spectacular sand sculptures, some 15 feet tall. Master artists from around the world compete for awards. The fun begins in early April with an opening weekend of special celebrations including a chance to meet the artists.

GET INSPIRED BY MASSIVE SAND SCULPTURES AT THE SPRINGTIME ART OF SAND FESTIVAL.

The gates stay open for a month with the works on display, along with entertainment, refreshments, and friendly competitions for company groups, families, and children. Admission: adults $8; seniors, military, children under 12 $4.

𝒮 **Easter Weekend: Ron Jon Easter Surfing Festival** (Cocoa Beach Pier and Shepard Park, www.easter surffest.com) In 1964 a Cocoa Beach community group held an Easter surf festival to attract crowds. The tradition continues as more than 100,000 fans gather to watch the best surfers in the world compete for top prizes in men's and women's championship shortboard and longboard events. Amateurs from age 6 to 60 compete in traditional events as well as fun categories like body surfing. The Pro/Am family-friendly festivities begin on Friday and include concerts, beachside movies, exhibits, kite surfing and skimboarding clinics, an Easter egg hunt, and sunrise services on Easter morning. Beach registration for the **Florida State Paddleboard Championships** begins at 7 AM Saturday at Shepard Park. The 7-mile race is a paddle, run, and swim event. On Saturday night the Cocoa Beach Surf Museum hosts an **Easter Extravaganza** where guests can mingle with professional surfers and enjoy a new exhibit. Everything is free; everything is fun.

Images in Art (321-615-8111; Manatee Sanctuary Park, Cape Canaveral) Beautiful Manatee Sanctuary Park, along the banks of the Banana River, is the perfect backdrop for this showing of fine art and creative crafts. Held the first Saturday and Sunday in April, the event is hosted by the City of Cape Canaveral and the Central Brevard Arts Association.

May/June: **Memorial Day Weekend: Beachfest** (Cocoa Beach Pier) Beach culture blends with the military heritage of Florida's Space Coast for three days of food, fun, music, activities, and contests. More than 500 military and law enforcement personnel, firefighters, and lifeguards compete in events such as an ocean relay race, a paddleboat race, and a volleyball tournament. Members of the armed forces hold exhibits and demonstrations, and on Monday they join together for a special tribute to the military. The event ends with a bugle rendition of "Taps."

Waterman's Challenge Surf Contest Weekend (International Palms Resort, Cocoa Beach) Since 2001 the East Coast Surfing Hall of Fame has presented this summertime, family-friendly surfing competition. Held over two days, the event is designed to highlight the history of surfing, encourage participation in the sport, and provide amateurs with a less-intense forum for competing. In keeping with the broad definition of a waterman (a term from the 1950s used to describe surfers, lifeguards, swimmers, and others who lived and played on the water), activities such as paddling might also be included as part of the festivities. A luau is held on Saturday night. The weekend is sponsored by Ron Jon Surf Shop and hosted by International Palms Resort.

July: **Fourth of July on the Beach**. Bring a blanket, a picnic basket, and some patriotic tunes on your iPod for spectacular fireworks staged from an ocean barge off Shepard Park in Cocoa Beach. The show begins just after sunset.

September: **Doctors, Lawyers, and Weekend Warriors** (Sebastian Inlet, www.doctorslawyersweekendwar-riors.com) Local lawyer Jack Kirschenbaum is all grown-up but still passionate about surfing. So every fall he invites professionals from throughout the country to trade in their business suits for bathing suits and head for the waves. Surfers raise money for children's charities in Brevard County, send a positive message about the sport, and have a great time.

Labor Day Weekend: National Kidney Foundation of Florida Pro-Am Surf Festival (Shepard Park and Cocoa Beach Pier, www.nkfsurf.com) This surfing event, which started in 1985, is the largest event of its kind to benefit a charity. Professional surfer Rich Salick was at the peak of his career when his kidneys failed. His twin, and fellow pro surfer, Phil, was a tissue match and donated a kidney, and Richard was able to return to competition. Both brothers remain involved in this popular surfing competition and family festival that raises money for the National Kidney Foundation of Florida.

October: **Cocoa Beach Air Show** (www.cocoabeachairshow.com) It's a bird, it's a plane . . . an extravaganza of planes! This two-day salute to the area's military and aerospace heritage is an awesome display of precision formation flying and aerial acrobatics. VIP seating is available or pull up your beach chair to enjoy the show for free. Shepard Park at the end of SR 520 in Cocoa Beach is the central location for most events.

International Sea-Bean Symposium (Cocoa Beach Public Library, 550 N. Brevard Avenue, Cocoa Beach, www.seabean.com) This two-day event combines education and fun with activities, speakers, and dis-plays to draw attention to ecological topics and the joy of collecting sea beans. Also known as drift seeds, the beans fall from plants and trees around the world, drop into water-ways, and are swept by the ocean to distant shores. Saturday morning begins with a Bean-a-Thon beach-combing trek.

Port Fest/Pink Ribbon Walk (www.visitportcanaveral.com; The Cove, Port Canaveral) Expect fun, feasting, and your favorite tune at this one-day event sponsored by the Port Canaveral Association. Activities go from sunrise to sunset and conclude with fireworks. A crowd favorite is the Bed & Bathtub Race, with teams representing the major restaurants and bars in the port.

November: ⚓ **Space Coast Art Festival** (www.spacecoastartfestival.com; intersection of A1A and Minutemen Causeway, Cocoa Beach) Thanksgiving weekend, the streets of downtown Cocoa Beach open to display the works of nearly 250 juried artists, most from Florida and many from Brevard County. The weekend takes off with a 5K Turkey Trot early Thursday morning, followed by the art show on Friday and Saturday. Enjoy exhibits, a student art display, children's craft and activities, music, and a street party into the evening. Eat, drink, and have a very merry time.

World Skin Cancer Foundation Slater Brothers Invitational (Coconuts, 2 Minutemen Causeway, Cocoa Beach, www.worldskincancer foundation.com) Sean Slater is chief organizer for this event that brings together world-class surfers and hometown heroes, like Kelly Slater and the Hobgood brothers, and upcoming local talent in the sport. At this event that raises money for the World Skin Cancer Foundation, teams of young, local surfers get the chance to join the pros for a weekend of contests, exhibitions, and fun. Watch top-notch surfing, attend parties and concerts, get screened for skin cancer by volunteer doctors, and support a great cause.

December: ♂ **Cocoa Beach Christmas Boat Parade** (Cocoa Beach) Santa Claus is escorted into this island town by a flotilla of large and small boats decorated for the season. At sunset, boats embark from the south-western shore of the Banana River at FL 520, parallel the causeway as they cross the river, then hug the shore heading south to the Cocoa Beach Country Club. Two favorite viewing spots are Bicentennial Park, midway along the Cocoa Beach Causeway, and Sunset Grill restaurant, at the eastern point where the boats begin their turn south. Good viewing spots fill up early for this very popular event. Check the newspaper schedule for seasonal boat parades held in other venues throughout the county.

Central Brevard 2

CENTRAL BREVARD

The town of Cocoa, reportedly named after a can of chocolate powder sitting on the shelf at a general store, is just a short drive from Cocoa Beach. Originally a trading post alongside the Indian River, it has evolved into one of the county's major communities. Visitors will enjoy strolling down the tree-lined streets of Historic Cocoa Village, where buildings from the steamboat era now house a quaint collection of restaurants, shops, and art galleries. Riverfront Park is a gathering spot for events and celebrations. Century-old homes lining the river road in Rockledge, to the south of Cocoa, reflect the golden age of this community.

Brevard Community College has a campus in Cocoa, and the world-class Astronaut Memorial Planetarium and Observatory is located there. The Brevard Museum of History and Natural Science is right next door.

Viera is a planned community west of I-95. The centerpiece is The Avenue Viera, the county's largest entertainment, retail, and dining complex. The Brevard Zoo and Space Coast Stadium—featuring the Washington Nationals during baseball's spring training season and the minor league Brevard Manatees in the summer—are located nearby.

GETTING THERE To get to Cocoa Village, take FL 520 west from Cocoa Beach for 7.5 miles, crossing the Banana River and Indian River. Turn left at Brevard Avenue, 2 blocks west of the Indian River. To reach Viera, continue on FL 520 to I-95 southbound. Space Coast Stadium is at exit 195/Fiske Boulevard; The Avenue Viera and the Brevard Zoo are near exit 191/Wickham Road.

✳ To See

Brevard Community College Astronaut Memorial Planetarium and Observatory (321-433-7373; www.brevardcc.edu/planet) 1519 Clearlake Road, Cocoa 32922. Open: Wednesday 1:30–4:00, Friday and Saturday 6:30–10 PM. Admission: Free for observatory and exhibits; shows: adults $7, seniors and students $6, children under 13 $4, combo tickets available. Glimpse distant galaxies and imagine the adventures awaiting future space travelers. On Friday and Saturday evenings, staff and volunteers help visitors identify key stars through the observatory's state-of-the-art telescope. Discover space memorabilia and meteorites in the exhibit hall. Like the stars in the night sky, show choices in this modern facility are always in motion. Tour the heavens or enjoy a laser show inside the world-class planetarium. View images captured by the Hubble telescope. Follow the constellations to learn the stories of ancient gods and heroes. A concert-level sound system blends rock music with laser effects for a powerful musical experience featuring acts like Pink Floyd, the Beatles, and a special Halloween rendition of monster favorites. The Iwerks Movie Theater presents the sights and sounds of nature on a three-story-high screen.

HISTORIC PLACES Cocoa Village began as a small riverside community and trading center for steamboat travelers. Just south of Cocoa, the town of Rockledge opened resort hotels and developed into a popular stop for visitors arriving by water and later by railroad. The river used to be much wider at Cocoa. About 40 years ago the city deepened the channel, and a dredge was used to expand the shoreline and add Riverfront Park.

The **S. F. Travis Building** at 300 Delannoy Avenue in Cocoa was built in 1907 for Col. Samuel Travis. Conveniently located next to the town wharf, Travis Hardware remains as the oldest existing business in Cocoa. Inside you'll find the original tin ceilings, wood shelving, and hardwood floors.

The **Porcher House** at 434 Delannoy Avenue was the home of prosperous citrus farmer Edward Porcher. This prestigious estate, originally on the banks of the Indian River, was built in 1916 using local coquina shell rock. Its turn-of-the-20th-century Classical Revival style, location, and grandeur make it a popular location for weddings. The bride enters from the upstairs balcony and floats down the wide central staircase.

St. Mark's Episcopal Church, 4 N. Church Street, reflects nautical touches by the local shipbuilder who designed the building. The first Cocoa Village community service held in the completed church was a Thanksgiving service in November 1887. Originally christened as St. Michael's, the church's name was changed in 1890 in recognition of help received from St. Mark's parish in New Jersey. A coat of stucco was added atop the wooden frame in 1925.

At 401 Delannoy Avenue, the **Taylor Bank Building** was home to the first bank of Cocoa, opened by Albert Taylor in 1892. Today it's a Ryan's Pizza, but BANK is still visible, etched in brick just below the middle window of the flat-front Masonry Vernacular structure popular at this time. In an interesting twist, Ryan's makes their pizza dough in the room-sized vault once used to secure the bank's paper dough.

Looking a little out of place, the ornate marble building at 114 Harrison Street was built in 1925 by the newly arrived **Brevard County Bank & Trust Company.** Inside are the original vaults and chandeliers. The building outlasted the bank, which closed in the crash of 1929.

In 1925, **Trafford and Field Real Estate Firm** remodeled an old garage at 316 Brevard Avenue, turning it into a Mediterranean Revival–style office building. Their mark, T&F, still stands above the entry of what is now the Ossorio

Central Brevard: Cocoa Village

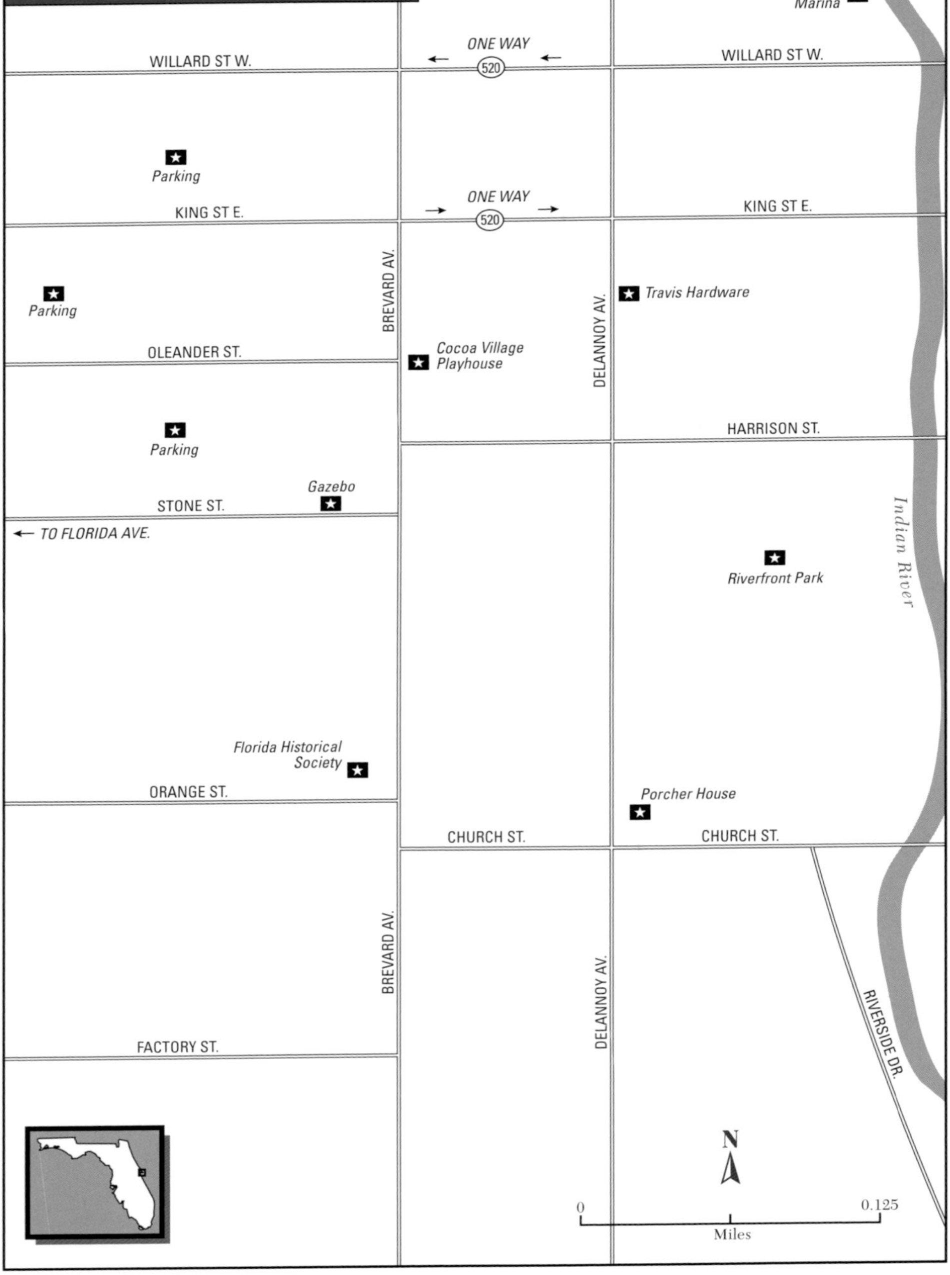

Cocoa Village Marina ★

WILLARD ST W.

ONE WAY
← 520 ←

WILLARD ST W.

★
Parking

KING ST E.

ONE WAY
→ 520 →

KING ST E.

BREVARD AV.

★ Travis Hardware

★
Parking

DELANNOY AV.

OLEANDER ST.

★ Cocoa Village Playhouse

★
Parking

HARRISON ST.

Gazebo
★

STONE ST.

← TO FLORIDA AVE.

★
Riverfront Park

Indian River

Florida Historical Society ★

ORANGE ST.

Porcher House
★

CHURCH ST.

CHURCH ST.

BREVARD AV.

DELANNOY AV.

RIVERSIDE DR.

FACTORY ST.

N
↑

0   0.125
Miles

bakery and sandwich shop. The unusual and distinctive pecky cypress ceiling is original.

The **Aviles Building,** directly across the street at 310 Brevard Avenue, is another example of the Mediterranean Revival style of 1925. The building was the home of Campbell's Drug Store in the 1950s. Imagine grabbing a stool at the lunch counter, enjoying a burger and a Coca-Cola, and catching up on local news.

Cocoa Village Playhouse at 300 Brevard Avenue is a magnificent four-story Italian Renaissance building that originally opened as the Aladdin Theatre in 1924, hosting live performances. Motion pictures moved in during the 1940s. For more than a decade, this performing-arts center has been home to *Broadway on Brevard* and other theatrical productions. The building is on the National Register of Historic Places.

Next door, the cream walls of the **Bellaire Arcade** encircle an outdoor courtyard filled with potted plants and tables. Bellaire is French for "beautiful air," and the arcade was originally built in 1925 with stores on the ground floor and offices upstairs.

Walk 2 blocks west and 2 blocks south to the intersection of Florida Avenue and Lemon Street. **The Julia Roberts House**, originally located at 415 Delannoy Avenue, was built in 1888 as a home and business for the city dressmaker, and is the oldest existing commercial building in Cocoa. The two-story cedar house with a tin roof has been restored and painted sky blue with white trim.

Rockledge Drive is a scenic byway and a National Historic District. Cocoa and Rockledge have long been considered sister cities, and Cocoa's downtown served both in the early years. Drive, bike, or walk from Cocoa Village via Riverside Drive at the end of Church Street. In just a few blocks the name of the road changes, and a sign marks the transition to the City of Rockledge. A mile down the road, pillars on the right lead into **Valencia Historic District,** a community of homes built during the land boom and designed by local architect Richard W. Rummell. Travel 2 blocks west, turn left on Osceola Drive, and come back east on Orange Avenue. When Henry Flagler brought the railroad to town, he built a spur line to transport visitors to the doors of nearby riverside resorts. The grand Hotel Indian River, on Rockledge Drive between Orange Avenue and Barton Avenue, once hosted President Grover Cleveland. The aging property was bulldozed in the 1950s to make room for condos, but the river view, framed by stately live oaks draped in hanging moss, remains. The original City Hall near the corner of Orange Avenue and Rockledge Drive is being converted into a Museum of Rockledge History. The **Barton Avenue Residential Historic District,** immediately south on Rockledge between Orange Avenue and Barton Avenue, features stately Queen Anne and Victorian homes from the turn of the 20th century. Most are privately owned. Brevard County has purchased and is renovating **Lawndale** at 1219 Rockledge Drive. Hiram Williams built his home in 1880 and one of the first schools in the area was held there.

LIBRARIES Brevard County Historical Commission (321-433-4415; www.brevardcounty.us/history) 801 Dixon Boulevard, Suite 1110, Cocoa 32922.

Explore the rich and colorful past of Brevard County online or by stopping by this historical archive. Historians and families with ties to the area can delve into video clips, newspapers, and maps that tell the life stories of Spanish explorers, early settlers, and builders of the space program. A three-volume *History of Brevard County* is available for review or purchase at their office. Hours may vary, so call ahead to arrange a visit.

Central Brevard Library and Reference Center (321-633-1792) 308 Forrest Avenue, Cocoa 32922. Open: Sunday 1–5, Monday, Wednesday, Friday, and Saturday 9–5, Tuesday and Thursday 9–8. Located just a few blocks from historic Cocoa Village, this is the largest library in the Brevard County system and a great resource for studying the past. Michael Boonstra, certified genealogist and historian, oversees an extensive collection of Brevard County records, including newspaper archives; marriage, real estate, and probate records; maps; and some city directories. Records from around the world are also available, as well as online access to the more popular family-history search engines.

Florida Historical Society Library of Florida History (321-690-1971; www .florida-historical-soc.org) 435 Brevard Avenue, Cocoa 32922. Open: Tuesday through Saturday 10–4:30. This statewide society has been collecting, preserving, and publishing Florida history for more than 150 years and they now occupy the site of the first Cocoa post office in historic Cocoa Village. An extensive collection of manuscripts, papers, maps, and other materials are available for on-site research. The **Florida Books and Gifts** shop offers publications about Florida or by Florida writers, including a large selection for children. Join the Discover Florida Lecture Series, with talks on Florida life and culture by contributors from many disciplines, at 2 PM. Events are scheduled on two Saturdays each month. The East Central Region of the Florida Public Archaeology Network, under the direction of Dr. Rachel Wentz, is located at the library. They host lectures and are available to answer questions about the area's valuable resources and discoveries.

Mosquito Beaters (www.mosquitobeaters.org) 435 Brevard Avenue, Cocoa 32922. Speedy Harrell is the founder and record keeper for this group of long-time Brevard County residents, who are dedicated to researching and recording the history of the area once called Mosquito County. Photographs, books, maps, and recorded stories are available to researchers. Find Speedy behind his desk inside the Florida Historical Society Library of Florida History.

MUSEUMS ✐ **Brevard Museum of History and Natural Science** (321-632-1830; www.brevardmuseum.org) 2201 Michigan Avenue, Cocoa 32926. Open: Tuesday through Saturday 10–4, Thursday through Saturday 10–4 (May–August). Admission: Adults $6, seniors and military $5.50, ages 5–16 $4.50. Every community has a few hidden gems, and this museum, with a goal of making history come alive, is such a find in Brevard County. Everyone in the family will enjoy the interpretive exhibits, historic artifacts, and scientific specimens that guide you through the natural and social evolution of the area. An Ais Indian village display (based on findings from the Windover archaeological discovery in North Brevard) provides a look at how the earliest settlers lived. A Cracker house and furnishings re-create a time when cowboys carried and cracked long, leather whips to herd cattle, kill rattlesnakes, and communicate danger with a Morse-code-like pattern. Dioramas show Brevard's ecosystems and creatures, and illustrate the interdependence of man and his environment. Outside, learn about native plants and wildlife while strolling through 22 acres of nature trails. To get to the museum, take FL 520 to US 1, head north 2.6 miles to Michigan Avenue, and then turn left 1.1 miles to the museum.

✳ To Do

BIRDING Rich Grissom Memorial Wetlands at Viera (321-637-5520) 10001 Wickham Road, Viera 32940. Thousands of ducks winter here—such as green- and blue-winged teals, mallards, and northern pintails. Black-necked stilts nest in spring and summer, and a bald eagle nest is visible from the road. Around one corner discover a neighborhood of herons, ibis, and other wading birds. Expect surprises. The most sought-after sighting may be the crested caracara.

BOATING: MARINAS AND RAMPS Cocoa Village Marina (321-632-5445; www.cocoavillage marina.com) 90 Delannoy Avenue, Cocoa 32922; ICW mile marker 897.5. Located in a protected basin at the north end of Cocoa Village, this first-class marina is a great stop for day guests, and boaters wishing to tie up for a longer stay. Dockage is available up to 110 feet, and amenities include showers, laundry facilities, ice, wireless Internet, cable television, and a sauna. If you're just stopping for lunch in the village, your stay is complimentary. Be advised: They don't sell fuel.

James G. Bourbeau Memorial Park (321-633-1874; www.brevard parks.com) 8195 King Street (FL 520), Cocoa 32926. The park has a dock and a two-lane public boat ramp, an airboat ramp, parking for 115 cars and boat trailers, a barbecue grill, and a pavilion. Here you'll have 24-hour access to the St. Johns River, and it's a stop along the Great Florida Birding Trail. Leroy Wright Recreation Area, directly across the road, has a launch for non-motorized boats.

AT BREVARD MUSEUM OF HISTORY AND NATURAL SCIENCE: DEPICTION OF EXCAVATION OF WINDOVER NATIVE AMERICAN ARCHEOLOGICAL SITE.

Lone Cabbage Fish Camp (321-632-4199) 8199 King Street (FL 520), Cocoa 32926. Use the launch ramp, and purchase bait and tackle. This genuine old Florida fish camp has a restaurant and airboat rides.

BOATING: TOURS AND RENTALS Grasshopper Airboat Eco Tours (321-631-2990; www.airboatecotours.com) Lake Poinsett Road, Cocoa (off FL 520, 0.5 mile west of I-95). U.S. Coast Guard Master Captain Rick takes passengers for a thrill ride and eco-tour on comfortable and stable state-of-the-art boats, providing up-close access to alligators and wildlife that abound in the St. John's River. Children age eight and older are welcome. $45 for 90-minute ride; group rates are available. Launch is from Lake Poinsett Lodge and Marina, at the end of Lake Poinsett Road.

Indian River Cruises (321-223-6825; www.indianrivercruises.com) Cocoa Village Marina. 90 Delannoy Avenue, Cocoa 32922. The wide stretch of the Indian River alongside the communities of Cocoa and Rockledge is a perfect spot for Brevard County's only sailing excursion, an unforgettable getaway that locals and visitors enjoy. Captain Mark and First Mate Joe host a maximum of six guests on a personalized cruise aboard the S/V *Double ShAAfted*, a luxury 47-foot catamaran with staterooms, two heads, and a wide deck with comfortable chairs and a trampoline lounger. Sail at 11, 2, or just before sunset. $50 per person for a two-hour tour. Romantic dinner-for-two or private dinner cruises for up to six can be arranged.

Island Boat Lines (321-454-7414; www.indianriverqueen.com) Take a trip back in time aboard the fully restored *Indian River Queen*, a romantic triple-decker paddlewheel riverboat. Food, drink, and live musical entertainment set the stage for a cruise down the Indian River. Catered charter excursions are perfect for family reunions, weddings, and other group functions. The schedule (available on their Web site) varies for general public cruises sailing on Friday nights, Sunday afternoons, space launch days, and holidays. Cruises depart from the east end of the dock at Cocoa Village Marina, at 90 Delannoy Avenue in Cocoa. $30–40 per person, plus tax.

Twister Airboat Rides (321-632-4199; www.twisterairboatrides.com) FL 520 at St. Johns River, Cocoa. Coast Guard-certified deluxe airboats, which launch onto the marshy St. John's River from Lone Cabbage Fish Camp (8199 King Street) in Cocoa, twist and turn at speeds up to 45 mph, with slowdowns so guests can capture amazing photos of wading birds, cypress trees, and alligators. Children ages 12 and older are welcome. For a 30-minute ride: adults $22, children $15. A minimum of four can book a longer ride for $45 for adults, $25 for children.

FAMILY FUN AND FITNESS Ace of Hearts Horseback Riding (321-638-0104; www.aceofheartsranch.com) 7400 Bridal Path Lane, Cocoa 32927. Life-long horse lover Sandra Vann carved the Ace of Hearts Ranch out of the scrub so visitors could experience the Florida habitat at a leisurely pace. Knowledgeable guides lead one-hour eco-tours on horseback through oak hammock, pine forest, palmettos, and wildflowers. Gentle horses accommodate riders over 10 years of age. Rides are offered daily, but times vary based on season; reservations are required. Trail rides $25. The ranch is located north of FL 528, about 25 miles from Cocoa Beach.

Baseball at Space Coast Stadium (321-633-9200; www.washingtonnationals .mlb.com, www.manateesbaseball.com) 5800 Stadium Parkway, Viera 32940. Every seat is a great seat in this red, white, and blue facility, which hosts Major League Baseball's Washington Nationals for spring training during March, and the Brevard County Manatees, a minor league affiliate of the Milwaukee Brewers, in the summer. Spring training games are a great chance to see professional players in a small venue. Minor league season runs from April to early September. General seating tickets can be purchased on game day; $7, $5 for military and students with ID, free for children under two. Pose outside by a mock-up of a space shuttle donated by the Kennedy Space Center.

✍ **Brevard Zoo** (321-254-9453; www.brevardzoo.org) 8225 N. Wickham Road, Melbourne 32940. The Brevard Zoo opened its gates in 1994 and has quickly gained a reputation as a premier regional zoo, a small zoo that does amazing things. Animals from around the world are showcased, with a special focus on the wildlife and nature of Florida and the habitats of Brevard County. Children love the Paws On exhibit with child-sized exhibits and experiences. A short train ride offers a quick chance to get your bearings and learn a little more about the native residents. Special programs like kayaking and the rhino encounter enrich the experience. The zoo is wheelchair accessible and has wheelchair and stroller rentals, free parking, a snack bar, and a gift shop. Open daily 9:30–5, with the last admission at 4:15. Adults $13.50, seniors $12.50, children 2–12 $10; animal exhibits and Paws On are included with admission. Train Ride $3 ages two and older; kayak tours $6 per person; rhino encounter $15 per person. Admissions support the zoo as well as wildlife conservation and education projects throughout the world. The zoo is located just off I-95 exit 191, near Viera. Here's a snapshot of what to expect: **Animal Exhibits:** Experience wildlife from around the world. See primates, gazelles, rhinos, and giraffes in Expedition Africa; wallabies, kangaroos, and Indonesian fruit bats, as well as exotic birds in a free-flight aviary, from Austral/Asia; and monkeys, tapirs, and giant anteaters from La Selva, the jungles of South America. Closer to home, the Wild Florida exhibit is a guaranteed spot to encounter alligators, red wolves, white-tailed deer, otters, and a bald eagle. Feeding the giraffes in Africa, and the lorikeets (parrots) and cockatiels in the aviary are perfect photo opportunities. Treats are available for a small charge. **Paws On:** Children are invited to build, explore, splash, and touch in this wonderland of fun. The petting zoo features alpacas, pigmy goats, and armadillos; a large aquarium and water play area offers a look at marine wildlife. Children can stay outside and build animal homes from natural resources

SPRING TRAINING GAMES AT SPACE COAST STADIUM ARE FUN FOR ALL AGES.

TICKLED PINK BY THE COLORFUL BIRDS AT THE BREVARD ZOO FREE-FLIGHT AVIARY.

like palm fronds, or go inside to a pretend veterinary lab with small animals. Parents will find ample seating and shading within easy view of their youngsters at play. **Kayaking:** Guided kayak tours take visitors down the Nyami Nyami River into Expedition Africa, or on a paddle through restored natural wetlands near Wild Florida. Children must be age 5 or older, and children 12 and under must be accompanied by an adult. Cost is $6 per person in addition to zoo admission.

FISHING See the "Recreation" chapter.

GOLF

Duran Golf Club (321-504-7776; www.durangolf.com) 7032 Stadium Parkway, Viera 32940. Price: Expensive. Designed to be playable for golfers of all abilities, this par 72, semiprivate, championship 18-hole course features plush-surface fairways and large, undulating greens. An equally well-maintained 9-hole, par 3, lighted course is open every night until 10. Amenities include a clubhouse with restaurant, lounge, and snack bar; driving range; and putting greens.

> **GREENS FEES**
> Inexpensive: Under $25
> Moderate: $25–50
> Expensive: More than $50

Turtle Creek Golf Club (321-632-2520; www.golfturtlecreek.com) 1279 Admiralty Boulevard, Rockledge 32955. Price: Moderate. Fairways meander through pines, oaks, and palms on this 18-hole course. The friendly semiprivate club welcomes guests for daily play or to join special events such as the shootout, a competition held every Saturday at 11:30 for players who maintain a handicap of 24 or less. Amenities include driving range, putting greens, rental clubs, restaurant, and bar.

NATURE PRESERVES AND PARKS James G. Bourbeau Memorial Park
(321-633-1874; www.brevardparks.com) 8195 King Street (FL 520), Cocoa
32926. Five miles west of I-95 on FL 520. Open: Daylight hours; boat ramp 24
hours. Admission: Free. Activities: Birding, boating, fishing, paddling. The winding St. Johns River flows south to north through Florida and forms much of the
western border of Brevard County. Nature writer Bill Belleville describes the
path of this liquid highway as "an indigo snake working its way through the tall
rushes and reeds." Outdoorsmen, boaters, and bass fishermen love gliding out
on this American Heritage river, thick with sawgrass and alligators. This park,
near the intersection of Lake Poinsett and FL 520, provides easy access to the
river. Across the street, the Leroy Wright Recreation Area has additional parking
for cars and boat trailers. Rest rooms, boat ramps, and docks are ADA accessible.

🐾 Rich Grissom Memorial Wetlands at Viera (321-637-5521) 10001 Wick-
ham Road, Viera 32940. The entrance is off Wickham Road, 2 miles west of
I-95. Open: Sunrise–Sunset. Activities: Birding, hiking, biking, photography. The
man-made habitat known informally as Viera Wetlands has quickly grown from
Brevard's best-kept secret to a popular ecosystem known throughout the world.
Park to walk or bike the perimeter, or drive slowly around the narrow 2-mile
path that winds through a wonderland of ponds, grasses, trees, and wildlife.
Keep the camera ready to capture the amazing variety of birds. Drivers get close
by using their car as a blind. An observation tower and gazebo provide a birds-
eye view. Pets must be on a leash at all times.

🐾 Riverfront Park at Cocoa Village (321-639-3500; www.cocoafl.org) Harrison Avenue, Cocoa Village. On the west side of Indian River at FL 520. Open:
Daylight hours. Admission: Free. Activities: Boating, fishing, family fun. Enjoy
an outdoor break from shopping in Cocoa Village at this 10-acre recreational site
bordering the Indian River that includes Lee Wenner and Taylor parks. The area
has an amphitheater, water feature, playground, boardwalk, and facilities for fishing and boat launching. Rest rooms are ADA accessible.

* Lodging

Hotels and Motels

**♂ Crowne Plaza Melbourne
Oceanfront Resort & Spa** (321-777-
4100, 1-800-227-6963; www.cp
melbourne.com) 2605 N. FL A1A,
Melbourne 32903. Price:
Expensive–Very Expensive. Wheelchair Access: Yes. Bask in beachside
luxury and exceptional service at this
eight-story hotel located just south of
the Eau Gallie Causeway. Standard
rooms, two-room suites, and kitchenette suites are decorated in relaxing

LODGING PRICES
Inexpensive: Up to $100
Moderate: $100–150
Expensive: $150–200
Very Expensive: Over $200

tones of deep sky blue, soft sunrise
yellow, and rich maroon. Guests
receive a delivered newspaper in the
morning, in-room movies, coffeemaker, microwave, small refrigerator, and

DINE IN AN INTIMATE, ROMANTIC
SETTING AT BLACK TULIP.

posh bedding at the end of the day. There's a choice of technology options, including high-speed Internet, a wireless data connection, and Internet browser TV. A Quiet Zone Floor caters to business travelers. Settle in a chair by the large pool and oceanside deck, or on a chaise lounge by the shore. Rejuvenate at the full-service Ocean Reef Spa. Coquina Restaurant serves fine dining indoors and out, and there is room service from early morning until late evening. Languages spoken by hotel staff include English, Hindi, Portuguese, and Spanish. Complimentary transportation is provided to Melbourne International Airport. The facility has received a Green Lodging designation from the state of Florida.

Holiday Inn Melbourne-Viera Conference Center (321-255-0077, 1-800-554-5188; www.ichotels.com) 8298 N. Wickham Road, Melbourne 32940. Price: Moderate. Wheelchair Access: Yes. This comfortable property in Viera has a history of providing attractive accommodations and exceptional guest service. Room options

include a standard, with a king or two double beds, and business suites, which add a seating area, sleeper sofa, workspace, microwave, and refrigerator. The RendezVous Restaurant and Lounge is open for casual dining every evening except Sunday, and several restaurants and fast-food outlets are located close to the hotel. Relax by the pool or take advantage of nearby recreation, including golf courses, shopping, baseball games, and the Brevard Zoo. The King Performing Arts Center is just 5 miles away, making this a convenient place to stay when in town for a performance.

✳ Where to Eat

Black Tulip (321-631-1133; www.blacktuliprestaurant.com) 207 Brevard Avenue, Cocoa 32922. Price: Expensive. Cuisine: European. Meals Served: L, D. For more than two decades owner Daniel Cazoni has provided Brevard epicures with the

Price codes are based on an appetizer, dinner entrée (or lunch if dinner is not served), and dessert, but they do not include tax, tip, or beverages.

Inexpensive: Up to $15
Moderate: $15–25
Expensive: $25–35
Very Expensive: $35 or more
The following abbreviations are used to identify what meals are served:

B: breakfast
L: lunch
D: dinner
SB: Sunday brunch

best of fine dining at the classy but comfortable Black Tulip restaurant in the heart of Cocoa Village. The signature dish for dinner is the inspired Tulip crisp roast duckling covered with a semi-sweet apple and cashew sauce. Each evening the chef also prepares a creative dish to recommend, but favorites like chicken breast Florentine and grouper in puff pastry are always available. The lunch menu has a light offering of soups, sandwiches, and salads, such as a shrimp salad-stuffed avocado served with fruit and vegetables, as well as smaller portions of entrées. The chilled gazpacho soup is perfect when dining on the covered patio on a pleasant summer day. The restaurant has a full bar. Closed Sunday and Monday; reservations are recommended.

Café Margaux (321-639-8343; www .margaux,com) 220 Brevard Avenue, Cocoa 32922. Price: Expensive. Cuisine: European/French. Meals Served: L, D. This jewel of a place, tucked away in a corner of the Bellaire courtyard, has won several dining awards and was selected by Zagat as one of the most popular restaurants on the Atlantic coast. French cuisine fuses with Mediterranean and Asian influences, reflecting the international training of Chef Erol Tugrul. Romantic dining rooms are decorated with elegant drapes and sparkling dinnerware. Waiters provide attentive service. Exotic hors d'oeuvres include baked Brie coated in macadamias and cashews with orange merlot sauce, and fine duck liver and peppercorn pâté. For lunch, enjoy a blackened red snapper sandwich on warm French bread served outside in the courtyard. Dinner entrées include

pastas, seafood, and meat dishes, including a traditional chicken breast Coq au Vin, along with some adventurous choices like spice-rubbed seared ostrich tenderloin. Several dishes will appeal to vegetarians, and there is a separate menu for young adults. Cocktails, beer, and premium wines are available by the bottle or glass. Closed Sunday; reservations are recommended for dinner.

Café Unique Amish Deli & Coffee Shop (321-504-0823; www.unique creationscourtyard.com) 607 Florida Avenue, Cocoa 32922. Price: Inexpensive. Cuisine: American-Casual. Meals Served: B, L. This charming establishment is truly unique as the name suggests, and as much a neighborhood gathering spot as an eatery. Food is simple, fresh, often organic, and heavy on vegetarian offerings. Although they have lots of items on the menu, the truth is they will usually combine what they have to prepare what you want. Breakfast is served all day and includes the standards along with Pennsylvania Dutch scrapple as an alternative meat choice. Pair with espresso, a latte, or one of their daily flavored coffees like blueberry. For lunch choose from salads, sandwiches, and wraps. Add a sweet treat—shoofly pie or ice cream. They are open to 6 PM on weekdays to accommodate early diners or provide evening take-out.

🍴 **Cara Mia Riverside Grill** (321-639-3388; www.caramiariversidegrill .com) 11 Riverside Drive, Cocoa 32922. Price: Moderate–Expensive. Cuisine: Italian. Meals Served: L (Monday through Friday), D. After an afternoon in the shops and galleries of historic Cocoa Village, stroll down to the water and drop in at this pleasant, casual eatery, with a romantic view of the wide Indian River. Service and satisfaction are high priorities for this family-run business, which serves northern and southern Italian dishes. Chefs prepare the food in an open kitchen. Start with an antipasti such as mussels Cara Mia, the New England variety served in a white wine or marinara sauce. Chicken, veal, and seafood are cooked to order or combined with fresh pasta, seasonings, and a myriad of sauces and vegetables to create delicious entrées. The wine list includes Italian and Californian varieties; house wines are available by the glass. Reservations are recommended for dinner.

Five Guys Burgers and Fries (321-633-0033; www.fiveguys.com) 2230 Town Center Avenue, Viera 32940. Price: Inexpensive. Cuisine: American-Casual. Meals Served: L, D. Sometimes you just want a really good burger—Five Guys is the place to go! The limited menu serves up burgers, dogs, fries, soda, and water. Everything is fresh and cooked-to-order in the open kitchen. Sloppy, juicy burgers are topped with any or all of 15 toppings, and then partnered with a bag full of hot, crispy fries. Vegetarians can select a grilled cheese or a grilled, melted combo of the 15 toppings.

Lone Cabbage Fish Camp (321-632-4199) FL 520 at St. Johns River, Cocoa 32922. Price: Inexpensive. Cuisine: Casual fare. Meals Served: L, D. A meal at this rustic camp is about as close as you'll come to catching your own fish and frying it in the pan. Try catfish, a house favorite, or something more adventurous, such as gator tail or frog's legs. Everything is served in a basket with fries, hush puppies, slaw, or baked beans. Sit on a picnic bench on the outside deck overlooking the beautiful St. Johns River. The best time to visit is on the weekends, when you can enjoy an afternoon of bluegrass or country tunes, always held on Sunday and sometimes Saturday, too. Dessert is simple: Just pick your favorite from the Good Humor wagon. Beer, wine, and soft drinks are available, or go with a real Southern treat—sweet tea poured over a tall glass of ice. Airboat rides take off about every 30 minutes. Families, bikers, young, and old gather here for a good time and a taste of old Florida. No wheelchair access in rest rooms.

The Melting Pot (321-433-3040) 2230 Town Center Avenue, Viera 32940. Price: Very Expensive. Cuisine: American-Gourmet. Meals Served: D. Gather around the fondue pot and dip in for fun, filling, and delicious food. Select your favorites from four courses. Start with a cheddar or Swiss cheese dip and a signature salad such as mushrooms and greens with a Parmesan Italian dressing. For the entrée, chunks of seasoned chicken, sirloin or filet mignon, seafood, and vegetables are gently lowered into hot oil or a vegetable bouillon base. For dessert, fruit, pound cake, and marshmallows are coated in milk or dark chocolate, which can be flavored with a liqueur such as amaretto or Baileys. To accompany your meal, choose from a full bar and extensive wine list. This is a leisurely dining experience equally perfect for an intimate evening for two or a festive group outing. The restaurant opens at 4 PM daily and 1 PM on the weekend; reservations are recommended.

Murdock's Bistro and Char Bar (321-633-0600; www.murdockscocoa village.com) 600 Brevard Avenue,

Cocoa 32922. Price: Moderate–Expensive. Cuisine: Eclectic. Meals Served: B, L, D. A grocery store back in 1940, this building has been renovated into a bright and airy restaurant with historical remnants from throughout Cocoa Village—windows from the old Hotel Brevard, rustic doors reclaimed for the bar top, and stained-glass windows on the ceiling. Dine inside, on the back porch, or at umbrella-covered sidewalk tables, where your doggie can tag along. Live music is played Wednesday through Saturday evenings. The fried pickles make an unusual and tasty appetizer, and hamburgers come in five different combinations. They also have soups, salads, and sandwiches. Dinner specials include old-fashioned dishes like chicken fried steak, pork chops, and meat loaf, served with Southern sides such as fried okra, black-eyed peas, and grits. A full bar can handle any wine, beer, or cocktail request. Reservations are recommended for groups. They open for breakfast at 9 AM weekdays; 10 AM weekends.

🐾 **Ossorio** (321-639-2423) 316 Brevard Avenue, Cocoa 32922. Price: Inexpensive–Moderate. Cuisine: American-Casual. Meals Served: B, L, D. When locals say, "Where should we meet?" this delightful diner is often the answer. Windows and bright colors transform this 1925 building in the center of historic Cocoa Village into an ideal spot for a break from shopping or to linger over a meal with friends. Behind the serving counter you'll find an array of delicious offerings, including breakfast baked goods, French pastries, flatbread pizza, sandwiches and salads, and an assortment of homemade, creamy ice creams. Each day they offer a creative soup or croissant sandwich. Seating spills onto the sidewalk, with an outside serving window and umbrella-covered tables where your dogs are welcome to tag along. The coffee shop uses fresh-roasted beans to brew tempting lattes and cappuccinos. Wine and beer are available.

Pizza Gallery & Grill (321-259-7598; www.pizzagalleryandgrill.com) 2250 Town Center Avenue Suite 113, Viera 32940. Price: Moderate. Cuisine: American-Casual. Meals Served: L, D, SB. Food becomes art at this roomy, colorful, and casual restaurant located at The Avenue Viera. The walls are lined with local artwork that's available for sale, and your meal is served on an artist's paint palette. Pizza is the main attraction, and they carry the largest gourmet pizza menu in Brevard. Combine any of the 60 toppings in a style just your own, or pick one of the chef's masterpieces like the Picasso Crab Cake pizza. Other food choices include sculpted salads and surreal sandwiches.

OSSORIO IS A WONDERFUL CAFÉ AT THE HEART OF COCOA VILLAGE; DOGS ARE WELCOME AT OUTDOOR TABLES.

Seafood, chicken, and pasta entrées are also available, and they have a full bar and outdoor patio. Sunday brunch includes complimentary mimosas and a sweet breakfast pizza with fruit, cinnamon cream sauce, powdered sugar, and a honey butter glaze. Reservations are recommended for groups.

Ryan's Village Pizza (321-634-5555) 405 Delannoy Avenue, Cocoa 32922. Price: Inexpensive. Cuisine: Italian. Meals Served: L, D. There's an Irish lad in town and he makes a perfect pizza with a crispy thin crust, a sweet tomato sauce, and piles of mozzarella cheese. The dough and sauce are freshly made every day. Stromboli, calzone, and submarine sandwiches are also on the menu, as well as light pasta dishes. Add wine and beer, a tropical fruit drink, or an iced mocha blend of espresso and chocolate. The word BANK etched in stone above the door is a reminder that this 1892 building was originally the first bank in Cocoa.

Ulysses' Prime Steakhouse (321-639-3922; www.ulyssesprimesteak house.com) 234 Brevard Avenue, Cocoa 32922. Price: Very Expensive. Cuisine: Steakhouse. Meals Served: D. This cozy establishment has taken fine dining up a notch in Brevard County with a reputation as one of the best restaurants in central Florida. It's a true gourmet steakhouse with a nod to the Greek heritage of owners Alex and Pamela Litras. *Florida Today* restaurant critic Gene Cate dubbed it "the area's fine dining mecca." Culinary skill, artistic presentation, and impeccable service weave together for a truly exquisite and unforgettable evening. The Avgolemono soup, a traditional Greek chicken soup blended with egg, lemon, and orzo pasta, makes a great starter. Most entrées are beef, prepared to melt-in-your-mouth perfection. A tender filet mignon is filled with roasted plum tomatoes, spinach, kalamata olives, and feta. End the evening with the macadamia-pecan baklava, a sweet, flaky treat flavored with Mt. Rainier fireweed honey and a tangerine glaze. Fine wines and cocktails complement your meal. Be prepared for sticker shock: Most entrées are about $40; sides are à la carte. Closed Sunday; reservations are recommended.

CAFÉS AND COFFEE SHOPS

Lea's Bistro (321-504-4004) 313 Delannoy Avenue, Cocoa Village 32922. Pick from a generous selection of soups, sandwiches, and salads. Foods like empanadas, Cuban sandwiches, and café con leche reflect the Cuban heritage of owners George and Lea.

Oleander Village Bakery and Cookie Factory (321-504-4301) 10 Oleander Street, Cocoa Village 32922. A tempting assortment of salads, canapés, and baked goods are available at this tiny shop, reminiscent of a European patisserie. Try smoked salmon on a breakfast bagel, with a salad, or in a sandwich made from fresh-baked bread. Homemade desserts such as almond croissants and carrot cake are as pretty as they are delicious. Open for breakfast and lunch.

Sunny Side Up Cafe (321-208-7951) 630 Brevard Avenue, Cocoa 32922. Breakfast is served all day at this charming spot at the south end of Cocoa Village. For lunch choose from a variety of healthy, homemade sandwiches, salads, soups, and sides.

ICE CREAM AND SWEET TREATS **The Village Ice Cream and Sandwich Shop** (321-632-2311) 120 Harrison Street, Cocoa 32922.

Pick up a quick lunch to go from the menu board of sandwiches and combine it with an old-fashioned grape or orange crush. Finish up with a cone from one of 35 flavors.

✳ Entertainment

MOVIES Satellite Cinemas (321-777-3778; www.satellitecinemas.com) Atlantic Plaza, 1024 A1A, Satellite Beach 32937. Atlantic Shopping Center Plaza is located on the west side of A1A, 12 miles south of FL 520.

Rave Motion Pictures Avenue 16 (321-775-1210; www.ravemotion pictures.com) The Avenue Viera, 2241 Town Center Avenue, Viera 32940. Take FL 520 westbound to I-95; go south on I-95 to exit 195. Turn right onto Wickham Road and then right onto Town Center Avenue.

MUSIC AND NIGHTLIFE Cocoa Village is taking baby steps to attract and keep crowds into the evening hours. **The Shamrock Room**, above Ryan's Pizza (105 Harrison Street) offers jazz, classical, and Irish music in a relaxing setting. Enjoy beer or wine, and order food from Ryan's. Great spot for a casual date or evening out with friends. Open Thursday through Saturday, 6–the wee hours. **The Dog 'n' Bone** (9 Stone Street) is just what you'd expect an English pub to be. Smoky rooms are crowded with 20-somethings enjoying conversation, darts, and live music on the weekends. Upstairs in the **Hippodrome Club**, they have a DJ or live music 6 nights a week. Patrons must be 21 years old, and the bar is open until 2 AM.

Café Unique (607 Florida Avenue, 321-504-0823, www.uniquecreations courtyard.com) presents dinner, danc-ing, and shows in their glitzy ballroom most Friday and Saturday nights. Call for reservations, or event-only tickets are available at the door.

Enjoy indoor and outdoor seating around the fountain at The Avenue Viera. Chuck and Maribeth, your hosts at **World of Beer** (2290 Town Center Avenue, 321-633-6665), serve over 500 imported and domestic brews from micro and craft breweries. Catch sporting events on big screen televisions. Acoustic musicians perform on Thursday, Friday, and Saturday evenings. Across the plaza, the **Pizza Gallery & Grill** offers a full liquor bar and features contemporary music on Friday and Saturday nights.

PERFORMING ARTS Brevard Theatrical Ensemble (321-676-0697; www.brevardensemble.com) Lady Gail B. Ryan leads this troupe of storytellers, who blend enchanting tales with Renaissance music and theater. Performances are held in venues throughout the area. Reserve ahead for recurring shows that sell out, including *Celtic Tales & Elegant Tea* in March, and *The Haunting of River House*, a Halloween season favorite. An evening with the *Dickens Christmas Carolers* adds a candy cane of fun to holiday plans.

Historic Cocoa Village Playhouse (321-636-5050; www.cocoavillage playhouse.com) 300 Brevard Avenue, Cocoa 32922. This elegant venue has had many reincarnations since opening in 1924. Today the restored 500-seat facility features Brevard Community College's *Broadway on Brevard* Series, bringing entertaining, top-quality musicals to the local community, along with performances by the Brevard Ballet Theatre. Attending one of their holiday productions has become an annual tradition for many area families. The youth drama group Stars of Tomorrow stages plays for young audiences.

✳ Selective Shopping

Historic Cocoa Village

It's difficult to tell where art ends and merchandising begins at this attractive, relaxing, and dog-friendly outdoor marketplace. Yesterday's riverside trading post has blossomed into a landscape of colorful shops interspersed with benches, fountains, and outdoor art. If shopping is part of your vacation itinerary, this is your destination.

HISTORIC COCOA VILLAGE PLAYHOUSE.

ANTIQUES AND COLLECTIBLES

Antique Emporium Mall (321-631-8377) 625 Florida Avenue, Cocoa 32922. This turquoise and yellow warehouse on the outskirts of Cocoa Village holds a vast collection of antique, vintage, and contemporary jewelry, clothing, books, housewares, artwork, and furniture. Multiple dealers participate, some with a booth and others with a separate room, like the hippie-dippy corner with bright-colored clothes and memorabilia from the 1960s. An auction is held every Thursday at 6:30 PM.

Caroline's House of Records (321-633-4600) 402 E. Brevard Avenue, Cocoa 32922. Step back in time and move to the tunes of the past. The racks contain over 30,000 vinyl memories, as well as posters and accessories like record sleeves and frames for album covers. Shipping is free for orders over $50.

Horse Feathers Antiques and Gifts (321-631-4959) 17 Stone Street, Cocoa 32922. Make this your lucky day. Pick up an old horseshoe from the bluegrasses of a Kentucky farm, or meander through a nostalgic display of vintage jewelry, fine porcelain, glassware, and sterling jewelry.

Stone Street Antiques (321-632-9924) 115 Harrison Street, Cocoa 32922. Three large rooms display all manner of antiques in a clutter-free and organized setting. Dishes, textiles, and other household items are sorted by room, a small alcove holds old sporting goods like golf clubs, boxing gloves, and baseball mitts. Select a historic postcard from this area for easy-to-pack souvenir.

CLOTHING, SHOES, AND ACCESSORIES

Downtown Divas (321-433-0727) 411 Brevard Avenue,

Cocoa 32922. Take a cruise, enjoy a night on the town, or just make a statement while wearing this daring metropolitan-style clothing for young women on the go.

Green Apples (321-635-8728) 111 Harrison Street, Cocoa 32922. The bright setting perfectly frames this fun, upscale collection of contemporary and comfortable women's clothing and accessories made from natural fibers that are wrinkle-resistant and ideal for warm climates. Stylish jewelry, bags, belts, hats, and shoes are also available, along with Life is Good merchandise in adult and children's sizes.

Mangos Fashion Boutique (321-639-3292) 319 Brevard Avenue, Cocoa 32922. Women of every age and size will have fun mixing and matching casual pants, skirts, shirts, and jackets in bright fabrics, then completing the outfit with a selection from the assortment of complementary jewelry, belts, shoes, and bags.

New Look Boutique (321-289-9145) 12 Stone Street, Suite 1, Cocoa 32922. A very small shop with a sur-

prisingly large and affordable collection of casual and resort wear appealing to every age and size. Start with a simple, sleeveless dress or top and enhance it with a delicate lace and beaded shrug, and finish the look with a tropical purse large enough for camera, sunscreen, and your favorite book.

Rare Essentials (321-633-6211) 415 Brevard Avenue, Cocoa 32922. Women's clothing, gifts, and accessories from the Vera Bradley and Brighton lines are the specialty of this establishment.

Season Tickets Boutique (321-690-1919) 301 Brevard Avenue, Cocoa 32922. Appropriately located directly across from the Cocoa Village Playhouse, this well-respected shop has been helping the women of Brevard County step out in fashion for nearly two decades with an unusual selection of international fashions, evening wear, sports and business clothes, shoes, and handbags.

VernaFlora Boutique (321-636-5532) 10 Stone Street, Cocoa 32922.

TREE-LINED STREETS OF HISTORIC COCOA VILLAGE.

Roger Scruggs

This cozy shop is brimming over with fanciful clothing and lingerie, bright and bold jewelry, and purses with flair, many handmade by local artists. Complete the outfit with a flowered scarf and matching shades.

A Village Home (321-633-1040) 212 Brevard Ave, Cocoa 32922. Find a special gift just for you in this charming boutique located in the French-inspired Bellaire Arcade. Choose from attractive lingerie, perfumed bath products, and scented candles like the Voluspa French lavender in a decorative tin. One set of shelves is home to a collection of soft, stuffed bears, perfect for a special child.

GIFTS AND SOUVENIRS Annie's Toy Chest
(321-632-5890) 405 Brevard Avenue, Cocoa 32922. Once upon a time, there were small, enchanting shops brimming with delightful toys for young boys and girls. This magical emporium harkens back to that time and will bring out the child in you. They carry collectible dolls, including Madame Alexander.

Bath Cottage (321-690-2284) 425 Brevard Avenue, Cocoa 32922. Create a world of pleasure and relaxation with a selection of soaps, bath salts, lotions, essential oils, and other pampering products from Crabtree & Evelyn and Thymes, along with soft, silky bamboo bedding and sleepwear.

Candles by G (321-638-4131) 402 Brevard Avenue, Cocoa 32922. The soybean Beanpod candles that are the specialty of this little shop in the Threadneedle Street Mall smell wonderful and burn longer than traditional candles. Wick cutters and decorative gifts are also available.

Coco's (321-433-0403) 402 Brevard Avenue, Cocoa 32922. The soothing scent of burning Soy Delicious candles invites visitors to relax and meander through an assortment of eco-friendly, contemporary, and high-quality jewelry and gifts. Moisturize your hands with a dab of the luke-warm candle wax.

From Olives & Grapes (321-205-1740) 12 Oleander Street, Cocoa 32922. Connoisseurs will enjoy sampling from a collection of balsamic vinegars and extra virgin olive oils from around the world. Gift-sized bottles are available premixed or you create your own special blend, like tangerine balsamic and Meyer lemon olive oil.

Gingerbread House (321-639-4694) 15 Oleander Street, Cocoa 32922. Proprietors John and Kelly have gathered a collection of crafts, gifts, collectibles, and home décor, along with Florida-themed items ranging from inexpensive magnets to higher priced hand crafted furniture.

Handwerk Haus (321-631-6367) 401 Brevard Avenue, Cocoa 32922. Traditional craftwork and fine collectibles fill this charming old-world shop from floor-to-ceiling, including Heartwood Creek painted figures by Jim Shore and pieces from the Nao collection by Lladro.

The Irish Shop (321-638-0608) 118 Harrison Street, Cocoa 32922. For Irishman Mike Blawn this wee shop celebrating his ancestral homeland is a labor of love. Discover products from Ireland like Belleek china and Galway crystal, teapots, jewelry, and other offerings that are just for fun. His books, music, and maps take visitors on an imaginary trip across the ocean. Erin go bragh!

Pear Tree (321-632-5432) 310A Brevard Avenue, Cocoa 32922. Slip down the rabbit hole into a shop of fun, functional, and unusual home accessories like wall clocks by designer and artist David Scherer, small fans hiding behind whimsical animal faces, and seashell or surfboard-shaped toilet flush handles.

Sand & Sea Gifts & Gallery (321-632-2745) 304 Brevard Avenue, Cocoa 32922. Male and female shoppers will all find something to like among the tropical and nautical décor, apparel, food treats, and art available at this island-themed shop. The tiki bar display is lined with cute signs, like WALK A DAY IN MY FLIP-FLOPS and colorful parrots in hanging swings. Collectors can buy assembled models of sailing vessels or a kit to make their own.

Space Coast Crafters (321-632-6553) 410 Brevard Avenue, Cocoa 32922. Pick up some great ideas for creating memorable pieces, or purchase already-completed handmade dolls, jewelry, woodcarvings, and ceramic pieces.

Sundancer Gallery (321-631-0092) 6 Florida Avenue, Cocoa 32922. Owner Jim McCarthy, of Blackfoot descent, carries on in the tradition of generations of Indian reservation traders at this Southwestern-style post. Most of the Native American art and artifacts are created and produced by tribes throughout North America, including authentic carved and painted Hopi kachina dolls. The gallery also serves as a Brevard County gathering place for local Native Americans and others interested in learning about the culture and participating in special events.

The Toy Box (321-632-2411) 419 Brevard Avenue, Cocoa 32922. Welcome to a miniature and magical world of dollhouses, available in kits or preassembled, along with an amazing selection of furnishings and accessories, even wallpaper and flooring materials.

HOME AND GARDEN Rendez-Vous & Something Different (321-633-0113) 121 Harrison Street, Cocoa 32922. Browse through a cornucopia of upscale, European-design home furnishings, including vases, floral arrangements, lamps and shades, custom-made pillows, bedding, quilts, duvet covers, draperies, and local art.

Travis Hardware Store (321-636-1441) 300 Delannoy Avenue, Cocoa

FIND NATIVE AMERICAN WORKS OF ART—LIKE THESE HAND-CRAFTED DRUMS—AT SUNDANCER GALLERY.

32922. Repeat visitors to Cocoa Village usually find their way to this friendly old-fashioned hardware store, where you can just browse or get help from the knowledgeable staff to find exactly what you need. Mac "Travis" Osbourne is the fourth generation of his family to operate this business, which opened in 1885 at the peak of the steamboat era. Today the store helps meet the hardware needs of NASA, the Air Force, and the next generation of rocket launchers.

Ventana al Mundo (321-633-5151) 402-F Brevard Avenue, Cocoa 32922. Owners Lynn and Tom offer a window to the world in their shop brimming with home accessories and wall hangings from Peru, Nicaragua, and Mexico, including pottery, pewter, candles, and hand-blown glass. They work with the Fair Trade Federation dedicated to creating opportunities for artisans and indigenous populations in developing areas.

JEWELRY Contemporary Concepts (321-632-9505) 216 Brevard Avenue, Cocoa 32922. Jewelry maker Janne Etz blends gold and silver wires with gemstones to handcraft chic, unique, and affordable jewelry, like her signature creation, ear sweeps, a strip of multiple jewels that slips into a single pierced hole and playfully climbs up your ear. Her small shop is tucked into the corner of the beautiful and historic Bellaire Arcade.

Jon's Fine Jewelry (321-631-0270) 215 Brevard Avenue, Cocoa 32922. Master jeweler Jon Miller creates stunning custom jewelry pieces, carries a showcase of diamond and colored gemstones, and features classic collections like Hearts on Fire diamond pieces, and newer lines such as Pandora, with interchangeable beads that quickly transform a piece from casual to formal.

SUNDRIES AND EXTRAS
Freida's Kritter Boutique
(321-639-8206) 116 Harrison Street, Cocoa 32922. Follow the paw prints—and bring your pet along if you like—to a pint-sized marketplace

THE FOUNTAIN IS AN OASIS AMID THE SHOPS AT THE AVENUE VIERA.

of toys, apparel, sunglasses, bandanas, and other goodies for the pampered pooch.

Nature's Spirit (321-632-1221) 405 Florida Avenue, Cocoa 32922. Owner Doreen invites you to try a holistic approach to healing the body and spirit with aromatherapy from natural, organic, and botanical products and oils. Books and music calm the mind. She also carries a small selection of apparel in natural fibers and holds weekly events.

What You Love to Do (321-504-0304) 602 Brevard Avenue, Cocoa 32922. This health and spiritual center at the southern end of Cocoa Village offers a selection of products and services designed to reduce stress, increase energy, and improve health. Select from gift and bath products, insightful books, and soothing music, or get a chair massage, Tarot card reading, or a detox footbath.

The Avenue Viera

The Avenue Viera (321-242-1200; viera.shoptheavenue.com) Viera 32940. Conveniently located off I-95, The Avenue Viera is a regional marketplace encompassing more than 50 department and specialty stores, 10 restaurants, coffee and ice cream stops, a 16-screen movie theater, and a park for special events or just relaxing amid fountains and plants. Some of the many shops here include: Coldwater Creek, Ann Taylor Loft, Glad Rags, Jos. A. Banks, Chico's, Old Navy, and Lane Bryant for clothing and accessories; Justice for young teen girls and Baby Zak's for children; World Market, Yankee Candle, and Bed, Bath & Beyond for the home; Books-A-Million and Belk department store; and Francesca's Collections and World of Beer for fun and unusual gifts.

February: ✤ **Space Coast Mardi Gras** (321-639-3976; www.spacecoast mardigras.com; Cocoa Village and Riverfront Park, Cocoa) The spirit of carnival comes to Brevard with an event drawing partiers to the banks of the Indian River. The family-friendly midway of rides, games, and concessions opens at 5 PM on Friday and 11 AM on Saturday and Sunday. Two stages at the nearby River Park Amphitheatre provide continuous music. When the sun goes down on Saturday, the streets of Cocoa Village light up with a boisterous and spirited crowd celebrating the masquerade party, and a parade with floats, stilt walkers, and local celebrities reigning as the king and queen. Sunday festivities include Paws in the Park, presented by the Central Brevard Humane Society. Dogs participate in contests and demonstrations, with one lucky pair picked as the king and queen dogs. Many of the events are ticketed.

July: **Fourth of July Concert & Fireworks** (www.cocoavillage.com/events; Riverfront Park, Cocoa) Cocoa Village turns red, white, and blue at this free celebration featuring the Brevard Symphony Orchestra. The concert of patriotic and pops classics begins at 8 PM.

November: ✤ **Space Coast State Fair** (321-639-3976; www.cocoa expo.com/fair; Cocoa Expo Sports Center, 500 Friday Road, Cocoa 32926) For 10 days, old-fashioned family fun runs rampant at the Cocoa Expo Center. One daily admission price covers name-talent concerts, thrill rides and midway, monster truck and motocross, bake-offs and pie-eating contests, and rodeo acts.

GALLERIES

In historic Cocoa Village, art is everywhere: Building murals set a scene of days gone by, colorful signs and decorated benches line the sidewalks, and galleries mimic the personality of the artists. No matter what the medium, expect expressions of nature from studios in this riverside locale.

BadBirds Gallery (302-218-6204; www.badbirdsgallery.com) 318 Delannoy Avenue, Cocoa 32922. Open: Tuesday through Saturday 12–6. Artist John Kalinowski has brought a bodacious bird to the Village, the Florida icon pink flamingo, and captured it drinking and dancing in witty, wonderful paintings and prints. Occasionally the bird emerges to parody famous works, like the artist's rendition of Whistler's Flamingo. In contrast, his gallery (in a restored 1920s fish house) also features WWII airplane-nose art and military posters. Visitors should try not to ruffle the artist's feathers if he is working and browse until he reaches a stopping point.

✍ **Carolyn Seiler Studios** (302-637-0444; www.carolynseiler.com) 318 Delannoy Avenue, Cocoa 32922. Open: Tuesday through Saturday 12–6. Carolyn Seiler's studio in the Village is easy to find—just follow the color. Working in oils, pastels, and acrylics, this versatile artist reflects the world around her in delightful, multi-hued paintings and sketches, as well as furniture, photo frames, and even the floor of her studio, where dolphins glide through swirls of the deep blue sea. Many of the works are original; others are reproduced in very low-priced posters and note cards. Seiler's passion is art education and she offers workshops and camps for children, including a drop-in class at 10 AM on most Saturdays.

The Clay Studio (321-636-4160) 116B Harrison Street, Cocoa 32922. Open: Monday through Saturday 7–4. This small pottery workshop tucked between two larger buildings is easy to miss. Wrought-iron gates swing open to a brick-lined path winding past a tropical bamboo garden and goldfish pond. A small green turtle peeks over a rock, but this turtle is imaginary. Here, artisan Harry Guthrie Phillips combines his passions for pottery and scuba diving to create nautical sculptures and functional pieces. Potter Eyca Moticska works and exhibits hand-thrown vases, chimes, and other pieces in blended earth shades of blue, green, cream, and brown.

Kurt Zimmerman Gallery & Studio (321-633-6514) 119 Harrison Street, Cocoa 32922. Open: Tuesday through Saturday 10–noon, 1–2:30. An assignment with the Apollo Moon Project brought Kurt Zimmerman to this area. Today, the works of this nationally renowned folk artist reflect his personal perspective of the universe. In his small upstairs gallery, Zimmerman enjoys challenging the senses and "making viewers aware of the greater dimensionality of life, a view very different from the normal day-to-day reality we perceive."

⚡ **Locklear Studio** (321-637-0061; www.loysannelocklear.com) 120 Harrison Street, Suite 2, Cocoa 32922. Open: Tuesday through Saturday 11–6. Potter Loys Anne Locklear molds clay pieces with natural materials and designs to create distinctively different works of art. Locklear is a member of the Lumbee Indian tribe and works entirely by hand, combining traditional Indian styles such as pinch, coils, and slabs, with contemporary techniques. Visitors must walk up a narrow staircase to reach her bright and roomy second-floor studio, with a small gallery adjoined to her work and classroom space. No guest leaves without a small token of her appreciation.

Miss Bailey's Curiosity Shoppe (321-636-1005) 404D Brevard Avenue, Cocoa 32922. Art for the home and for you best describes this shop's assortment of old and new treasures from around the world, including furniture, jewelry, glassware, décor, and one-of-a-kind purses and bags. One corner of the shop is devoted to the Black Dog Gallery and the works of longtime local artist Lori, whose whimsical style is immediately recognizable on the amusing wood paintings scattered throughout the village.

R. L. Lewis Gallery (321-433-0145; www.rllewisartist.com) 224 Forrest Avenue, Cocoa 32922. Open: Tuesday through Saturday 10–4. The door of the R. L. Lewis Gallery opens into a world of Florida landscapes and coastal scenes. Lewis, a Cocoa native, was one of the legendary Florida Highwaymen—a group of African American artists who traveled the state selling art from their cars because they were denied access to galleries. Today this retired art teacher and member of the Florida Artists Hall of Fame sells his own original works, as well as paintings from fellow Highwaymen. The gallery is a few blocks north of Cocoa Village but well worth the detour.

ARTISTS JOHN KALINOWSKI AND CAROLYN SEILER SHARE STUDIO AND GALLERY SPACE IN COCOA VILLAGE.

WILDLIFE PROFILE: PELICAN

The big, bulky brown pelican is an odd-looking bird, with dull gray-brown feathers and a white head. A long, flat bill scoops up water, and an expandable black pouch holds the catch. On land, the pelican waddles on short legs and wide-webbed feet.

Everything changes when this amusing creature takes flight. Often flocks of pelicans form a V and glide and flap in unison like synchronized swimmers dancing in the blue waters of the sky. A single bird may coast for a long distance, just skimming the water's surface. In its most daring move, a pelican soars up to 60 feet high, suddenly diving headfirst into the water to grab a fish.

A more attractive cousin, the American white pelican, with white, black-tipped wings, arrives annually from the north to winter along Florida's shallow, fish-filled coastal lagoons. In spring both species of pelicans roost in colonies in the mangroves of the Indian River Lagoon, where eggs can be protected from predators and food is more readily accessible. Immature birds are distinguishable from adults by a brown head that turns white at three or four years of age.

The brown pelican is one of the most entertaining birds in the area. The adult eats 4 pounds of fish daily and is busy and visible even during the hottest hours. Pelicans track fishermen as well as fish. When boats return to the docks at Port Canaveral in late afternoon, the birds patiently queue up like theme-park visitors in line for the next attraction. Once the catch of the day is unloaded, pelicans sift the water for remnants of the day's catch. Remember that pelicans are wild and should not be directly fed.

Space Coast Sightings: Brown pelicans are always near the water—at the beach and in inland waterways. Spot them up close on fishing piers and docks. The best places to see white pelicans (November to March) are Merritt Island National Wildlife Refuge, Cocoa Beach Thousand Island, and the Port Canaveral locks.

BROWN PELICAN (*PELECANUS OCCIDENTALIS*)

Jim Angy

North Brevard 3

NORTH BREVARD

The old, the new, and the natural converge in north Brevard County. The city of Titusville on the Indian River Lagoon is the oldest settlement in the county, and once flourished as a docking site for 19th-century sailing vessels. Today, Space View Park along the river faces Kennedy Space Center. Monuments to the Mercury, Gemini, and Apollo programs echo with the cheers of crowds who gathered by a giant countdown clock to watch over 130 space shuttle missions soar into the vast waters of the universe. Historical Downtown Titusville is restored with shops, eateries, and galleries.

More than 50 years ago, the government purchased thousands of acres of scrubland at the north end of Merritt Island (just across the Indian River) for military and space programs. NASA owns the land and operates on about one-third of it. The remainder is protected and maintained by the Department of the Interior. How ironic that space-age technology, which brought significant and sometimes unwelcome development to the area, also ensured that two large adjacent parks, Merritt Island National Wildlife National Refuge and Canaveral National Seashore, would remain in much the same pristine condition as when the Ais Indians roamed the area.

GETTING THERE Plan on a drive time of 30 to 60 minutes to reach most of the attractions in this area. Kennedy Space Center is about 30 miles from Cape Canaveral. To get there, follow FL 528 west and exit north on US 1. FL 405 eastbound leads directly over the NASA Parkway to Kennedy Space Center. To reach historic downtown Titusville, continue a few miles north to the intersection of US 1 and Main Street. Garden Street, FL 406, is 3 blocks north of Main Street. Go east over the bridge to reach the Merritt Island National Wildlife Refuge and Canaveral National Seashore.

✴ To See

✎ **Kennedy Space Center Visitor Complex** (321-449-4444; www.kennedy spacecenter.com) NASA Parkway, Merritt Island 32899 (off FL 405, 0.5 mile east of US 1). Open: Daily at 9; closing times vary. Closed Christmas. Admission: Adults $38, children ages 3–11 $28. The John F. Kennedy Space Center opened in 1962 as the launch facility for NASA and the last stop on Earth before astronauts headed into space. This all-day theme park, operated by Delaware North Companies Parks & Resorts, Inc. on behalf of NASA, blends entertainment and technology with authentic equipment and operations to tell the story of our nation's past, present, and future space exploration. Learn about each chapter of the manned space program through interactive exhibits, rides and attractions, IMAX movies, and a variety of special tours. Take your time selecting the ticket you want. Regular admission covers most of the center, or you can choose combo tickets that fold in tours and special activities. All attractions are wheelchair accessible, and complimentary strollers and wheelchairs are provided. Whether you're mildly interested in space or over the moon about the topic, a visit to the Kennedy Space Center Visitor Complex is fun, educational, and awe-inspiring for all ages. If you don't get to see it all the first day, a second day is included in the admission price. In addition to life-sized rockets, actual moon rocks, a space exploration play dome for children, and the largest space merchandise shop on the planet, here are some highlights, most included with the regular ticket.

Climb aboard the exciting **Shuttle Launch Experience** ride and experience the out-of-this-world thrill of flying aboard a shuttle as it launches into space. Astronaut testimonials prepare you for the trip, and then veteran astronaut Charlie Bolden conducts a pre-flight briefing. Everything is go for launch, so buckle up and prepare for liftoff as your shuttle rumbles, roars, and soars skyward. Once in orbit, the peaceful silence of space settles in, and the payload bay doors slide open to provide a breathtaking look back at planet Earth. At nearby **Space Shuttle Plaza**, walk through a full-sized mockup of a space shuttle. The shuttle program is set to retire soon. Now the adventure is captured for all time.

THE KENNEDY SPACE CENTER TOUR STOPS AT THE INTERNATIONAL SPACE STATION CENTER, STAGING AREA FOR THE SPACE LABORATORY COMPONENTS BEFORE THEY ARE DELIVERED VIA THE SPACE SHUTTLE.

Courtesy NASA

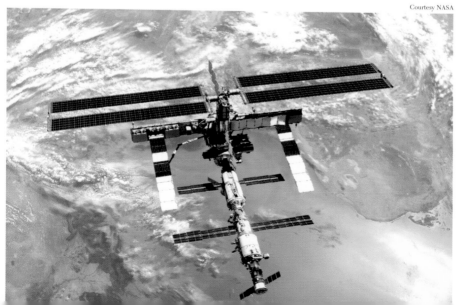

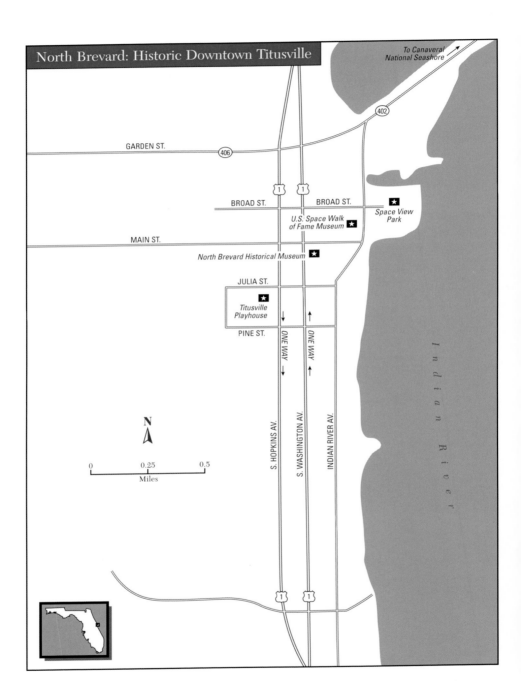

North Breavard: Historic Downtown Titusville

To Canaveral
National Seashore

402

GARDEN ST. — 406

1 1

BROAD ST. BROAD ST.

★ Space View Park

U.S. Space Walk of Fame Museum ★

MAIN ST.

North Brevard Historical Museum ★

JULIA ST.

★
Titusville Playhouse

PINE ST.

ONE WAY ONE WAY

ONE WAY ONE WAY

S. HOPKINS AV.

S. WASHINGTON AV.

INDIAN RIVER AV.

Indian River

N

0   0.25   0.5
Miles

1 1

Just over 500 privileged men and women have actually traveled into space. With the **IMAX Experience,** viewers join them through video, special effects, and a wall of sound that moves the audience into the exciting and challenging world of space exploration. Much of the film footage for *Magnificent Desolation: Walking on the Moon 3D,* narrated by Tom Hanks, was shot during actual NASA missions. Leonardo DiCaprio narrates *Hubble 3D,* which recounts the amazing journey to photograph the farthest depths of the universe, The IMAX 3D camera that recorded the stunning images of an astronaut walking in space to repair the telescope, flew from Kennedy Space Center in May 2009 aboard Space Shuttle *Atlantis.* **Eye of the Universe: The Hubble Telescope** exhibit is just outside the IMAX theatre and takes guests down a pathway of images and models of ancient stars, nebulae, and galaxies captured by Hubble cameras.

On the **Kennedy Space Center Tour,** a short bus ride takes you to NASA operations while a video explains the sights. Get great photos at the historic Launch Complex 39 observation gantry with a panoramic view of Kennedy Space Center. Drive by the Vehicle Assembly Building, where vehicles are prepared for launch, and then stop and tour the **International Space Station Center**, where components of the space station were processed and prepared for the trip into orbit. See how crew members live, sleep, and work in a full-scale mock-up of the Habitation module. Next stop is the **Apollo/Saturn V Center** and **Apollo Treasures Gallery**. The main attraction is a fully restored, 363-foot-tall *Saturn V* moon rocket lying on its side for an up-close view of how it was assembled and stacked. This 6.5-million-pound engineering marvel roared into the heavens on November 9, 1967. Less than two years later, on July 20, 1969, Neil Armstrong took "one small step for man, one giant leap for mankind" as he planted an American flag on the lunar surface.

Check the **Astronaut Encounters** schedule when you first arrive to plan around this opportunity to visit with an astronaut. For a half hour you'll hear stories and have a chance to ask questions. For a more personal experience, join an astronaut for lunch. The buffet is a great midday meal and is accompanied by a video about life in space. Over dessert, an astronaut joins the group, shares personal comments, and answers questions. Each guest gets a signed picture of the host and a few minutes for a personal photo opportunity. The cost is $60.99 for adults and $43.99 for children, and it includes regular park admission.

For a more in-depth look at the space program facilities, sign up for one of the guided **special-interest tours.** *NASA Up Close* brings you the closest to the launch pads and swings by the shuttle landing strip—which is so long that it's visible from space. *Cape Canaveral: Then and Now* goes back in time with a visit to **Canaveral Air Station and the Air Force Space & Missile Museum,** site of the first successful satellite launch in 1958. Both bus excursions take three to four hours. The ticket price for each is $59 ($43 for children), which includes regular admission. Unless you're a space buff, you may not want to spend the extra time and money.

In 1984 the six surviving Mercury program astronauts and others formed the Mercury 7 Foundation to honor space travelers and provide scholarships to strengthen America's leadership position in science and technology. The group, now the Astronaut Foundation, is still giving scholarships and is also the driving force behind the **U.S. Astronaut Hall of Fame.** At the museum, visitors learn the human story behind space travel and discover the largest collection of astronaut artifacts and mementos ever assembled. Those who want to put themselves through the paces that separate NASA's best from the rest can try out the interactive simulators that offer a true taste of space, like the G-Force Trainer, which simulates the pressure of four times the force of gravity. The Hall of Heroes celebrates astronauts inducted into the Hall of Fame. This entertaining and interactive facility is 6 miles from the visitor complex.

Take your space visit to the edge with the **Astronaut Training Experience (ATX)**, one- or two-day interactive immersion programs that include education, hands-on training exercises, and a team-based simulated mission. Children ages 8 to 14 can get a head start on the dream of a future in space at **Camp Kennedy**, week-long daytime sessions held during the summer. Special programs are available for individuals, families, and student groups. Check the Web site for more details.

✎ STAR LIGHT, STAR BRIGHT: VIEWING A SPACE LAUNCH

A thunderous rocket liftoff is the best show in town. A streamer of white smoke blazes a trail across a clear blue sky. At night the fiery craft fades in the distance until resembling a single bright star. Traffic is heavy, so arrive early and plan on delays heading home. Consider access to refreshments and rest rooms when parking on the side of the road. Kennedy Space Center, Merritt Island National Wildlife Refuge, and Canaveral National Seashore are closed before launches.

Viewing Sites

1 Port Canaveral has outstanding views from Jetty Park and the restaurants and bars along Glen Cheek Drive.

2 The beaches of **Cape Canaveral and Cocoa Beach** are ideal spots, especially to the north around the Cocoa Beach Pier.

3 On FL 528, the **Bennett Causeway over the Banana River** has off-road parking space, and several boat tour operators schedule special outings.

4 US 1, north and south off FL 50, has parks right along the Indian River.

5 US 1 at FL 406 in Titusville is directly across from the launch pads. Sand Point Park and Space View Park make accommodations for crowds, and parking is plentiful in the downtown Titusville area.

6 Kennedy Space Center Visitor Complex offers a bus ticket that will get public visitors as close to the launch pads as possible.

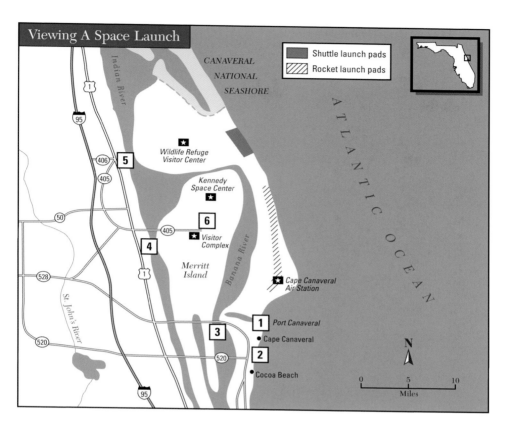

Viewing A Space Launch

CANAVERAL
NATIONAL
SEASHORE

Shuttle launch pads
Rocket launch pads

ATLANTIC OCEAN

Indian River

95

1

406

405

5

Wildlife Refuge
Visitor Center

Kennedy
Space Center

6

405

4

Visitor
Complex

*Merritt
Island*

Banana River

Cape Canaveral
Air Station

50

528

1

520

St. John's River

520

3

1

Port Canaveral

Cape Canaveral

2

Cocoa Beach

95

N

0   5   10
Miles

Space Walk of Fame and Astronaut Memorial at Space View Park (321-264-5105; www.brevardparks.com/parks/index.htm) 101 N. Washington Avenue, Titusville 32796. Open: 7 AM–dark. Admission: Free. This expansive waterside park in the heart of historic Titusville honors space workers who built a path to the moon through the Mercury, Gemini, and Apollo programs. Monuments mark the completion of successful missions, and handprint plaques from Hall of Fame astronauts line the walkways. Built on three separate sites, the park is directly across the Indian River from Kennedy Space Center and offers the absolute best off-property spot for viewing space launches. Downtown Titusville has plenty of parking, rest rooms are available, and a giant clock counts down to blast-off.

✦ **U.S. Space Walk of Fame Museum** (321-264-0434; www.spacewalkoffame .com) 4 Main Street, Titusville 32796. Open: Monday through Friday 10–5. Admission: Free. Step behind the scenes at this museum that honors the men and women who made the dream of space travel a reality, along with the astronauts who flew the missions. Retired workers dedicated to preserving America's space history have compiled a collection of artifacts, scale models, rare photos, and other exhibits. Personal tales are woven into the tours by volunteer docents like Sam Beddingfield, who was recruited by Gus Grissom to join NASA as an engineer in 1959, just as the manned space flight program was gearing up. By the time he retired in 1985, 23 shuttle launches had flown. Pint-sized astronaut suits and detailed scale models of rockets and the shuttle are among the unusual offerings found in the gift shop.

Valiant Air Command Warbird Museum (321-268-1941; www.vacwarbirds .org) 6600 Tico Road, Titusville 23780. Open: Daily 9–5; closed Thanksgiving, Christmas, and New Year's Day. Admission: Adults $12; seniors, military $10; ages 4–12 $5. A warbird is an airplane once used by the armed forces of any country that is now privately owned. At this museum, such aircraft dating from before World War I until today are restored and displayed to preserve aviation history and honor their courageous pilots. The *Tico Belle*, a C-47 from the D-Day invasion shares space with a Grumman F-14 like the one shown in the movie *Top Gun*. The museum includes a gift shop and library, and it is located next to Space Coast Regional Airport. Check the Web site for dates of the spring Tico Warbird Airshow, a three-day extravaganza of flying exhibitions, and the November Veteran's Day Open House with free admission for all active and retired military, and Brevard County residents.

Zero G Weightless Flights (954-756-1000; www.gozerog.com) Price: $5,000 and up. The future of space tourism is here. A modified Boeing 727 flies multiple parabolic arcs, each one allowing you and a group of family or friends to levitate in weightlessness for up to 30 seconds at a time. Fly across the cabin or do a backflip. This is truly an out-of-this-world vacation adventure. "Space, here I come," was physicist Stephen Hawking's reaction after his brief flight from Cape Canaveral. Call or check the Web site for schedule and booking.

HISTORIC PLACES The roots of the Brevard County family tree are planted in the rich soils and marshes of north Brevard. In 1837, during the Seminole Wars, the U.S. government built Fort Ann to guard the strategic strip between Mosquito Lagoon and the Indian River, and a small center of trading developed nearby. Growth really took off in 1885 when Titusville became a transportation hub, with a railroad spur line connecting inland travelers to steamboats for a scenic excursion down the Indian River. Passengers lining up at the city wharf could not have imagined that less than a century later that sandy spot would be a front-row seat for history in the making—a trip to the moon.

The starting point for a walk through **historic downtown Titusville** is the intersection of Washington Avenue and Broad Street. The first rail service came east down Broad Street and linked to steamboat traffic at the river wharf. By the turn of the 20th century, the East Coast Railway depot was built 2 blocks south on Julia Street. This was the center of commerce. Most of the buildings on Washington Avenue date from around 1910 to 1920 and are a simple masonry design constructed following a fire that destroyed earlier wood structures. Stores, banks, and businesses lined the east side; hotels and boardinghouses were across the street. The **Washington Hotel** was on the corner, and you can still see balconies, once shaded with bright awnings. Kloiber's Cobbler Eatery at

337 S. Washington Avenue, once **Denham's** dry goods and clothing store, has been restored inside and out to bring back much of the original design features. The **Emma Parrish Theater** on the corner of Julia Street and S. Hopkins Avenue opened as a venue for silent movies in 1912 and quickly became the community's cultural center. Today it is commonly known as the Titusville Playhouse. Many of the furnishings are original.

St. Gabriel's Episcopal Church, at the corner of Pine Street and Palm Avenue, was built in 1887 with old stand longleaf pine, native to the area. This renovated and expanded neo-Gothic-style church maintains its original character. Names below the stained-glass windows tell the story of the area's early families. Across the street is the **Brevard County Courthouse,** built in 1913 to replace a small wood structure erected in 1882 when Titusville was designated as the county seat. Four large classical columns are at the entrance; the jail was on the third floor. On the opposite corner is the **oldest government building** still standing in the county, a brick and concrete facility built in 1903 for the Clerk of the Court. The 1891 **Pritchard House,** at the corner of Washington Avenue and Pine Street, was home to Captain James Pritchard and his wife, leading citizens in the growing town. The stately two-story residence built with heart pine is an example of Queen Anne architecture popular in Florida during this period. The upstairs porch on the southeast corner of the second floor would have provided a magnificent view of the Indian River, just a block away at that time. Pritchard family members lived in the home until 2005. It now belongs to the county and is being renovated as a house museum, with original period furnishings throughout.

The historic **LaGrange Church** is just a short drive north to the intersection of Dairy Road and Old Dixie Highway. Built in 1869, it is the oldest Protestant church south of St. Augustine and is restored to its original condition, except for the addition of electricity. Colonel Titus and civil rights activists Harry and Harriette Moore are among those buried in the older front section of the shaded church cemetery.

MUSEUMS ✇ **American Police Hall of Fame and Museum** (321-264-0911; www.aphf.org) 6350 Horizon Drive, Titusville 32780 (west of the entrance to the Kennedy Space Center Visitor Complex). Open: Daily 10–6; closed Thanksgiving, Christmas, and New Year's Day). Admission: Adults $12; seniors, military, and children $8; free under four years old. Law enforcement officers and family members of those killed on duty are admitted free to this museum, which pays homage to America's police force. A memorial to officers killed in the line of duty since 1960 includes a dedicated exhibit to personnel who perished on September 11, 2001. Entertaining exhibits trace the history of law enforcement, crime, and punishment from the days when bad behavior was punished with a visit to the guillotine. Reality and mythology mix with displays about the mobsters of the 1920s next to cars and memorabilia from television and the movies. Learn how a crime lab works or hop on a police motorcycle. The entire facility is kid-friendly, and in the Discovery Zone youngsters can practice dialing 911, hear tips for staying safe, and make their own police officer badge to take home. The

$35 Big Ticket covers museum admission, instruction, and ammo on the gun range. Gun range restricted to U.S. citizens age 13 and older.

Harry T. & Harriette V. Moore Cultural Center (321-264-6595; www .brevardparks.com/htm/index.php) 2180 Freedom Avenue, Mims 32754. Open: Monday through Friday 9–6, Saturday 10–6, Sunday 2–6. Admission: Free. The story of civil rights pioneers Harry T. and Harriette V. Moore is the lodestar for this center that illuminates the path of African American history in America. The Moore's were killed on this site when a planted bomb exploded under their home Christmas night, 1951. Working closely with their daughter, Evangeline, builders have created a replica of the home and furnishings as they were at that time. Inside the museum, a narrative and timeline of photographs place their experience in the context of the struggle for civil rights. Knowledgeable staffers are available to conduct tours of the home and answer questions. This young nonprofit organization is just beginning to build a collection of documents, memorabilia, and artifacts. Performing-arts programs and classes are offered at the facility. To get there, follow US 1 for 2.6 miles north of Main Street in downtown Titusville. Turn left on Parker Street. Freedom Road is 0.4 mile farther on the left.

North Brevard Historical Museum (321-269-3658) 301 S. Washington Avenue, Titusville 32796. Open: Tuesday through Saturday 10–3. Admission: Free; donations appreciated. The rooms of this cozy facility, located in the center of historic Titusville, are chock-full of books, artifacts, furnishings, and photographs telling the stories of north Brevard. The museum displays vintage uniforms representing every service branch. The collection includes memorabilia from Titusville's beginnings, including items belonging to city founding father, Henry Titus. Visitors will enjoy a visual trip through the late 19th and early 20th centuries. Residents or others with roots in this area may find pictures of themselves or ancestors in school yearbooks and records of local organizations. Call ahead to request guided tour.

✳ To Do

BIRDING Black Point Wildlife Drive (321-861-0667; www.fws.gov/merritt island) Merritt Island National Wildlife Refuge, North Merritt Island. The 7-mile Black Point Wildlife Drive loop is one of the premier birding spots in the country. The refuge has documented more than 320 species of birds, including wood storks and bald eagles, gulls, terns, sparrows, and raptors. A flock of roseate spoonbills provides a breathtaking sight. Seven walking trails branch off from the loop and lead through a variety of habitats. A birding guide and loaner binoculars are available at the visitor center, and field trips take place during peak times. Call ahead for reservations.

Canaveral National Seashore (321-267-1110; www.nps.gov/cana) 212 S. Washington Avenue, Titusville 32796. The undeveloped coast of the national seashore features an abundance of shorebirds, especially during the fall and winter. Elevated platforms provide a venue for scoping gannets and jaegers out at sea. Along the road to the beach there are ponds that attract wading birds and waterfowl.

BOATING: MARINAS AND RAMPS **Bair's Cove** Haulover Canal, Merritt
Island National Wildlife Refuge (321-861-0667; www.fws.gov/merrittisland),
North Merritt Island. Encounter birds, manatees, and dolphins, as well as barges
and yachts, in the Intracoastal Waterway connecting Mosquito Lagoon and the
Indian River. A natural sandy beach launch for kayaks and canoes is at the end of
the dirt road heading west across from the manatee viewing deck.

Eddy Creek Canaveral National Seashore (386-428-3384, ext. 10; www.nps.gov/
cana) 212 S. Washington Avenue, Titusville 32796 (local office). There is an
access launch available for motor and non-motorized boats entering the south-
ernmost part of Mosquito Lagoon. Amenities include parking and rest rooms.
There is a $3 per person fee to enter the national seashore.

Marina Park Near US 1 and Garden Street, Titusville, past Titusville Marina.
There is a public launch for non-motorized boats, as well as a a two-lane boat
ramp. Open 7 AM–dark.

Parrish Park Max Brewer Causeway (FL 406, on the east side of the Indian
River), Titusville. Has a public launch on south side for paddlers heading south
on the Indian River.

Titusville Municipal Marina. (321-269-7255) 451 Marina Road (south of
marker 27), Titusville 32796. This marina has 195 slips in a protected basin with
floating docks. Transients are welcome. Ship's store, gas, and fuel.

BOATING: TOURS AND RENTALS **A Day Away Kayak Tours** (321-268-
2655; www.adayawaykayaktours.com) First-timers and experienced paddlers
alike will enjoy Mike and Elizabeth's two-hour guided tour into the Haulover
Canal and Merritt Island National Wildlife Refuge. Multi-day, overnight, and
more challenging tours can be custom planned. For an unforgettable experience,
sign up for a moonlight paddle, or the bioluminescent night tour offered during
the summer season. This is a great family experience. Children three and older
are welcome, but consider the capability and patience of the child. $24–32 per
person; reservations required. Single, double, and fishing kayaks are also available to rent. Fee includes paddle, life jacket, whistle, and equipment to secure
boat to your car. $20 half day, $30 full day for single; $35 half day, $45 full day
for double.

Brevard Zoo (321-254-9453; www.brevardzoo.org) Trained naturalists from the
Brevard Zoo guide groups on kayak eco-tours through the Haulover Canal at
Merritt Island Wildlife Refuge, Manatee Cove on Merritt Island, and Samson's
Island on the Banana River. $30–50 per person.

Kayaks by Bo (321-689-3404; www.kayaksbybo.com) 515 Garden Street,
Titusville 32796. Owners Tom and Lynn have transformed their passion into
their work. The local couple loves the nature and beauty of the Indian River
Lagoon. Visit their store where boats are also for sale, or give them a call.
"Deliver to the river" is their motto. Single kayaks are $29 for a half day and $39
for a full day; two-seaters are $35 and $45 respectively, with a $5 delivery fee.
Life jackets and safety whistles are included.

CAMPING AND RVING Canaveral National Seashore (386-428-3384, ext. 10; www.nps.gov/cana) 212 S. Washington Avenue, Titusville 32796 (local office). The National Park Service offers backcountry camping along the beach from November 1 through mid-April, and year-round on designated islands in Mosquito Lagoon. Campsites are $10 per night, and a permit must be picked up in person from the information center located at the north end of the seashore near New Smyrna Beach. Advance reservations are required. The sites are very primitive and have no fresh water or sanitation facilities. Island sites are only accessible by boat, canoe, or kayak. Campers are advised to bring a cell phone and plenty of bug repellent.

Manatee Hammock Park (321-264-5083, fax 321-264-6468; www.campspace coast.com) 7275 S. US 1, Titusville 32780. This 26-acre site, located on the banks of the Indian River about halfway between the Beachline Expressway and Titusville, offers 147 shaded RV spots with water, electric, and sewer, and 35 campsites with water and electric. Hot showers are available. Other amenities include shoreline fishing, laundry facilities, a fishing pier, a small swimming pool, and a perfect view of space launches. Operated by Brevard Parks.

❦ **Titusville KOA** (321-269-7361, 1-800-562-3365; www.koa.com) 4513 W. Main Street, Mims 32754. KOA Kampers will be pleased to discover this location, a perfect base for exploring Merritt Island National Wildlife Refuge and Kennedy Space Center attractions. The shady, rural setting has a clubhouse, swimming pool, and convenience store; free wireless Internet; and bicycle rentals. Rent a tent or RV site, or reserve an air-conditioned cabin or lodge with a kitchenette and enough beds to sleep six (with your own linens). Pets are permitted, with restrictions for some large dogs.

FAMILY FUN AND FITNESS Space Coast Geocachers (321-459-1050; www.spacecoastgeocachers.com) 55 Goodwin Drive, Merritt Island 32952. Fans of treasure hunting through geocaching will find this is a great tool for exploring many of the parks and recreational spots in Brevard County. Grab your GPS navigator and hit the road, but be careful not to disturb or be disturbed by wildlife that might be sharing a hiding place with a cache. A permit is often required to plant a cache. For local advice contact Dale and Barb at Space Coast Geocachers.

FISHING See the "Recreation" chapter.

GOLF Walkabout Golf & Country Club (321-385-2099) 3230 Folsom Road, Mims 32754. Price: Moderate. This course is a little out of the way, but it has become one of the more popular in north Brevard. Perry Dye designed the 18-hole championship course, along with LPGA star Jan Stephenson, and it is an undulating landscape with lakes and native vegetation. There is a bonus 19th hole—a par 3 green

GREENS FEES
Inexpensive: Under $25
Moderate: $25–50
Expensive: More than $50

shaped like the continent of Australia. Amenities include a snack bar, driving range, and putting greens.

SALONS AND SPAS La Bella Spa (321-453-1510; www.labellaspa.com) 3505 N.Courtenay Parkway, Merritt Island 32953. Rejuvenate your mind, body, and soul at Brevard County's most elegant destination spa. Located just minutes from the beach, La Bella offers a complete menu of personal services, including hair care, nail treatments, waxing, facials, massages, medical skin care, and reflexology. Call for an appointment.

✳ Green Space and Beaches

BEACHES Playalinda Beach at Canaveral National Seashore (321-267-1110) FL 402, Titusville. From US 1, head east on FL 406/402 to the coast. Open: Daylight hours; closed for space launches. Entrance fee: $3 per person; free age 15 and under. Lifeguards: Memorial Day through Labor Day. Playalinda Beach remains much as it might have looked when European sailors landed here nearly 500 years ago—4 miles of undeveloped, wild coast at the southern end of Canaveral National Seashore. The pristine dunes and beach are a sanctuary for birds and wildlife. There are no amenities other than rest rooms at each of the parking areas. Lot 8 has wheelchair-accessible parking and a beach ramp. If nudity offends you, consider stopping before you get to Lot 13 (the farthest lot), which has become a popular spot for natural sunbathers. Pets are not permitted, but alcohol is allowed in non-glass containers. Also see below for information on the national seashore.

NATURE PRESERVES AND PARKS Canaveral National Seashore (321-267-1110; www.nps.gov/cana) 212 S. Washington Avenue, Titusville 32796 (local office). Go east on FL 406/402 from Titusville. Open: Daylight hours. Admission: $3 per person; free age 15 and under. Activities: Birding, camping, fishing. Canaveral National Seashore is the longest stretch of undeveloped, unspoiled beachfront on Florida's east coast. Sunbathe, swim, surf, and fish along an ocean shore virtually unchanged from when it was inhabited by ancient settlers. From the refuge, enter on FL 402. Playalinda Beach (see above), at the southern end, is accessible from FL 402, where a paved road leads to several parking areas with rest room facilities. There are no other amenities. Eight magnificent vistas in the lagoon and dunes are great spots to view plants and wildlife, as well as the Kennedy Space Center launch complexes. Wheelchair access is available at parking lot 8.

☙ Enchanted Forest Sanctuary (321-264-5185; www.eelbrevard.com) 444 Columbia Boulevard, Titusville 32780. On the north side of FL 405;

Lifeguard coverage is defined as Year-round (every day from 10 to 5) and Seasonal (weekends beginning in late March, every day from Memorial Day weekend to early August, and weekends again until late October). These dates are always subject to change. For more timely information call 321-637-5777. Dogs are not permitted on any Brevard County beaches.

0.5 mile west of US 1. Open: Tuesday through Sunday 9–5. Admission: Free. Activities: Birding, trails. Long a local favorite, the Enchanted Forest Sanctuary was acquired by the Environmentally Endangered Lands (EEL) program in 1990 and is their flagship preserve in Brevard County. The Management and Education Center has hands-on exhibits and interpretive displays. Several short trails, 5 miles when combined, weave through the 465-acre park that is enhanced with benches, bridges, and overlooks. Five uniquely different habitats host an abundance of wildlife. The operation is subsidized by donations and purchases from the charming gift shop, operated by the Friends of the Enchanted

VISITOR INFORMATION CENTER AT MERRITT ISLAND WILDLIFE REFUGE.

MERRITT ISLAND NATIONAL WILDLIFE REFUGE

(321-861-0667; www.fws.gov/merrittisland) North Merritt Island. Take US 1 or I-95 north to FL 406, then head east over Indian River Lagoon. Open: Refuge is open during daylight hours; sections may close for space launches. The visitors center is open Monday through Friday 8–4:30, Saturday and Sunday 9–5; closed Sundays from April through October and federal holidays. Admission: Free. Activities: Birding, boating, fishing, paddling, trails.

Merritt Island National Wildlife Refuge is one of the most accessible and diverse natural habitats in America. When NASA acquired land to build a space center, 140,000 acres on north Merritt Island were set aside as a buffer and are protected by the U.S. Department of Interior as a national wildlife refuge and seashore. Many habitats commingle and are home to more than 500 species of wildlife and the highest number of endangered and threatened species found in any national wildlife refuge.

Forest. Pets, bikes, and smoking are prohibited. The parking lot, garden, amphitheater, and one trail are ADA accessible. Cart tours, group tours, and guided Saturday morning walks are offered, but call ahead to ensure staff is available.

Haulover Canal & Mosquito Lagoon (321-861-0667; www.fws.gov/merritt island) Merritt Island National Wildlife Refuge. US 1 or I-95 north to FL 406; 10.5 miles from visitor center. Open: Daylight hours; sections may close for space launches. Admission: Free. Activities: Birding, boating, fishing, paddling. The Haulover Canal links Mosquito Lagoon to the Indian River Lagoon and is

First-time guests should begin at the ADA-accessible **Refuge Visitor Information Center**. From there, every area of the refuge is within a 15-mile drive, and you will appreciate the orientation and information provided. The center's interpretive exhibits and habitat models offer an excellent overview of the habitat and its residents, and movies and programs are often held in the small auditorium. The center is about 5 miles east of US 1 in Titusville. To get there, stay on FL 406 as it merges to the right into FL 402.

Five **walking trails** are identified on the refuge map, and the shortest is a 0.25-mile picturesque walk behind the Visitor Information Center. The raised boardwalk path, which meanders through oak and palm hammocks, includes a gazebo for resting and is ADA accessible. Other trails range from 0.75 mile up to the 5-mile Cruickshank Trail and Tower at the halfway point of Black Point Wildlife Drive.

Black Point Wildlife Drive Allow about an hour to follow this 7-mile, one-way loop and self-guided tour through diverse habitats teeming with wildlife. Everywhere you look there are great photo opportunities. Take shots from your car, or stop at one of the many parking pullovers. The least active season is the summer, but you will almost always see alligators basking in the sun. Portable rest rooms are located along the drive.

Cruickshank Trail Get a little closer to nature on the 5-mile walking path that begins from the back half of the Black Point Wildlife Drive and circles a shallow marsh. Parking and rest rooms are available at the beginning of the trail.

Haulover Canal and Manatee Observation Deck The Haulover Canal is a narrow, short, serene passage connecting Mosquito Lagoon and the Indian River Lagoon. Motorboats can launch into the Indian River from nearby Blair's Cove, but it's most popular with paddlers. The ADA-accessible parking area and observation deck are great places to see manatees, especially during the spring and fall.

an incredibly beautiful, peaceful waterway where birds, manatees, and dolphins mingle with boaters, paddlers, and fishermen. A manatee observation deck is on the east side of FL 406, and a significant number of these docile creatures swim in the Haulover Canal year-round. The platform is ADA accessible. Novices will find paddling in the deeper Indian River Lagoon is a little more challenging than in the Thousand Islands at Cocoa Beach. Mosquito Lagoon is a pristine, shallow waterway that is thick with sea grasses and redfish. The lagoon is aptly named, so bring bug repellent.

✷ Lodging

Hotels and Motels

⚲ **Casa Coquina Bed & Breakfast** (321-268-4653, 1-877-684-8341; www .casacoquina.com) 4010 Coquina Avenue, Titusville 32780. Price: Moderate. Wheelchair Access: No. Built as a private home in the 1920s, this very colorful landmark overlooking the Indian River has been recently renovated and provides adult guests with an alternative to more traditional lodging. Each of the seven suites is named after a jewel and decorated in the appropriate color scheme and has a different design—pick the passionate Ruby or the more restful Sapphire. An executive suite is available for longer stays. The home is an eclectic mix of angels, flowers, antiques, brocade, and lace. Common areas for guests include a bar, library, gardens, and sundeck. A full breakfast is served each morning. The backyard garden and gazebo are popular spots for weddings and renewing vows. Avoid traffic delays and simply walk across the street to a nearby park for a perfect view of a space launch.

🐾 **Fairfield Inn & Suites** (321-385-1818; www.marriott.com) 4735 Helen Hauser Boulevard, Titusville 32780. Price: Moderate–Expensive. Wheelchair Access: Yes. The bold yellow, green, and blue colors of this new Titusville hotel reflect the hues found in the flora and fauna of the nearby Merritt Island Wildlife Refuge, Canaveral National Seashore, and Mosquito Lagoon. In fact, special rates are available to nature lovers who are in the area for fishing or birdwatching. The convenient location just off I-95 makes it a great stop for families and business travelers just passing through or staying for a few days. Rooms are spacious and comfortable. Amenities include a complimentary continental breakfast, pool, nearby jogging trail, fitness room, and business center. Small pets are welcome.

Hampton Inn Titusville (321-383-9191; www.hamptoninn.com) 4760 Helen Hauser Boulevard, Titusville 32780. Price: Moderate–Expensive. Wheelchair Access: Yes. The Hampton Inn is conveniently located directly off I-95, about 10 minutes from both downtown Titusville and the Kennedy Space Center. Choose from standard rooms, with one king or two double beds, or suites, which add a sleeper sofa and bar sink. The studio suite includes a small refrigerator and microwave. A complimentary hot

LODGING PRICES
Inexpensive: Up to $100
Moderate: $100–150
Expensive: $150–200
Very Expensive: Over $200

breakfast is part of every stay. Smoking rooms are available.

✳ Where to Eat

Caffe Chocolat (321-267-1713; www.caffechocolat.com) 304 S. Washington Avenue, Titusville 32796. Price: Moderate. Cuisine: European. Meals Served: B, L, D. Tickle your taste buds in this European-style café, decorated in comfortable cream and espresso tones. The menu choices are what you'd expect—muffins, scones, and eggs for breakfast; sandwiches, soups, and salads for lunch; with hot entrées like Chicken Pot Pie for dinner along with coffee drinks, and chocolate desserts. The difference is the cornucopia of flavors that proprietors Joe and Huberta Davis add to the mix: Partner a pineapple muffin with a butter toffee latte. Drizzle feta cheese and Aegean dressing over a salad, and top pita chips with sesame, garlic, and lemon-seasoned hummus. Finish with an elaborate dessert or one exquisite piece of chocolate fused with hazelnut, or cappuccino. The prices are reasonable and the servings are plentiful, with lots of choices for vegetarians. Chocolate concoctions are available to take home, and the adjoining gallery sells themed gifts. Closed Sunday; reservations are recommended for groups.

Dixie Crossroads (321-268-5000; www.dixiecrossroads.com) 1475 Garden Street, Titusville 32796. Price: Moderate. Cuisine: Seafood. Meals Served: L, D. Situated at the intersection of Garden Street and the path of the original Old Dixie Highway, this local landmark's signature is ocean-grown seafood served with a side of Southern hospitality. Their specialty is melt-in-your-mouth rock shrimp.

Price codes are based on an appetizer, dinner entrée (or lunch if dinner is not served), and dessert, but they do not include tax, tip, or beverages.

Inexpensive: Up to $15
Moderate: $15–25
Expensive: $25–35
Very Expensive: $35 or more
The following abbreviations are used to identify what meals are served:

B: breakfast
L: lunch
D: dinner
SB: Sunday brunch

Other shrimp varieties, such as red, pink, and Canaveral white, are available in season. Every meal starts with a basket of warm corn fritters sprinkled with powdered sugar. The menu

CASA COQUINA'S BREAKFAST ROOM.

is simple, with seafood, chicken, and steak cooked to order, and a list of side dishes that includes fries, fresh vegetables, and a cinnamon-topped baked sweet potato. Since you order your shrimp by the dozen, you know just what to expect on your plate. The kids' menu has fish, shrimp, and clams, as well as the usual hamburger and chicken nuggets. Prices are reasonable, and most entrées are available in a small, medium, or large portion. This popular, don't-miss family restaurant often has a wait during peak times, so order a drink at the gazebo, enjoy the murals depicting native birds and animals, or feed the fish in the outdoor pond. Call ahead for priority seating.

Kloiber's Cobbler Eatery (321-383-0689) 337 S. Washington Avenue, Titusville 32796. Price: Inexpensive. Cuisine: American-Casual. Meals Served: L, D. In the heart of historic downtown Titusville, the building that now houses this diner was originally Denham Department Store, built in the 1890s. Exposed brick and broad wooden beams retain the rustic feel.

DIXIE CROSSROADS HAS GOOD FOOD IN A CASUAL SETTING.

The menu includes salads, quiche, sandwiches, and their specialty, fruit cobbler, served warm and topped with a scoop of rich, creamy vanilla ice cream. There is a small art gallery on the upper level. Closed Sunday.

✦ **Paul's Smokehouse** (321-267-3663) 3665 S. Washington Avenue, Titusville 32796. Price: Expensive. Cuisine: Barbecue. Meals Served: D. The cow on the front sign is evidence that beef is the star at this popular local restaurant. Over the last quarter century, owner and Kentuckian Paul Salisbury's original riverside barbecue shack has grown into a three-story restaurant with a hybrid menu of home cooking and fine dining. Three dining rooms and a screened-in porch offer a stunning view of the Indian River and the towering Kennedy Space Center vehicle assembly building. Try the prime rib, a filet mignon, or New York strip steak along with an exceptionally soft and creamy baked potato. Fresh seafood is also on the menu, often as part of a surf-and-turf combo. The sentimental house favorite is tasty smoked barbecue by the plate or on a sandwich. The chefs enjoy preparing simple dishes, including grilled steak and shrimp scampi, as well as more unusual offerings, such as mahi-mahi covered with avocado salsa. Finish your meal with a juicy slice of pie. Closed Monday; reservations are recommended for groups.

CAFÉS AND COFFEE SHOPS
Sunrise Bread Company (321-268-1009) 315 S. Hopkins Avenue, Titusville 32796. By the time this bright and welcoming shop opens its doors at 6 AM, the bakers have spent several hours preparing fresh-baked, all-natural breads, scones, bagels, and

FISHING—AND DINING—RUN IN THE FAMILY

Fishing has always been good on Florida's Space Coast. Captain Rodney Thompson, whose father operated the Titusville fishing pier, made his living from the fruits of the sea. He was already a master shipbuilder when he decided to try his luck at catching shrimp in the coastal waters. The biggest hauls came from rock shrimp, known locally as poor man's lobster. The tiny, hard-shelled crustaceans were nearly impossible to sell because they were so difficult to open and prepare. Thompson and his daughter Captain Laurilee teamed up to develop a machine to split the shells and then butter and broil the tender, tasty meat that is now considered a regional specialty. Seafood is still the family business: Thompson's daughter Sherri operates Wild Ocean Seafood market at Port Canaveral, and Laurilee serves boatloads of rock shrimp to guests at Dixie Crossroads, a Titusville landmark.

muffins, most without any preservatives, fats, or oils. Locals arrive early to be sure and get their favorite, like cranberry orange walnut, rosemary garlic, or nine grain. Baked goods are supplemented with a rainbow of coffees, teas, and smoothies. Two stories provide plenty of seating, so relax a while, or grab and go. Free WiFi for patrons.

SPECIALTY MARKETS Wild Ocean Seafood Market (321-269-1116) 688 S. Park Avenue, Titusville 32796. Take home Florida's wild-caught seafood and ship gifts to family and friends anywhere in the continental United States.

✳ Entertainment

PERFORMING ARTS Titusville Playhouse at Emma Parrish Theater (321-268-1125; www.titus villeplayhouse.com) 301 Julia Street, Titusville 32796. This lovely and well-designed venue is steeped in nearly a century of tradition. Enjoy musical comedies like *Guys & Dolls*, and

children's favorites like *The Velveteen Rabbit,* in the main auditorium, with floor and balcony seating, and great acoustics. Upstairs in Emma's Attic, edgier works offer an alternative theater experience. The facility is a popular spot for presentations by local musicians and other community groups.

✳ Selective Shopping

Historic Titusville is a quiet town, reminiscent of a summer afternoon spent sipping sweet tea on a breezy wraparound porch. The old downtown area sometimes seems on the fence, trying to decide whether to roll up the sidewalks or kick up its heels.

Turn-of-the-20th-century buildings have been restored, and many have been converted to antiques emporiums. Galleries display the themes and colors of nature, and sport shops prepare outdoor aficionados with equipment and information about recreation on the Indian River Lagoon.

ANTIQUES AND COLLECTIBLES

Banana Alley Antiques (321-268-4282) 106 Main Street, Titusville 32796. The steady tick-tock of an assortment of wind-up clocks accompanies visitors while they browse through estate jewelry, china, silver, and collectibles. Look for the banana sign hanging over the door.

Dusty Rose Antique Mall (321-269-5526) 1101 S. Washington Avenue, Titusville 32780. For more than 25 years, Dusty Rose has built a loyal following of antiques lovers throughout central Florida. More than 40 dealers share 7,000 square feet of air-conditioned space, providing variety in product and a steady change of inventory. The mall is located near the entrance to the Titusville historic district, on US 1 as it divides into 2 one-way roads.

Revive (321-268-4171) 5 Main Street, Titusville 32796. Longtime resident Reva Harris has done a remarkable job of converting the old Titusville post office into an attractive salon of upscale clothes, used and antique furnishings, and vintage household items and apparel.

River Road Mercantile (321-264-2064) 219 S. Washington Avenue, Titusville 32780. Dixie operates this quaint storefront, where the collectibles of four dealers represent a varied assortment of kitchen, glassware, vintage textiles, toys, dolls, and more. The garden center features yard implements and decorations.

GALLERIES **Downtown Gallery**

(321-268-0122) 335 S. Washington Avenue, Titusville 32796. Open: Monday through Friday 10–5, Saturday 11–3. This cheerful gallery is an ideal backdrop for works by local artisans, including paintings, sculptures, photographs, and handcrafted jewelry. Much of the collection features the birds, wildlife, and natural beauty of the area. Exhibits showcase the innovative techniques and talents of young north Brevard artists.

NATURE IS THE THEME FOR MANY WORKS DISPLAYED AT DOWNTOWN GALLERY IN TITUSVILLE.

The Greenwood Gallery (321-268-3362) 1520 Garden Street, Titusville 32796. Open: Tuesday through Friday 10–5. German artist Helene Greenwood came to Titusville with her husband when he was recruited as a participant in the build-up of America's space program in 1964. For more than 30 years she has operated a first-class gallery displaying original fine art along with etchings, serigraphs, and limited-edition posters. Custom framing and art supplies are available. Weekend visits may be made by appointment.

Peggy Gunnerson Studio & Gallery (321-268-3388; www.gunner son.com/peggy) 11 Main Street, Titusville 32796 (in the Gaslight Mall). Open: Monday through Saturday 9–11:30 and 3–5, by appointment. Three artists, Peggy Gunnerson, Jon R. Miller, and Mary Lou Antes, share this space. All work in acrylic but with very different styles. Many of their large paintings are featured as scenery for Titusville Playhouse productions. Displayed works are always changing. Plan to spend time absorbing this array of thought-provoking works. The artists are all in the studio on Thursday afternoons.

R. Merrill Gordon, Artist (321-720-3938) 11 Main Street, Titusville 32796 (in the Gaslight Mall). Open: Monday through Saturday 11–5. After just a few minutes in this tiny Art, Inc. gallery, you're inspired to pick up a brush and create. Award-winning artist Rosemary Gordon displays her own works, as well as those of others she coaches in exploring bold new directions in fine arts. In collaboration with contemporary poet Doug Clow, Gordon brings words to life on the canvas. Natural materials such as seashells, bamboo, and feathers are incorporated into many of the paintings, giving the scenes a three-dimensional perspective.

Vessels in Stoneware (321-720-0783) 113 Broad Street, Titusville 32796. Oregon native Jo Chapman uses a midrange firing temperature to infuse pottery with trendy, vivid tones of periwinkle, plum, and sage. Her specialty is utilitarian stoneware for the home, such as dinnerware and ovenware, serving dishes, wine coolers, and olive-oil dipping plates. Small berry bowls with drain holes are a beautiful and practical way to store and serve fruit.

SPORTS Action Bait & Tackle (321-264-0996) 425 Garden Street, Titusville 32796. Open daily and conveniently located near the bridge leading to Merritt Island National Wildlife Refuge, this small and friendly shop sells fishing gear and live bait.

Captain Hook's Bait & Tackle (321-268-4646) 103 Max Brewer Memorial Parkway, Titusville 32780. This is the last stop for bait and fishing goods before heading over the causeway to the Merritt Island National Wildlife Refuge. They carry a full line of fishing equipment, as well as navigational maps and some last-minute supplies.

The Fly Fisherman (321-267-0348) 1114 S. Washington Avenue (US 1), Titusville 32780. Inside this impressive store, knowledgeable staff guides novice and experienced fishermen in selecting equipment and services. Often local fishing legends are around, ready to share fish stories and offer advice. As the name suggests, fly-fisherman will find tackle, line, weights, rods, and reels, and custom rigging. Conventional fishing gear is also available. Clothing, hats, sunglasses, maps, books, and a large selection of kayaks round out the inventory.

SUNDRIES AND EXTRAS

Chocolate Salon (321-267-1713) 304 S. Washington Avenue, Titusville 32796. Chocolatiers offer a wide selection of flavorful fudge and delectable chocolates, many in space and nature-themed molds. Choose just one perfect piece or create an assortment of personal favorites. Gift and special-occasion baskets are made while you wait. Yum!

Prop'a Place Hobby Shop (321-267-5999) 329 S. Washington Avenue, Titusville 32796. Enthusiasts who enjoy assembling aviation and boating vehicles will find kits for both here. Ready-to-fly remote-control planes and flight-simulation software are also available.

DESIGN YOUR OWN RIGGING WITH THE HELP OF THE FLY FISHERMAN.

✳ Special Events

Monthly: **Titusville Art Walk** (Washington Avenue and Broad Street, Titusville) Browse through galleries offering an evening of art discovery. Many of the works reflect the dual influences of nature and space travel. The event held on the third Friday of each month is a great opportunity to visit with the artists who sometimes have light refreshments in their studio. Local musicians perform.

January: **Space Coast Birding & Wildlife Festival** (1-800-460-2664; www.nbbd.com/fly; Brevard Community College Campus, 1311 N. US 1, Titusville 32796) Since the idea was hatched in 1998, birders and environmentalists from around the world have gathered in north Brevard for a week dedicated to showcasing how science and technology benefit wildlife. Rated as the nation's top birding and wildlife event, the SCBWF is held in January, when the bird population is at its peak and rare species are in the area. Renowned experts offer classes and demonstrations covering every aspect of the hobby, and guided field trips throughout Central Florida begin at daybreak. Mingle with other birders at an opening reception, or pick up new ideas and information at the exhibit center.

March: **Harry T. & Harriette V. Moore Heritage Festival of the Arts & Humanities** (321-264-6595; www.harryharriettemoore.org/festival) Activities are held throughout Brevard County celebrating the lives of Harry and Harriette Moore and their important contributions to America's civil rights movement. Educational sessions, theater performances, and a black-tie dinner highlight the event. Activities conclude at a

WILDLIFE PROFILE: GREAT BLUE HERON

One of the most engaging members of the beach community is the great blue heron. The lanky blue gray birds wade in the surf at dawn and dusk, waiting to snatch fish caught by a surf fishermen. Each heron works alone and usually has a specific territory where it shows up on a regular basis. The majestic birds stand picture-perfect without much concern about the humans around them.

At a height of 4 feet, the great blue heron is the tallest and most common North American member of the long-necked, long-legged heron family, which includes numerous species of herons, egrets, and bitterns. The wading birds thrive in the shallows and marshes of the Indian River Lagoon and set up breeding colonies on the mangrove islands. There they find sturdy branches to support their nests, a barrier of water to dissuade predators, and prime fishing waters. The common names given to the birds generally relate to their color and size. Several types live in this habitat: great and small, snowy, blue, reddish, green, and even a tricolor, with a bright blue head, gray feathers, and a black-tipped beak.

Many great blue herons prefer the banks of the lagoon waters, where they will patiently and slowly walk in the shallow mud until they spot a fish, snake, or shrimp. Then they dip their long, pointed bills into the water with great speed and precision and seize the prey, which they swallow whole. Because they are so tall, they can fish in deeper water than other wading birds. Like any good angler, the great blue heron is an early bird—most active at dawn and again at dusk when the fish are biting, or ready to be bitten.

Space Coast Sightings: Cape Canaveral and Cocoa Beach beaches, Ramp Road Park, Kelly Park, Rich Grissom Memorial Wetlands at Viera, Merritt Island National Wildlife Refuge, most piers and docks.

GREAT BLUE HERON *(ARDEA HERODIAS)*

Jim Angy

Sunday afternoon street festival featuring gospel music, mingling, good food, and tours of the museum.

St. Patrick's Day Parade & Street Party (321-952-5510; www.meg omalleys.com; downtown Melbourne) Irish and the Irish at heart wear the green proudly at this daylong party centered around Meg O'Malley's in historic downtown Melbourne. Start the day with an Irish buffet breakfast. The streets close to traffic for the parade that steps off at 11 AM, and is followed with a day of traditional music, food, and drink. Enjoy family activities throughout the afternoon; an adult street party into the wee hours of the evening. 'Tis said that God needed laughter in the world, so he made the Irish. Enjoy the party!

TICO Warbird Airshow (321-268-1941; www.vacwarbirds.org; Space Coast Regional Airport, US 1 and FL 405, Titusville) For three days in March, the skies over Titusville come alive with aircraft. The lineup changes each year, but expect everything from vintage planes to powerful fighter jets. The closing show on Sunday is always the Missing Man Formation. Purchase a ticket for each day or a pass for the entire event.

April: ✈ **Indian River Festival** (321-615-8111; www.brevardproductions .com; Sand Point Park, Titusville) Sand Point Park comes alive with rides, games, concerts, an arts and crafts show, and tasty treats. This is one of Brevard County's longest-running events, kicking off on Thursday and running through Sunday. Families and children will enjoy the pint-sized midway rides and special children's activities. Adopt a "lucky duck" to participate in the race and help a local organization.

South Brevard 4

SOUTH BREVARD

South Brevard is a technology hub—home to the Florida Institute of Technology and cutting-edge corporations like Harris, DRS Tactical Systems, and Northrop Grumman. Many of the county's largest communities, including Melbourne and Palm Bay, are in the south. Along the south Brevard coast are the quieter beaches and towns of Satellite Beach, Melbourne Beach, and Indialantic. Sebastian Inlet defines the southern boundary of the county. The drive down A1A to Sebastian Inlet is one of the most scenic routes in the county.

Eau Gallie was one of the area's earliest river ports and retains a unique identity, although it is technically part of the city of Melbourne. The Brevard Art Museum is the centerpiece of the Eau Gallie Arts District featuring galleries, antiques shops, and cafés. Just south, the original settlement of Melbourne lies at the strategic waterway intersection of the Indian River and Crane Creek. Historic Downtown Melbourne, alongside the Crane Creek promenade, is now a shopping and dining center with most of the old buildings still in use.

GETTING THERE Eau Gallie is about 20 miles from Cocoa Beach. Take A1A south to FL 518 at Indian Harbour Beach. Go west across the Indian River. Highland Avenue is the second street after the bridge and the focal point of old Eau Gallie. To get to downtown Melbourne, continue on FL 518 to US 1 (S. Harbor City Boulevard) and turn left. Continue 1 block past US 192 and turn right onto New Haven Avenue.

✳ To See

HISTORIC PLACES Development of southern Brevard centered around two inlets, the Eau Gallie River bordering the town of Eau Gallie, and Crane Creek, the Melbourne harbor area. Eau Gallie is the older settlement, dating from 1859. The name Eau Gallie means "rocky water," referring to the coquina rocks that line the riverbank. By 1885 a boatyard and basin had been built, and the inlet had a reputation as one of the safest deepwater harbors on the east coast. Melbourne settlement began around 1870 when three black men, freed slaves, set up homesteads near Crane Creek. By 1880 the town had a small number of families, who gathered together and voted for the name of Melbourne, after the city in Australia that was once home to the English postmaster.

Eau Gallie Landmarks: The **James Wadsworth Rossetter House,** 1320 Highland Avenue in Eau Gallie, was built in the 1860s and purchased by Rossetter in 1902. Daughters Caroline and Ella lived in the home until they donated it to the Florida Historical Society in 1992. The back section of the house was one of the original buildings when there was a pineapple and sugar plantation on the land. Tours of the period home, furnishings, and botanical gardens are conducted daily. Learn about paranormal observations in the home and nearby pioneer cemetery during a Ghost Tour beginning at 7 on the first Friday of each month. Call ahead for reservations.

Directly across the street, the **Roesch House** was the home of William R. Roesch, the town's first mayor. The house, a turn-of-the-20th-century Frame Vernacular design common to early Florida, has been restored by the Florida Historical Society and serves as a museum for period pieces of furniture, household goods, and photographs.

Two other homes are of interest. The **Winchester Symphony House** at 1500 Highland Avenue is a Florida Cracker frame home built with a wide front porch typical of Eau Gallie homes in the 1890s. Today the offices of the Brevard Symphony Orchestra are located here. The Queen Anne style **William H. Gleason house** at 1736 Pineapple Avenue was built around 1892 and is now a private bed-and-breakfast.

Melbourne Landmarks: **Front Street,** the site of the original town of Melbourne business district, runs along a small peninsula between the Indian River and Crane Creek. A fire destroyed most structures in 1919, and the downtown was resurrected along nearby New Haven Avenue. Spared from the flames was the **John and Nannie Lee House** atop a bluff at the corner of Strawbridge and

MELBOURNE HOTEL.

Courtesy Brevard County Historical Commission

M-19—Melbourne Hotel, Melbourne, Fla.

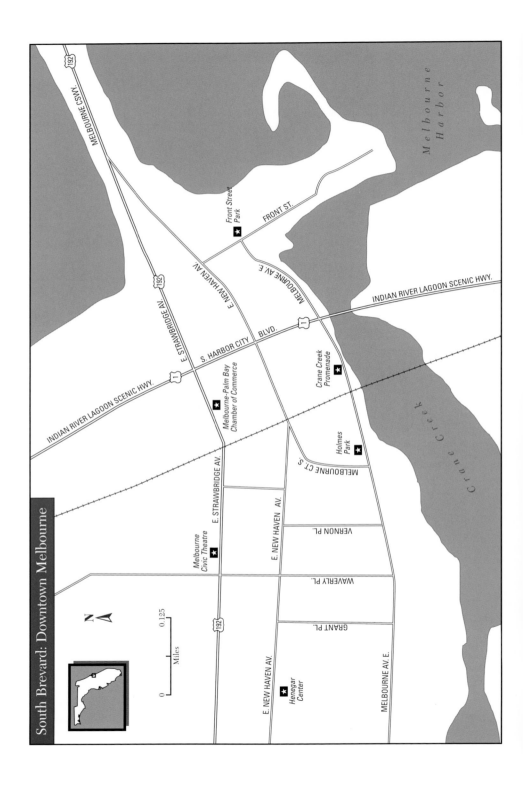

South Brevard: Downtown Melbourne

Melbourne Harbor

Melbourne Cswy.

192

Front Street Park

FRONT ST.

E. NEW HAVEN AV.

MELBOURNE AV. E.

INDIAN RIVER LAGOON SCENIC HWY.

INDIAN RIVER LAGOON SCENIC HWY.

E. STRAWBRIDGE AV.

S. HARBOR CITY BLVD.

192

1

1

Melbourne-Palm Bay Chamber of Commerce

Crane Creek Promenade

Crane Creek

Holmes Park

MELBOURNE CT. S.

E. STRAWBRIDGE AV.

E. NEW HAVEN AV.

VERNON PL.

WAVERLY PL.

GRANT PL.

MELBOURNE AV. E.

Melbourne Civic Theatre

192

E. NEW HAVEN AV.

Henegar Center

N

Miles

0   0.125

New Haven. Claude Beaujean, a talented carpenter and ferryboat operator, built the home in 1905.

At the intersection of New Haven and US 1, the **Melbourne Hotel,** also known as the 1900 Building, had businesses on the ground floor, such as shops and a barbershop, and rooms on the upper floors to serve northern visitors arriving mostly by train. The "strictly fireproof" building was erected in 1924 as down-town was developing west of the railroad tracks. **Campbell Park,** at New Haven Avenue and Melbourne Court, is named for C. J. F. Campbell, the town's first mayor, and was an early gathering spot for community activities.

The nearby and recognizable **Flat Iron Building** is typical of most buildings on New Haven Avenue. The structures were all built in the 1920s, and most still have at least some original exterior designs and interior features. The main building of the **Henegar School Complex,** at 625 New Haven Avenue, was built from 1919 to 1921 along what was then a dirt road. The high school was added in 1926. Today the facility is a well-used community performing-arts center.

Return east to Grant Place and walk a block south to Melbourne Avenue. Stately homes such as the Crane Creek Inn, built in 1925, are still private residences. **Holmes Park** is across the street, and then the road goes under the wooden railroad track bridge, constructed in 1921. Stop and relax at the **Crane Creek Promenade Manatee Observation Area.**

LIBRARIES Indian River Lagoon House (321-725-7775; www.mrcirl.org) 3275 Dixie Highway NE, Palm Bay 32905. Open: Monday through Saturday 9–5. The Marine Resources Council operates this resource center, which over-looks the Indian River Lagoon. Exhibits, photographs, and artifacts depict the development of Brevard County, and a large model provides a three-dimensional look at the lagoon. The council library contains extensive data and information about the history of the lagoon and the natural resources of Brevard County. To get there, take US 1 southbound (Dixie Highway NE) to Stephen Drive, 1.8 miles past US 192 in Melbourne.

MUSEUMS Brevard Art Museum (321-242-0737; www.brevardartmuseum .org) 1463 Highland Avenue, Melbourne 32935. Open: Tuesday through Satur-day 10–5, Thursday 10–7, Sunday 1–5. Admission: Adults $5, seniors $3, chil-dren and students with ID $2, free on Thursday. Brevard's premier fine arts museum is the centerpiece of the Eau Gallie Arts District. Throughout five gal-leries, works from permanent holdings are blended with outstanding special exhibits to present a constantly shifting landscape of visual arts designed to enlighten and inspire visitors. The museum collection is an eclectic mix of con-temporary and traditional, playful and dignified, and represents a myriad of cul-tures through artifacts such as Chinese porcelain, Egyptian statuettes, and Tibetan costumes. The viewer-friendly museum frequently stages creative exhi-bitions like Navel Gazing that invited artists to share their fresh-squeezed inter-pretations of Florida, with unusual and often amusing results, and Razzle Dazzle featuring imaginative and artistic tabletops for holiday entertaining. Take a

BREVARD ART MUSEUM

leisurely self-guided tour or join a docent-led group. Call ahead for information on special events such as receptions and lectures. The museum and most events are free to museum members. To get there, take A1A to FL 518 and turn right on Highland Avenue.

✑ **Brevard Art Museum School** (321-242-0737; www.brevardart museum.org.) 1520 Highland Avenue, Melbourne 32935. Open: Tuesday through Saturday 10–5, Sunday 1–5. Admission: Included in admission to the museum. Adults and children are invited to explore their creative side through classes in painting, photography, pottery, sculpture, and drawing. The Brevard Art Museum mission is committed to encouraging and promoting arts education, and this quality school is part of their outreach to the community. Works are displayed and sold in the Museum School store.

✳ To Do

BIRDING North Tidal Pool (321-984-4852; www.floridastateparks.org/sebastian inlet) Sebastian Inlet State Park, 9700 A1A, Melbourne Beach 32951. Early morning at the North Tidal Pool, before the crowds arrive, is a bonanza. The cove is a feeding ground for shorebirds and waders, such as American oyster-catchers and reddish egrets. A nearby wooded area attracts woodpeckers and songbirds, and at dawn you may see a great horned owl.

BOATING: MARINAS AND RAMPS Inlet Marina (321-724-5424; www .sebastianinletmarina.com) 9502 S. A1A, Melbourne Beach 32951. This full-service marina and gateway concessionaire is located about 1 mile north of Sebastian Inlet State Park. Boat slips are available for $20 to $25 per night or $100 to $125 per week. Rent skiff boats accommodating up to 4 passengers, or a pontoon boat with capacity for 8–12; hourly rates range from $100 to $150, and full day from $200 to $300. Launch from paved ramps: $5 for boats, $3 for canoes and kayaks. Canoes and kayaks are also available to rent. The Marina store carries refreshments, fishing gear, and other essentials.

BOATING: TOURS AND RENTALS Indian River Outfitters (321-779-4228; www.iroutfitters.com) 294 E. Eau Gallie Boulevard, Indian Harbour Beach 32937. Paddlers will find everything they need to explore the Brevard County waterways at this full-service shop convenient to both the Indian River Lagoon and the Atlantic Ocean. Kayaks, canoes, and fishing kayaks, along with equipment and accessories, are available. They also rent kayaks and canoes, and will attach them to your vehicle. Rates are $30 half day, $40 full day, $45 overnight for single kayak; $40 half day, $50 full day, $55 overnight for tandem kayak or canoe.

Inlet Marina (321-724-5424; www.sebastianinlet.com) 9502 S. A1A, Melbourne Beach 32951. Join a Florida naturalist and experienced guide on a two- or four-hour kayak tour through this area of the Indian River Lagoon. Groups are limited to a maximum of four, so the tour can be very personalized toward the capabilities and interests of the paddlers. The fee is $35 per hour in addition to a boat rental fee. Rent single, double, or triple kayaks, or canoes, for $18 to $40 for two hours. Two-hour private pontoon eco-tours accommodate up to six passengers for $200.

CAMPING AND RVING Long Point Park (321-952-4532; www.campspace coast.com) 700 Long Point Road, Melbourne Beach 32951. This rustic camp operated by Brevard Parks is located near Sebastian Inlet. All sites have water and electricity; some also include sewer. The island campground fronts the Indian River, and campers can launch small non-motor boats and fish right outside their front door. The 84.5-acre conservation spot has a boat ramp, showers, laundry facilities, nature trails, a playground, and a swimming pond. Cross a bridge to Scout Island, where primitive camping is offered to groups. The park is a roosting site for wood storks and home to a variety of wildlife.

🐾 Sebastian Inlet State Park Campground (ReserveAmerica: 1-800-326-3521; hearing disabled: 1-888-433-0287; www.floridastateparks.org/sebastian inlet) 9700 A1A, Melbourne Beach 32951. Reservations are in demand for the 51 tent sites in this premier location, just a short walk from the Indian River Lagoon or the Sebastian Inlet beaches. The campground accommodates RVs up to 40 feet long, and it has electrical hookups, fire rings with grills, picnic tables, full ADA-accessible rest room facilities, and a coin laundry. Fisherman will discover some of the best saltwater fishing on Florida's east coast. Pets are welcome. Reservations may be made up to 11 months in advance.

EXPLORING THE TIDAL POOL AT SEBASTIAN INLET STATE PARK

FISHING See the "Recreation" chapter.

GOLF Crane Creek Reserve (321-674-5716) 475 W. New Haven Avenue, Melbourne 32901. Price: Inexpensive. This 18-hole, par 71 public course was opened by the city of Melbourne in 1926. Some of the first golfers may have been part of the

> **GREENS FEES**
> Inexpensive: Under $25
> Moderate: $25–50
> Expensive: More than $50

crew that built a rocket and sent Alan Shepard to hit golf balls on the moon 45 years later. The well-kept course is flat, with water on almost every hole. PGA Professionals manage the club; pro shop, driving range, putting greens, and snack bar are available.

Spessard Holland (321-952-4530; www.golfspessardholland.com) 2374 Oak Street, Melbourne Beach 32951. Price: Moderate. Ocean breezes and distracting views create challenges on this Arnold Palmer Signature 18-hole, par 67 public course, tucked between the Atlantic Ocean and the Indian River. There is only one par 5, so accuracy is an advantage. Amenities include a mini driving range, putting greens, and a snack bar.

SALONS AND SPAS Ocean Reef Spa (321-777-4100; www.cpmelbourne .com) Crowne Plaza Melbourne Oceanfront Resort and Spa, 2605 N. A1A, Indialantic 32903. Relaxation and serenity surround you at this luxury spa, located inside the Crowne Plaza resort. Services range from massages, facials, and body wraps to hair and nail treatments. Massages are available in private treatment rooms or oceanfront cabana. And experienced and attentive staff promises a wonderful escape.

✳ Green Space and Beaches

BEACHES Sebastian Inlet State Park Lifeguards: Memorial Day through Labor Day. The 3 miles of beautiful beaches at Sebastian Inlet are a great compromise between minimal development and modest concessions. Beachgoers will find conveniently located rest rooms, eating/gift facilities, and bait and tackle shop. Sebastian Inlet has one of the best surfing breaks in Florida and is popular with experienced amateurs and professional surfers. Beach wheelchairs are available upon request. See *Nature Preserves*, below, for more information.

NATURE PRESERVES AND PARKS ⚘ **Barrier Island Sanctuary** (321-723-3556; www.eelbrevard.com/ep_recreation.php) 8385 S. Highway A1A, Melbourne Beach 32951. Fourteen miles south of US 192. Open: Tuesday through Sunday, 9–5. Admission: Free. Activities: Birding, trails, turtle walks. The diverse habitats of Brevard's south beaches are featured at the newly built Barrier Island Sanctuary stretching from dunes and coastal strands along the Atlantic Ocean, to maritime hammocks and tidal ponds bordering the Indian River Lagoon. The center includes interactive exhibits and a movie on sea turtles. This stretch of beach is one of the busiest sea turtle nesting spots and educating guests on the protection and preservation of these wondrous creatures is a key focus for the sanctuary. Guided sea turtle walks are held in June and July. Sanctuary trail is a 1-mile hike from the center to the lagoon, through natural brush where birds and occasional wildlife will be spotted. The site has a picnic pavilion and a kayak launch area. The charming gift shop is managed in partnership with the Caribbean Conservation Corporation and specializes in nature-based jewelry, artwork, children's books, and other souvenirs. The center and ocean boardwalks are handicap accessible.

Sebastian Inlet State Park (321-984-4852; www.floridastateparks.org/sebastian inlet) 9700 S. A1A, Melbourne Beach 32951. Located on A1A, 18 miles south of US 192. Open: 24 hours a day. Admission: $4 for single entry, $8 per vehicle up to eight people; $2 for pedestrians and cyclists. Activities: Birding, boating, camping, fishing, paddling, trails. Water, wilderness, and sunshine are the backdrop for this strikingly beautiful inlet connecting the Atlantic Ocean with the Indian River Lagoon. This Florida state park is a popular recreational area with trails, campgrounds, a marina, and coves ideal for paddling. Anglers can choose from two fishing jetties extending into the Atlantic Ocean. Picnic tables, a playground, rest rooms, bathhouses, showers, and a snack bar are available near the fishing jetties and beach. Children and families can cool off and get close to small marine wildlife in the shallow tidal pool on the north and west side of the inlet. Connected trails run from the ocean to the lagoon and are ideal for hiking and biking. Also see *Beaches*, above.

BARRIER ISLAND SANCTUARY IN MELBOURNE BEACH.

Courtesy Environmentally Endangered Lands (EEL) Program

✱ Lodging

HOTELS AND MOTELS 🐾 **Crane Creek Inn Waterfront Bed & Breakfast** (321-768-6416; www.cranecreekinn.com) 907 E. Melbourne Avenue, Melbourne 32901. Price: Moderate–Expensive. Wheelchair Access: No. This attractive 1925 home, at the heart of historic downtown Melbourne, provides a haven for adult guests who prefer a more homey and pampered setting. A backyard veranda, pool, hot tub, and hammock overlook picturesque Crane Creek, where manatees, dolphins, and water birds are likely to come calling. Each of the five rooms is furnished with antiques and includes a private bathroom, TV, and wireless Internet. Add romance to your stay with a candlelight dinner, followed by a play at the nearby Henegar Center and a moonlight stroll back to the inn. A full breakfast is served every day. Well-behaved pets are welcome, but there is an additional fee.

BALCONY OF THE ELLA BELLE SUITE AT PORT D'HIVER BED & BREAKFAST OVERLOOKS THE OCEAN.
Courtesy Port d'Hiver Bed & Breakfast

LODGING PRICES
Inexpensive: Up to $100
Moderate: $100–150
Expensive: $150–200
Very Expensive: Over $200

The Old Pineapple Inn (321-254-1347, 1-888-776-9864; www.oldpineappleinn.com) 1736 Pineapple Avenue, Eau Gallie 32935. Price: Expensive. Wheelchair Access: No. Step back in time when you walk through the door of this 1886 three-story Victorian mansion built by Eau Gallie pioneer William Henry Gleason. The stately home is filled with memories and memorabilia from the past: a porch swing swaying on a breezy veranda, a 1928 baby grand player piano, and a crystal pineapple chandelier. There are also modern touches like a swimming pool, media center, high speed WiFi, and Jacuzzi tubs. Three suites are decorated in a colorful and comfortable style. A fully equipped tropical guesthouse with four bedrooms, two baths, kitchen, living, and dining areas accommodates families or groups for extended stays. The Indian River is just across the street; the Eau Gallie Arts District is a short walk away; beaches are about 2 miles east.

⚥ **Port d'Hiver Bed & Breakfast** (321-722-2727; www.portdhiver.com) 201 Ocean Avenue, Melbourne Beach 32951. Price: Very Expensive. Wheelchair Access: No. In 1916 Melbourne resident Walter Brown built a sturdy cypress beach house as his winter port—Port d'Hiver. To get there he had to take a boat across the Indian River, but today guests simply cruise straight down A1A. The main house has matured into a captivating seaside retreat, with lush, tropical

WORTH A DETOUR

If visiting the Sebastian Inlet area, make a short detour to see two unusual attractions on the south side of the park.

The **Sebastian Fishing Museum,** on the right as you cross the Sebastian Inlet Bridge, is a replica of a fish house and dock, with exhibits and a video reflecting the rich cultural history of Sebastian's fishing industry. Open daily from 10–4; park admission applies.

✔ The **McLarty Treasure Museum** features artifacts, displays, and a movie about early Spanish ships that perished in storms and went down with their treasure while traveling off the east central Florida coast. An observation deck overlooks the Atlantic Ocean and stirs fantasies of joining salvagers who continue today on a quest to recover lost bounty. Open daily from 10–4:30; $2 admission, free for children under 6. Located on A1A 2 miles south of the Sebastian Inlet Bridge.

landscaping and a winding path connecting four buildings, a courtyard, and the pool. The rooms vary in size and each exquisitely reflects the color and style of a special theme. All accommodations are embellished with fresh flowers, soft robes, bottled water, and a flat screen TV and DVD player. The cozy Ella Belle's in the main house has French doors leading to a balcony overlooking the ocean. Or stroll across a garden bridge to the opulent Mangrove Suite with a separate living room, bath with spa tub, and large private porch. The day begins with a full breakfast served in the dining room, the garden courtyard, or your room. Expect fresh fruit and pastries, a choice of gourmet entrées like Italian Strata or vanilla custard French toast, and accompaniments such as a potato casserole, thick maple bacon, or crêpes. The chef easily accommodates vegan, gluten-free, and other dietary requests. Wine and light hors d'oeuvres are served in the main house

each evening, and the day ends with a sweet treat and turndown room service. While perfect for a romantic get-a-way, families are welcome with children 10 and older. Port d'Hiver is included as a member of the Select Registry of distinguished inns.

✔ 🐾 **Seashell Suites** (321-409-0500; 866-571-0500; www.seashellsuites .com) 8795 S. Highway A1A, Melbourne Beach 32951. Price: Very Expensive. Wheelchair Access: Yes. Immerse yourself in a natural cocoon of sunshine, soothing waves, soft sand, and protective scrub brush, along with visits from shore birds, dolphins, wildlife, and even giant sea turtles who bury eggs along this stretch of beach during their nesting season. Just north of Sebastian Inlet, owner and microbiologist Wendell Mazelow has created a first-class, secluded eco-resort designed to harmonize with the pristine natural setting. Guests can breathe easy knowing they are surrounded with toxin-free building materials and cleaning agents, a

A BIKE RIDE IS THE PERFECT WAY TO ENJOY THE NATURE TRAILS NEAR SEA SHELL SUITES.

healthy saltwater, soft water pool, and 100 percent cotton linens. The intimate boutique has only eight suites. Each comfortable and well-decorated unit has two bedrooms, a full, modern kitchen, and a wide-screen HDTV in the living room and bedroom. Complimentary beach chairs and umbrellas, bicycles, surf fishing supplies, and boogie boards are available. After a day of exercise and fun, take a nap in the hammock or rejuvenate in the sauna, and then join other guests on the ocean deck to toast the end of a wonderful day. The digital library features many favorites, as well as a collection of nature movies and documentaries. Rates are significantly reduced for weekly stays.

Tuckaway Shores Resort (321-723-3355, 1-800-820-1441; www.tuckaway shores.com) 1441 S. Miramar Avenue (A1A), Indialantic 32903. Price: Moderate. Wheelchair Access: Partial. Located on a quiet stretch of the south beaches, this charming motel offers the style and hospitality of old Florida, with a few modern twists like wireless Internet and flat-screen TVs in most of the rooms. The décor is clean, crisp, and comfortable. Every accommodation is a two-room suite, oceanfront or ocean view, has a full kitchen, and sleeps four. After a day in the sun, mingle with other guests in the Cabana Room or settle in one of the colorful Adirondack chairs out by the barbecue grills. A perfect choice that's a little off the beaten path but an easy walk or drive to the Fifth Avenue strip of shops and restaurants.

Windemere Inn by the Sea (321-728-9334, 1-800-224-6853; www .windemereinn.com) 815 S. Miramar Avenue (A1A), Indialantic 32903. Price: Moderate–Expensive. Wheelchair Access: Partial. Discover romance and relaxation at this luxury bed-and-breakfast on the south Melbourne beaches. Rooms, furnished in antiques and wicker, with plush linens piled high on four-poster beds, are available in the Main House and the Cottage; or choose the Carriage House Suite with two connecting guest rooms. Some accommodations offer ocean views and Jacuzzi baths. After a gourmet breakfast (included in the rate), grab a beach chair and towel and settle in for a day of sunshine and swimming on this very quiet stretch of beach. Small weddings can be arranged at the beachside pergola that frames the sunrise on each new day. Historic Downtown Melbourne with an array of shops and restaurants is just across the causeway.

✷ Where to Eat

Brio Italiano (321-676-8949; www .brioitaliano.com) 2003 Vernon Pl, Melbourne 32901. Price: Moderate–Expensive. Cuisine: Italian. Meals Served: L, D. Simple and flavorful Sicilian cooking is inspired by the many cultures that traveled by this Mediterranean island at the tip of the Italian boot. Sicilian Chef Danny Genna and his son, Richard, continue the tradition with an abundance of fresh and flavorful dishes based on their family recipes. Most begin with a rich and savory pomodoro sauce that is the trademark of Sicilian cooking, like traditional cacciatore with thin slices of chicken breast, sweet onions, celery, and green olives. Hungry seafood lovers might try the pescatore, a combination of clams, mussels, shrimp, calamari, and scallops in pomodoro sauce and served over pasta. Baked dishes like lasagna rollatini and eggplant parmigiana are made fresh and cooked to your order, so they take a little longer but are well worth the wait. They have a full bar and generous wine list. Finish the evening with an espresso and a locally baked cannoli with sweet chocolate chips and topped with a rich, mascarpone cream. Reservations are recom-

mended for dinner. Only dinner is served on Sunday, when they open at 5.

⨍ **Chart House Restaurant** (321-729-6558; www.chart-house.com) 2250 Front Street, Melbourne 32901. Price: Expensive. Cuisine: Seafood and Beef. Meals Served: D. This upscale steak and seafood restaurant sits at the edge of a point in Melbourne Harbor where the Indian River meets Crane Creek. The waterfront view is breathtaking and makes it a wonderful spot for a special occasion or romantic evening. Exceptional service begins with valet parking. A raw bar, an impressive salad bar, and appetizers such as calamari and crab-stuffed mushrooms are great starters. In addition to signature entrées such as Snapper Hemmingway–a sautéed snapper encrusted in a Parmesan and cracker mix and topped with jumbo lump crab–expect tender steaks cooked just as you like, and seasonal seafood specials. Dessert lovers will drool over the hot chocolate lava cake. Reservations are recommended.

Concepts on Highland (321-610-7987) 1437 Highland Avenue, Eau Gallie 32935. Price: Expensive–Very Expensive. Cuisine: Seafood and Beef. Meals Served: L, D. The only dough made in the old Eau Gallie bank building today is bread dough for the warm, crusty loaf served with every meal at this downtown restaurant. Owner and Chef Grant Heaslewood changes the menu frequently to take advantage of fresh, seasonal foods that are available. All dishes are made from scratch and tailored to deliver a wonderful dining experience. Lunch options are light and tasty, like a tuna salad mixed with celery, walnuts, and dried cranberries, or a pita with hummus, an assortment of fresh vegetables, and topped with a lemon-garlic sauce. Pork, veal, seafood, and chicken dinner entrées are creatively cooked and presented. Beef lovers can choose a filet mignon cooked au poivre style with a crust of cracked peppercorns, or splurge on a tender, juicy Kobe strip steak. Save room for dessert because a rich chocolate concoction is always on the menu. You can bank on that!

Continental Flambé (321-768-2445; www.continentalflambe.com) 936 E. New Haven Avenue, Melbourne 32901. Price: Moderate–Expensive. Cuisine: European. Meals Served: L, D. This stately establishment offers a relaxing and satisfying dining experience for a reasonable price. Order from the menu, or try the prix fixe meal that includes an appetizer, salad, entrée, and dessert. Start with baked Brie, escargots with garlic and hazelnut butter wrapped in puff pastry, or pita points with a goat cheese and edamame fondue. Entrées include pasta, seafood, chicken, and beef dishes, most prepared with an assortment of light, flavorful sauces. Flaming desserts such as crêpes Suzette and cherries jubilee are prepared at your table and end a pleasant evening with a dash of flair. Servers can help you choose from more than 800 wine selections. Dine inside or at outdoor tables. Closed Sunday; reservations are recommended.

Enigma (321-779-8202; www.enigma beachside.com) 1550 Highway A1A, Satellite Beach 32937. Price: Moderate–Expensive. Cuisine: American-Gourmet. Meals Served: L (Tuesday through Friday), D (Daily). Palm trees, waterfalls, murals of tropical gardens, and wicker furniture create

Price codes are based on an appetizer, dinner entrée (or lunch if dinner is not served), and dessert, but they do not include tax, tip, or beverages.

Inexpensive: Up to $15
Moderate: $15–25
Expensive: $25–35
Very Expensive: $35 or more
The following abbreviations are used to identify what meals are served:

B: breakfast
L: lunch
D: dinner
SB: Sunday brunch

the illusion of a relaxing meal on a Southern veranda, and the exceptional service makes you feel like a special guest. For lunch choose a soup, sandwich, or entrée salad such as greens mixed with steak and bleu cheese, and then sprinkled with dried cranberries and pumpkin seeds. Dinner appetizers range from simple lightly fried zucchini sticks to a zesty Mexican shrimp cocktail. Tasty entrées include the Enigma wrap, baked eggplant and three cheeses, rolled and topped with homemade tomato sauce, and a shrimp and chicken combination, sautéed with roasted red peppers in a mustard cream sauce and served over linguine. Finish up with a generous slice of their sweet, juicy Florida orange sunshine cake. Vegetarians will find lots of creative food choices. In addition to the main dining room, seating is available outside or in the comfortable bar. A full line of cocktails, martinis, and coffee drinks are offered. Live entertainment is presented on the weekends. Closed Monday; open for lunch Tuesday through Friday; walk-ins welcome.

Island Pasta Company (321-723-1584; www.islandpasta.com) 903 E. New Haven Avenue, Melbourne 32901. Price: Moderate. Cuisine: Caribbean. Meals Served: L, D. Bright, colorful décor and fresh, healthy dishes blend into a relaxing island getaway in the middle of shopping and gallery hopping. Try shrimp-and-crab cakes with a Key lime and pineapple tartar sauce, or the Blue Lagoon salad, with greens, candied walnuts, blue cheese, red onion, and grapes. Hawaiian pork is served with a spicy pineapple barbecue sauce. A delectable assortment of desserts, made on the premises, includes Puerto Rican Flan from an old family

recipe. This casual spot has a full bar and is perfect for a leisurely lunch or dinner. Seating is available indoors and out. Reservations are recommended for groups.

Long Point Cafe (321-723-8839; www.longpointcafe.com) 100 Long Point Road, Melbourne Beach 32951. Price: Moderate. Cuisine: Caribbean. Meals Served: B, L, D (dinner Friday and Saturday). Vacationers staying near Sebastian Inlet and visitors to the area for a day will love the convenience of this family-friendly café located on A1A just 1 mile north of the inlet. All will be surprised to discover really good food prepared with gourmet touches and presented with artistic flair. Lunchtime standards are available—sandwiches, salads, soups, and burgers, but every meal also features chef's specials, most built around fresh seafood. Select the sig-

THE STATELY ENIGMA RESEMBLES A SOUTHERN PLANTATION ALONG A1A IN SATELLITE BEACH.

nature dinner dish of Applewood bacon-wrapped scallops over a Caesar salad with poached egg, or try a platter of Florida cracker-style fried shrimp. Children's menu is available. They serve beer and wine. Stop next door at the seafood market and the convenience store catering to campers and fishermen. Closed Monday.

Matt's Casbah (321-574-1099; www.mattscasbah.com) 801 E. New Haven Avenue, Melbourne 32901. Price: Expensive. Cuisine: Asian. Meals Served: L, D, SB. Matt's Casbah is a downtown Melbourne oasis offering visitors hospitality, exceptional culinary creations, and tempting liquid refreshments. The expansive restaurant has become the neighborhood place to wine and dine, see and be

THE DÉCOR IS EXOTIC AT MATT'S CASBAH IN DOWNTOWN MELBOURNE.

seen. Chef Matt Nugnes creates entrées described as American with an Asian twist, like Moroccan Spiced Long Island duck breast, and pan-seared mahi-mahi fillet, and grilled shrimp with a blond miso, sake glaze. The sushi bar is among the best in Brevard with an amazing array of top quality seafood, including some unexpected choices like quail eggs. Traditionalists can savor the pot roast, a customer favorite, and vegetarians will discover plenty of tasty choices. For dessert, try the sweet and satisfying kiwi banana spring roll. Choose from a generous wine list or have them make up a signature cocktail. Guests are served in the main dining room, the sushi bar, or on the patio. Dress for a special night out if dining indoors, but more casual is fine for appetizers in the bar or dining on the patio. Enjoy live entertainment most evenings. Lunch is always casual. Sunday brunch begins at 11 AM. Reservations are accepted, and recommended for weekends when this hot spot gets pretty crowded.

Meg O'Malley's (321-952-5510; www.megomalleys.com) 812 E. New Haven Avenue, Melbourne 32901. Price: Moderate. Cuisine: Irish. Meals Served: L, D, SB. From lovely beginnings to happy endings, the leprechauns promise a good time at this friendly and popular restaurant and Irish pub. The food is first-rate. With a bow to tradition, a cup of the flavorful Irish Parliament bean soup is priced at 18 cents. Corned beef and cabbage with spicy grain mustard is served with colcannon, an Irish cabbage and potato dish, or boiled red bliss potatoes. The Ploughman's prime rib sandwich is tender, juicy, and seasoned to perfection, topped with grilled onions and farmhouse cheddar, and served on a Kaiser roll with lettuce and tomato. End with M.O.M.'s bread pudding, made fresh daily from an old Irish recipe and served with your choice of topping, perhaps Irish coffee cream sauce. Guinness on tap is just one of many domestic and imported beers, along with a full bar. Live entertainment lasts into the wee hours, with local music on Wednesday and Thursday, Irish music on Friday and Saturday. A traditional Irish breakfast is available as part of the Sunday brunch beginning at 11 AM. Reservations are recommended for groups.

Mezza Luna Italian Restaurant & Bar (321-254-6166; www.mezaluna melbourne.com) 1385 Highland Avenue, Eau Gallie 32935. Price: Expensive. Cusine: Italian. Meals Served: L, D. Bring family, friends, and a robust appetite with you to this wonderful neighborhood restaurant in the heart of historic downtown Eau Gallie. Choose an indoor table or dine alfresco in the sidewalk café area or on the cozy backyard patio. The setting invites you to linger—from appetizer to dessert. The menu offers an extensive array of flavorful Italian dishes from the simple, like classic spaghetti and meatballs, to the sublime, an impressive Zuppa di Pesce with clams, mussels, shrimp, calamari, and fish in a marinara, garlic, and white wine sauce. The chef creates unusual and delicious daily specials featuring fresh, seasonal ingredients. The lunch menu offers gourmet soups, salads, and sandwiches along with other dishes. Service is friendly and guests are easily accommodated if they want to modify a recipe, try a new wine, or split entrées. For

dessert, try the Cassata Cake, flavored with ricotta cheese, cherries, pineapple, and amaretto, and topped with a creamy chocolate icing. Enjoy jazz and easy listening musicians on the patio on Thursday and Friday evenings. Reservations are recommended for groups and on the weekend.

Nosh & Ganache (321-254-1451) 1540 Highland Avenue, Eau Gallie 32935. Price: Moderate–Expensive. Cuisine: French. Meals Served: L, D. Carlin is the proprietor and your host for a leisurely meal at this cozy bistro in the heart of the Eau Gallie Arts District. Dine at the delightful outdoor patio or in the comfortably formal inside dining room. Select from a variety of creative soups, sandwiches, salads, and hot entrées with a French flair. The chef offers daily and seasonal specials like a Cottage Pie with white-meat chicken and winter vegetables in a wine cream sauce and topped with a puff pastry crust. Complete your meal with one of their signature desserts, or a selection from their large assortment of handmade chocolates and a rich espresso. Lunch is served from 11–2:30; candlelight repast from 6 PM Thursday through Saturday evenings. Open 10–5 for retail sales of chocolates. Closed Sunday.

✔ Sand on the Beach (321-327-8951; www.pepajrestaurants.com) 1005 Atlantic Street, Melbourne Beach 32951. Price: Moderate. Cuisine: Seafood. Meals Served: B, L, D. Before the Melbourne Causeway was built, residents on the mainland would take a ferry to the Melbourne Beach Pier and ride or stroll 4 blocks east to the ocean. They had to bring a picnic lunch, but today food and drinks are available from sunup to long past sundown at this very casual restaurant located directly on the ocean. Come as you are and dine on the deck or grab a table upstairs in the Bikini Bar. Appetizer choices center around seafood selections, like crab cakes, shrimp, mussels, and a tangy fish dip. Burgers, a lobster Reuben, and other sandwiches are served in a basket with fries. For dinner, try tuna or mahi-mahi, grilled or blackened, along with mashed potatoes and veggies. The music and noise crank up after the sunset, so visit during the day or early evening if you want to bask in the breeze and have a relaxed conversation. The menu is simple, the food is good, and the view is amazing.

ᛣ Squid Lips Overwater Grill
(321-259-3101; www.squidlipsgrill
.com) 1477 Pineapple Avenue, Eau Gallie 32935. Price: Moderate–Expensive. Cuisine: Seafood. Meals Served: L, D. Locals selected Squid Lips, at the intersection of the Indian River and Eau Gallie Causeway, as the best restaurant with a water view. They may also have the best variety of seafood in the area. For an appetizer, try the cracked conch, sashimi-grade seared tuna, or oysters from the raw bar. Sandwiches like the Abaco fish with mango chutney are made-to-order. Traditional baskets with fries come with unusual choices, like Cajun crawfish. For dinner, dive into the seafood lasagna stuffed with blue crab meat, shrimp, and scallops. Save room for dessert. Mike's Key Lime Pie was featured on The Food Network. They carry a full selection of beers and wines—along with lots of meal choices for landlubbers. The view is magnificent; the food is extraordinary. Enjoy!

ᛣ Yellow Dog Café (321-956-3334;
www.yellowdogcafe.net) 905 US 1, Malabar 32950. Price: Very Expensive. Cuisine: Eclectic. Meals Served: L, D. The Yellow Dog Café is an exercise in contrasts: fine dining in a wooden shack; comfort food with gourmet touches. The restaurant is located on the west bank of the Indian River, and every table has a front seat for a parade of boats and birds. Owners Stuart and Nancy Barton oversee this award-winning fine-dining restaurant. One tasty appetizer could be called "not your grandmother's potato pancakes." The crunchy patties are topped with sour cream, smoked salmon, and a spoonful of caviar. Stuart's favorite entrée is onion-crusted chicken with a caramel citrus glaze. Vegetarians have several choices, including a grilled Portobello mushroom sandwich paired with roasted red peppers, artichoke hearts, spinach, and Havarti cheese. Meat lovers will enjoy the well-seasoned mixed grill with the chef's combination of meats, such as duck, chicken, sausage, and lamb. Complement your meal with a choice from their extensive wine list. For dessert, bite into a chewy brownie shaped like a dog bone and topped with vanilla ice cream and fudge sauce. The service is phenomenal. There are four dining areas: one is the library with floor-to-ceiling books and intimate tables, and another is the multi-level covered deck. Dress is Florida casual, or a little dressier for dinner. Bring a framed photo of your favorite pooch to add to their collection. Closed Monday; reservations are recommended.

CAFÉS AND COFFEE SHOPS
Depot Café (321-722-9050) 1929 Depot Road, Melbourne 32901. Located at the edge of downtown

Melbourne, right along the railroad tracks, this is a great choice for breakfast or lunch. They open at 7 and serve breakfast all day.

Le Bon Cafe (321-725-2600) 802 E. New Haven Avenue, Melbourne 32901. The aroma of fresh-brewed coffee—including more than 75 flavors, such as chocolate hazelnut and pumpkin spice—spills onto the sidewalk and draws you into this tiny diner. Enjoy Melbourne moonshine, a blend of cinnamon, Kahlúa, rum, and eggnog. Bagels and wraps are available.

905 Café (321-952-1672) 905 E. New Haven Avenue, Melbourne 32901. This quaint and cozy spot is perfect for meeting friends or grabbing a quick bite while shopping. Choose from the many flavors of coffee, or try an iced mocha with the popular Brie, apple, and walnut sandwich. Kid-friendly sandwiches are available.

☙ **The Sun Shoppe Cafe** (321-676-1438) 540 E. New Haven Avenue, Melbourne 32901. Patrons are usually waiting when this music, arts, and Internet café opens at 6 AM, and lingering at closing time. This casual, comfortable hangout attracts young and old, locals and visitors; families, first-daters, and friends. Enjoy soups, salads, and sandwiches, mostly homemade, and breakfast anytime of the day. Outside diners are welcome to bring their dogs. Local art lines the walls and local musicians entertain.

ICE CREAM AND SWEET TREATS Croissant Chateau Bakery (321-956-9009) 817 E. New Haven Avenue, Melbourne 32901. This old fashioned take-to-go shop is a nice place to stop by for a cookie

Courtesy Yellow Dog Cafe

A YUMMY CHOCOLATE DOG-BONE BROWNIE IS THE FEATURED DESSERT AT YELLOW DOG CAFÉ.

break, or pick up some bread or pastries to take home or back to your hotel for breakfast. Owner Karen bakes many of the desserts provided at area restaurants.

Grimaldi Candies (321-724-0535) 815 E. Strawbridge Avenue, Melbourne 32901. Visitors from other parts of Florida make side trips to this small shop to pick up a box or two of the legendary Florida-made Grimaldi candies. The most popular choice is probably the Chips 'N Chocolate, a deliciously delicate blend of sweet and salty.

Kilwin's of Melbourne (321-723-1141) 906 E. New Haven Avenue, Melbourne 32901. If you've forgotten what it feels like to be a kid in a candy store, come visit this bright, charming shop in historic downtown Melbourne. Rich, creamy chocolates are made daily using the same recipes that have made Kilwin's a favorite with chocoholics for more than 60 years.

Tin Roof Popcorn Company (321-723-0200) 924 E. New Haven Avenue, Melbourne 32901. Pick your favorite from more than 30 different flavors, such as Butterfinger-flavored Tin Roof Rusted, sweet red cherry, or cheddar cheese. Seasonal choices include gingerbread and candy cane in the winter, and for spring a mix of blue raspberry, strawberry, and banana. Flavored fudge also available.

SPECIALTY MARKETS The Green Turtle (321-773-2001) 855 E. Eau Gallie Boulevard, Indian Harbour Beach 32937. Grab a basket at the door of this gourmet to-go market, because you're going to find lots of goodies. Delicious and surprising fruit and vegetable salads are prepared fresh each day. Soups and sandwiches are available, or an entrée such as stuffed chicken breasts, ready for the oven. You'll find bakery goods, snacks, candies, and other tempting treats, as well as more than 800 wines. The market is located on FL 518, just a short distance from A1A.

✳ Entertainment

MUSIC AND NIGHTLIFE On Friday and Saturday nights, historic downtown Melbourne is transformed into a trendy, urban block party. **Mainstreet Pub** (705 E. New Haven Avenue) is a bright two-story outdoor bar catering to young professionals. The porch at **Matt's Casbah Patio** (801 E. New Haven) has jazz, and a late-night menu including sushi, drinks, and cigars. Relax and kick back at **Foo Bar & Lotus Gallery** (816 E. New Haven Avenue)—an indoor patio bar serving light snacks and cocktails. The **Executive Cigar Shop & Lounge** (832 E. New Haven Avenue) has an old-world feel. Cigar buffs will enjoy the walk-in humidor. The young and hip mingle at **Dondi's Downtown** (836 E. New Haven Avenue), a

comfortable indoor and outdoor spot offering fine wines, a full bar, and free pool. Get comfortable at **Florida Keys Piano Bar & Cocktail Lounge** (903 E. New Haven Avenue) while you enjoy the music of John Ryan and other guest entertainers while sampling a full bar, appetizers, and desserts. At upscale **Lexi** (924 E. New Haven Avenue) blend martinis and tapas with comfort and conversation.

Lou's Blues Upstairs (3191 N. A1A, Indialantic; 779-2299) is a two-story waterfront bar just south of A1A and FL 518. The view from the upstairs deck is one of the best on the beach. Live music plays every night at this good-time tavern and dance hall—mostly blues, but also rock classics, jam bands, and karaoke. Occasionally, special performances or fund-raisers will require a separate event ticket. A full menu is available. As you might guess, a popular choice is the "bluesburger" burger with blue cheese.

PERFORMING ARTS Brevard Symphony Orchestra Orchestra in Residence at King Center for the Performing Arts (321-242-2024; www .brevardsymphony.com) 1500 Highland Avenue, Melbourne 32936. More than 50 years ago, a group of Brevard musicians joined forces to accompany a presentation of *The Mikado*. Today, the Brevard Symphony Orchestra is one of the finest in the country. Maestro Christopher Confessore conducts talented musicians in an extensive repertoire of performances. The group offers a "teaching concert" for fifth-grade students each year, as well as a free family concert as part of their fall season. The orchestra's offices are housed in the historic Winchester Symphony House, built in 1886.

Brevard Symphony Youth Orchestra (321-254-9583) With the belief that music can excite the human spirit and stimulate the imagination, founders of this organization bring together 200 of the most talented young musicians in Brevard County. Orchestra members, from elementary level to high school, commit to a weekly schedule of rehearsals and performances. Professional and seasoned conductors lead a symphony orchestra, concert orchestra, and string ensemble.

Henegar Center for the Arts (321-723-8698; www.henegar.org) 625 E. New Haven Avenue, Melbourne 32901. This facility opened in 1919 as the Melbourne School. The building is named for Ruth Henegar, a teacher and principal, and is a learning center for creative workshops as well as a center for performing arts. Revolving art exhibits are hosted by members of the Strawbridge Art League, the cast of Red Carpet Productions stages musicals and comedies throughout the year, and other community organizations hold events and festivals here. The 500-seat theater is a perfect setting for intimate and eclectic presentations.

Maxwell C. King Center for the Performing Arts (321-242-2219; www.kingcenter.com) 3865 N. Wickham, Melbourne 32935. Concerts, Broadway musicals, plays, and presentations for children ensure this remarkable multi-use facility is busy almost every week. The 2,000-seat main stage hall features world-renowned performers in touring shows, concerts, and performances. The cozier 200-seat Studio Theatre offers offbeat productions. The lobby is a staging gallery for local art. The

King Center is also the resident venue for many of Brevard County's most talented artistic groups.

Melbourne Chamber Music Society (321-956-8775; www.melbourne chambermusicsociety.com) P.O. Box 033403, Indialantic 32903. Acclaimed musicians from around the world perform classical music at St. Marks United Methodist Church in Indialantic, 18 miles south of FL 520 and A1A.

Melbourne Civic Theatre (321-723-6935; www.mymct.org) 817 E. Strawbridge Avenue, Melbourne 32901. Brevard County's oldest community theater group stages several plays each season, some from early Broadway and others, more contemporary productions. Most are funny, and all are entertaining. The space is small, so this is a very intimate theater experience. The venue is located in La Galerie in Historic Downtown Melbourne, making it easy to begin your evening with dinner at one of many restaurants within walking distance. Acting classes are available.

Space Coast Ballet Most performances at King Center for the Performing Arts (321-253-0544; www.space coastballet.com). Former Kirov dancers Boris Chepelev and Janna Kirova direct the Space Coast's only professional ballet company. The troupe dances classical ballets, like their annual performance of *The Nutcracker*, as well as modern works developed by today's most talented choreographers. Young dancers are nurtured and trained through the Space Coast Ballet Academy.

Space Coast Pops Most performances at Merritt Island First Baptist Church (321-632-7445; www.space coastpops.com). Professional musicians entertain with lighter and more recognizable pops selections. Music director and flamboyant conductor Richard Hayman is a veteran of the Boston Pops and delivers arrangements and performances that delight his audiences. Ticketed concerts are held on Saturday afternoons during the winter/spring season. In addition, this longtime community group holds free concerts on the Fourth of July and during the holidays.

Space Coast Symphony Orchestra Most performances at Merritt Island First Baptist Church (321-536-8580; www.spacecoastsymphony.org). This newcomer to the area's cultural landscape initiated the inaugural season in 2009 with the dual goal of blending experienced and renowned professionals with talented young musicians, and reaching a wide audience by offering a reasonably priced ticket. The group is under the direction of conductor and composer Aaron Collins.

✳ Selective Shopping

Eau Gallie Arts District (EGAD!) Life imitates art on Highland Avenue where the stores are colorful and display local artwork along with specialty merchandise. Most shops are closed on Sunday and Monday.

Art Expressions (321-259-1492) 1404 Highland Avenue, Eau Gallie 32935. For years Jody Carter has been providing quality picture framing for fine art. Now she has expanded her shop to offer art, including delightful miniatures, original microprints strung on satin or leather cording, and other jewelry and gifts.

Eau Gallie Florist (321-254-2584) 1490 Highland Avenue, Eau Gallie 32935. Flowers flow out of the store

and into the courtyard at this bright spot on Highland Avenue. For Link and Alexis Johnson, a pot is the canvas and bright petals are the paint. They carry a selection of unusual home and garden accessories.

The Laughing Mermaid (321-368-7002) 1372 Highland Avenue, Eau Gallie 32935. Relax, renew, and restore your spirit at this delightful shop that carries organic and natural products for the body and hair. Whimsical art lines the walls. The Siren Boutique offers a collection of fun and affordable casual wear and accessories.

Ralph's Art Supply (321-255-3331) 1420 Highland Avenue, Eau Gallie 32935. Be inspired and discover your inner artist at the largest art supply store on the Space Coast. Choose from a rainbow of paints and pencils, as well as boards, sketchpads, and educational materials. One corner is stocked with creative kits and tools for youngsters.

Main Street Melbourne Stroll through the restored area of old Melbourne and enjoy a glimpse at what this avenue was like at the turn of the 20th century. Antiques and bric-a-brac vie for your attention, along with contemporary décor and colorful clothing and accessories. This is the place to find the perfect gift for yourself or someone back home. Many of the shops are open on Friday evening but are closed on Sunday.

ANTIQUES AND COLLECTIBLES
Betty's Antiques (321-951-2258) 2001 Melbourne Ct., Melbourne 32901. Betty specializes in estate sales, especially furniture, silver, jewelry, and glassware, and is a licensed appraiser.

Melbourne Antique Gallery (321-951-0151) 806 E. New Haven Avenue, Melbourne 32901. Poke around inside and discover a selection of furniture, vintage dishes, and oriental pieces, and porcelain.

CLOTHING, SHOES, AND ACCESSORIES

Albatross (321-723-2270) 826 E. New Haven Avenue, Suite 101, Melbourne 32901. Welcome to the islands. In this relaxed shop, men and women will discover tropical and stylish Tommy Bahama brand clothing and watches, perfect for watching time go by.

Baby Patch (321-676-7590) 800 E. New Haven Avenue, Melbourne 32901. For over 20 years this adorable shop has been outfitting pampered Brevard babies with layettes, cuddly gifts and toys, furniture, gift items.

Downtown Divas (321-733-0898) 847 E. New Haven Avenue, Melbourne 32901. Small and colorful shop features metropolitan clothing in a small town setting, with avant-garde styles and accessories meant to be noticed; a great place to stop before a night out on the town.

The Flop Shop (321-724-6740) 820 E. New Haven Avenue, Melbourne 32901. Step through the door and into a world of flexible footwear, stylish sandals, and colorful Crocs in a variety of styles for adults and children—everything from truly casual to flops sprinkled with bling.

Gabrielle (321-952-1177) 843 E. New Haven Avenue, Melbourne 32901. Specialty dress boutique featuring designers Joseph Ribkoff and Komarov, with selections perfect for daytime wear and special occasions.

The Gauzeway (321-723-0334) 818 E. New Haven Avenue, Melbourne

32901. Bright, breezy cloth is spun into delicate gauze skirts, tops, pants, and capris, all 100 percent cotton and made with natural fibers and dyes. Distinctive handmade jewelry by Treska and Susan Sorrentino complements the outfits.

Isabella's Ladies Apparel (321-952-4489) 845 E. New Haven Avenue, Melbourne 32901. Fashionable formal wear in traditional and daring designs, perfect for a special occasion, is available here. An entire wedding party can be accommodated with choices in bridal gowns, wedding party dresses, and accessories. They feature Brighton accessories.

Kiwi Seeds (321-723-4200) 826 E. New Haven Avenue, Melbourne 32901. Fans of Fresh Produce will find a wide range of colors, styles, and sizes from kids to adults. The shop also carries belts, bags, and jewelry, along with the Life is Good line.

Mirabella's (321-725-4983) 909 E. New Haven Avenue, Melbourne 32901. Find playful resort wear, jewelry, and accessories, with an emphasis on comfortable and carefree natural fabrics.

Unique Treasures (321-723-7290) 828 E. New Haven Avenue, Melbourne 32901. Browse through fun fashions and accessories at this one-stop-shop. Finish the outfit with a choice from their collection of gemstones and sterling jewelry.

Yapa (321-727-2300) 925 E. New Haven Avenue, Melbourne 32901. The name means "a little something extra" and this store delivers, with funky and fabulous clothes, jewelry, and bling for the home.

HOME DÉCOR AND GIFTS

The Chandlery (321-726-0192)

GALLERIES
Eau Gallie, Melbourne

The Eau Gallie Arts District (EGAD!) preserves and promotes the creative spirit of this historic riverside community. Highland Avenue is the main thoroughfare for a neighborhood where artists live and work; where early 20th-century buildings are transformed into attractive showroom galleries and working studios. In addition to regular hours, all the galleries are open during the First Friday Art Walk, and most plan special receptions and offer refreshments.

Art and Antique Studio (321-253-5553; www.artandantiquestudio.com) 1419 Highland Avenue, Eau Gallie 32935. Open: Monday through Friday 10, Saturday 9–4. Watercolorist and studio founder Therese Ferguson is inspired by the small group of award-winning artists that cooperatively display and give classes in this working studio and gallery adjoining an open-air courtyard. The garden décor frames a full range of mediums, including paintings, pastels, pottery, photography, and glass. An antique table doubles as an easel for displaying contemporary art, and sketches of historic Eau Gallie houses share a corner with bold, modern jewelry in this gallery reminiscent of a well-decorated home.

Fifth Avenue Art Gallery (321-259-8261; www.fifthavenueartgallery.com) 1470 Highland Avenue, Eau Gallie 32935. Open: Tuesday through Saturday 10–5, Sunday 1–5 (September through May). Together for more than 30 years, this cooperative of local artists has earned a nationwide reputation for exhibiting high-quality and collectible art. The spacious and bright gallery features an impressive and original array of artistic works, as well as one-of-a-kind jewelry and gift items. The gallery has marvelous sculptures, including many large pieces that hang from the ceiling like the mermaids that appear to float through an imaginary sea. New exhibitions are introduced at an opening reception held on the first Friday of each month. Refreshments are served, admission is free, and the public is invited to attend and meet the artist.

Highway Grrls and Studio (321-227-3075; www.highwaygrrlsgallery.com) 1414 Highland Avenue, Eau Gallie 32935. Open: Monday through Saturday 11–4, Sunday 1–4. Robin Rothrock has created a feast of color with her innovative visual art that uses acrylic paints on canvas, glass, ceramic tile, metal, and even lampshades. Water plays an important role in the works of the artist who grew up as a surfer girl in nearby Satellite Beach and, like the unpredictable currents of the ocean, Robin describes her method as "process art" which means she's unclear where she's going until she gets there. The works of other local artists are often featured.

Indian River Potters' Guild (321-543-3645) 1542 Guava Avenue, Eau Gallie 32935. Open: Monday through Friday 11–5. Local potters inspire each other and share

ideas and space in this renovated home located a block off Highland Avenue.
Founder Valerie Karas has designed and equipped the facility to ensure that
novices and master potters all have an opportunity to develop their art. The
beauty and diversity of the work is on display and for sale in the small gallery
connected to the studio.

New Haven Avenue, Melbourne
New Haven Avenue in historic downtown Melbourne draws talent from down
the street and around the world. The dynamic environment has been home to
some artists for many years, while others are new to the area.

Art Gallery and Studio LLC (321-729-9368) 822 E. New Haven Avenue, Melbourne
32901. Open: Monday through Saturday 11–5. A community of experienced
artists hopes to enhance interest in art through this enjoyable collection of
mixed media and styles. Each member has a completely different area of focus,
including watercolor, acrylic, jewelry, porcelain, stained glass, and more.
808 Art Gallery (321-890-3978) 808 E. New Haven Avenue, Melbourne 32901.
Open: Tuesday through Saturday 11–5. Lifelong Brevard County resident Jerry
Hooper developed a love for nature and an eye for detail as a landscape designer. Under the tutelage of accomplished local artists, his talent grew. Today this
award-winning Florida painter creates extraordinary abstracts, landscapes, still
lifes, and portraits that grace the walls of this bold and beautiful gallery. Expect
to find Hooper at his easel. Other artists and styles are also featured. The gallery
is often open on Sunday and Monday during the busy winter season.

LoPressionism Gallery (321-722-
6000; www.lopressionism.com)
1002 E. New Haven Avenue, Melbourne 32901. Open: Monday
through Saturday 10–5:30. This
sophisticated gallery is a little off
the beaten path but well worth the
detour. Music and outdoor paintings lead upstairs into what feels
like a metropolitan living room
decorated with contemporary fine
art from around the world. Talented artists working in all mediums
are featured in the regular collection and in rotating shows. The
boutique offers artistic glassware,
jewelry, and novelty items.

PAINTER JERRY HOOPER AT WORK AT 808
ART GALLERY.

911 E. New Haven Avenue, Melbourne 32901. Enhance the warmth of your home with candles and home fragrance accessories, such as oil lamps, scented candles, and decorative holders. Select from a full line of wedding candles and a rotation of seasonal selections.

Christmas Cottage (321-725-0270) 1002 E. New Haven Avenue, Melbourne 32901.Capture the holiday spirit any day of the year as you browse through seasonal collectibles, decorations, and gifts.

Creative Energy (321-952-6789) 835 E. New Haven Avenue, Melbourne 32901. Aromatherapy fills the air and sets the mood for exploring New-Age gifts for the mind, body, and soul, including books, music, jewelry, clothing, lotions, and oils. Tarot cards available and readings sometimes offered on Saturday.

From My Heart to Yours (321-914-3909) 819-4 E. Strawbridge Avenue, Melbourne 32901. This delightful shop tucked into the La Galerie Arcade offers local handcrafted jewelry, quilts, stained glass pieces, candles, Adirondack chairs, and more.

The Gourmet Garden (321-409-2999) 909 E. New Haven Avenue, Melbourne 32901. Experienced and casual gourmets alike will be taken with the tempting and delightful choices of kitchen, dining, and entertaining accessories, along with seasonings, mixes and sauces.

Indian River Soap (321-723-6464) 804 E. New Haven Avenue, Melbourne 32901. Nourish the body and the spirit with natural, wholesome skin products, soaps, soy wax candles, bath accessories, and gifts. Devotees of Crabtree & Evelyn will find all their favorite scents.

Irish Shop (321-723-0122) 818 E. New Haven Avenue, Melbourne 32901. Top of the morning to you! Owners John and Mary Nolan will help you find a pot of gold at the end of the rainbow with traditional products from Ireland, such as Belleek china, Galway crystal, Claddagh jewelry, scarves and throws, and wedding and baby gifts.

Lord Ravenswood Hall (321-768-8369) 909 E. New Haven Avenue, Melbourne 32901. Enjoy the flavor of olde England with comedy videos, bone china teacups, teapots and cozies, sweets and biscuits, and more imports from across the pond.

Sendala's (321-951-2110) 909 E. New Haven Avenue, Melbourne 32901. Indulge the senses with an array of bath and body products, and personal touches for the home, including a full line from Thymes.

JEWELRY Jessups (321-724-2201) 912 E. New Haven Avenue, Melbourne 32901. This family-owned store, which carries both estate and new fine jewelry, is also Melbourne's oldest licensed pawnbroker. They feature real roses dipped in gold and a selection of jewelry boxes.

Just for You Estate Jewelry (321-768-2636) 829 E. New Haven Avenue, Melbourne 32901. In addition to fine antique and estate items, the store has a complete line of Vera Bradley purses, watches, and belts.

SPORTS Harry Goode's Outdoor Shop (321-723-4751) 1231 E. New Haven Avenue, Melbourne 32901. Harry Goode, a member of one of Melbourne's founding families, opened this sporting goods store in

1946 with the motto, "fish more, live longer." Stop by for fishing supplies, paraphernalia, assistance, and a smattering of tall tales. Located at the intersection of the Indian River and Crane Creek.

✴ Special Events

Monthly: **Downtown Melbourne's Friday Fest** (New Haven Avenue near US 1, Melbourne) Join the street party beginning at 6 PM on the second Friday of each month, except December. Fun spills into the streets when New Haven Avenue is closed to traffic, bands set up on the sidewalks, and shops and restaurants open their doors.

First Friday Art Walk at Eau Gallie (Highland Avenue, downtown Eau Gallie) The Eau Gallie Arts District (EGAD!) rolls out the red carpet on the first Friday of each month. Galleries feature special exhibits and receptions, restaurants and shops stay open, musicians play in the park, and artists bring their work into the streets.

February: **Grant Seafood Festival** (321-723-8687; www.grantseafood festival.com) Nearly 40 years ago, the town of Grant, located 12 miles south of Melbourne off US 1, held a fish fry to raise money for the community center. Today, the residents of this still-small town sponsor this all-volunteer event, which has become the Southeast's largest and longest-running seafood festival—attracting nearly 50,000 people over two days. Expect live entertainment, handmade crafts, and special exhibits, but the main attraction is the seafood: clams, crab, scallops, shrimp, oysters, conch fritters, and all the fixin's! The festival is held the last weekend in February;

admission and parking are free.

Greek Festival (321-254-1045; St. Katherine's Greek Orthodox Church, 5965 N. Wickham Road, Melbourne 32940) For more than 35 years, St. Katherine's has sponsored a two-day celebration of Greek culture. Enjoy authentic foods, dance, music, and, of course, ouzo. Fantastiko!

Indiafest (720-8590; www.indiafest brevard.org; Wickham Park Pavilion, Melbourne) Sample the amazingly diverse foods and fashions of India, a country where more than a billion people speak a dozen languages. This weekend-long festival includes music and dance programs, yoga demonstrations, palm readings, and even advice on how to wear a sari. Organizers use the event to raise money for local and international charities.

March: 𝒮 **Habitat for Humanity Strawberry Festival** (321-728-4009;

A COLLECTION OF SOOTHING SOAPS FROM INDIAN RIVER SOAP.

WILDLIFE PROFILE: MANATEE

The manatee is an amusing and popular resident of the Indian River Lagoon. The odd-looking, docile sea creatures were probably the beautiful sirens that ancient sailors dubbed mermaids, although it would take distance and an active imagination to make such a mistake. Manatees have a mermaid's flat, paddle-shaped tail, but it's attached to a gray, wrinkled body. An adult Florida manatee, a subspecies of the West Indian manatee, is about 10 feet long, weighs 1,000 pounds, and has whiskers and bad breath.

Florida's state marine mammal is commonly referred to as a sea cow because this strict vegetarian spends most of the day grazing on grasses in shallow rivers and estuaries. It resembles a walrus but is actually most closely related to the elephant. The manatee never leaves the water, but because it is a mammal, it surfaces to take a breath every three to five minutes—with a noisy exhale.

The manatee is an endangered species but has no natural predators. Speedboats, plastic bags, and discarded fishing lines are its biggest threat. Area waters populated by manatees are designated no-wake zones so boaters can see and avoid the slow-moving swimmers. The manatee's reproductive process begins late and is infrequent, with a single birth every three to five years. Newborns are about 4 feet long and stay with their mother for two years.

The best way to see a manatee is from a pontoon boat, kayak, or canoe.

www.brevardhabitat.com; Wickham Park Pavilion, Melbourne) Bring family, friends, and a big appetite to this festive get-together. Musical entertainment, craft exhibits, and a classic car show are window dressing for the main event—fresh-picked, red, ripe strawberries piled high over shortcake, spooned over rich vanilla ice cream, or dipped in chocolate. The fun starts with a pancake breakfast each morning and continues until 5. The two-day event is held the first weekend in March. Admission is free.

April: **Melbourne Art Festival** (321-722-1964; www.melbournearts.org; downtown Melbourne) Art lovers will enjoy this juried art show, featuring more than 250 participants and ranked among the top 25 art shows in the country. The streets of historic downtown Melbourne are filled with exhibits and workshops. KidsWorld is dedicated to hands-on activities and free stage performances for children. Top this all off with an abundance of food and entertainment. This event is very crowded and does not allow pets (except service animals), roller blades, skateboards, or coolers.

September: **Family Salsa Festival** (Wickham Park, Melbourne) Follow the sounds of rhythmic salsa music, and the savory aroma of island seasonings to the Wickham Park pavilion. This one-day event features live

Tour operators guide guests to areas where they like to feed. Their gray brown skin blends with the water (hence the danger from boaters), so look for a tail flap as they propel forward or a snout poking upward. Manatees leave

MANATEE (*TRICHECHUS MANETUS*)   Jim Angy

a swirling "footprint" as they meander close to the water's surface. Once located, they're often clearly visible in the water. They can turn and tumble but never jump like dolphins—and they are almost impossible to photograph. The best picture you'll have is the one planted firmly in your memory.

Space Coast Sightings: Manatee Park in Cape Canaveral, Port Canaveral locks, Cocoa Beach Thousand Islands, Haulover Canal, Crane Creek in Melbourne.

music, culinary treats, children's activities, and a Miss Puerto Rico contest. United Third Bridge, an organization dedicated to Hispanic education and culture, sponsors the festival.

October: **Meg-O-Ween** (www.down townmelbourne.com; New Haven Avenue, downtown Melbourne) On the Saturday closest to Halloween, crowds of young and not-so-young adults spill onto New Haven Avenue for an outrageous and over-the-top good time. Families with children may want to head home as evening activities begin. The highlight is a risqué costume contest. The event is sponsored by Meg O'Malley's and has become a Space Coast tradition.

Melbourne Oktoberfest (321-328-4234; www.melbourneoktoberfest .com; 3865 N. Wickham Road, Wickham Park, Melbourne) In 1810 a celebration was held in Munich, Germany, to commemorate a royal marriage. Now mid-October is a traditional time to enjoy German music, dance, food, and beer, along with all-American, 21st-century fair rides. The party begins on Thursday and Friday evenings and continues through the weekend.

November: ✧ **ArtWorks Eau Gallie Fine Art Festival** (www.artworksof eaugallie.org; Highland Avenue, Eau Gallie) For two days in mid-November, the Eau Gallie Arts District is

WILDLIFE PROFILE: ALLIGATOR

After existing more than 150 million years and surviving the cataclysmic disaster that drove its dinosaur cousins to extinction, the American alligator species was nearly done in by love—the public's love for purses, belts, shoes, wallets, and other goods made from exotic alligator hide. In the late 18th century, naturalist William Bartram wrote of seeing so many alligators in the St. Johns River "it would have been easy to have walked across on their heads had the animals been harmless." A hundred years later, the population was significantly depleted, and the state stepped in to protect the species and reverse the decline.

The adaptable American is the official reptile of Florida, a curious, reclusive star in the state's ecological drama. These cold-blooded creatures spend long hours basking in the warm sun near canals, rivers, lagoons, and even ponds on the golf course. A shovel-shaped snout is trimmed with teeth; bulging eyes sit high on the head and scan for prey while the gator floats just beneath the water's surface. The hide is dark, scaly, and bony—reminiscent of prehistoric roots. The largest reptile in North America, the alligator is usually at least 8 to 10 feet long as an adult, including a thick powerful tail that propels it through the water and sideswipes adversaries. Alligators creep slowly across the ground on stubby, webbed appendages but can move very quickly if provoked.

Make no mistake, these normally timid creatures are the wildest of wildlife, and when mating or protecting their young, or when harassed, they can quickly become aggressive. It's illegal to feed alligators because they'll

transformed into an outdoor studio. More than 100 local artists display their works, while creating new works *en plein air* and demonstrating their technique at the same time. Community musicians and food vendors add to this hometown event.

Festival of Trees (www.kingcenter .com; King Center for the Performing Arts, 3865 N. Wickham, Melbourne 32935) A stroll through this forest of themed Christmas trees marks the unofficial start of the holiday season in Brevard County. The Junior

League of South Brevard sponsors this event, which benefits local organizations. Bid on a fully decorated tree, or just enjoy refreshments, crafts, and a visit with Santa.

Melbourne Independent Filmmakers Festival (www.3boys productions.com; Melbourne) This weekend of movie screenings, workshops, and activities promotes local filmmakers and a general interest in film. Buy a weekend pass or tickets to individual events, including a VIP reception and courtyard party for lose their fear, and the chance of an attack on humans or pets increases. The risk is so great that once an alligator has been fed, it will be captured and killed. For your protection and theirs, keep your distance as you admire these fascinating and fearsome survivors.

Space Coast Sightings: Black Point Wildlife Drive at the Merritt Island National Wildlife Refuge, St. Johns River airboat tour, Wild Florida exhibit at Brevard Zoo.

AMERICAN ALLIGATOR (*ALLIGATOR MISSISSIPPIENSIS*)

Jim Angy

adults and children. All proceeds support a local nonprofit organization.

Native Rhythms Festival (321-639-3561; www.nativerhythmsfestival.com; 3865 N. Wickham Road, Wickham Park, Melbourne) This three-day event held during Native American Heritage Month honors the culture of the indigenous peoples of the Americas through music, especially the flute. Musicians and storytellers invite people of all nations to enjoy concerts, workshops, and competitions; costumes, arts and crafts, and traditional foods.

SUGGESTED ITINERARIES

Often visitors have itineraries or intentions that make a stay on Florida's Space Coast a little difficult to navigate. Business travelers and cruisers may have only a few hours or a day to sample the area, while others want to extend their stay. The beach is a natural magnet for a special celebration or gathering, but presents planning challenges. Here are some suggestions to help you steer a steady course, grouped by the following areas of interest:

Celebrations and Special Occasions

If Time Is Short

Theme Parks

Visitor Resources

CELEBRATIONS AND SPECIAL OCCASIONS Florida's Space Coast offers ideal outdoor settings for family reunions, weddings, and other celebrations. The beach at sunrise or sunset is memorable and romantic. Brevard Zoo offers couples a change to invite some "wild" guests to their party. Historic sites like the Porcher House in Cocoa, the Rossetter Home in Eau Gallie, or the Indian River Queen paddleboat provide old-Florida ambience. Each facility can assist guests in locating local planners to help blend lodging, dining, and recreation and create a perfect stay for your small or large gathering.

Doubletree Oceanfront Hotel (321-783-9222; www.cocoabeachdoubletree .com) The staff at the Doubletree Hotel makes all the arrangements for a celebration to remember. Facility choices include the beach, pool deck, or elegant ballroom. The planning and service will be exceptional for intimate events or sit-down dinners for 300.

Dream Beach Weddings (321-271-0908; www.dreambeachweddings.com) Imagine exchanging vows against a backdrop of blue sky, soft breezes, and rolling surf. Relax and let the folks at Dream Beach Weddings guide you through every wedding planning detail—flowers, location, limousines, photographers, and more.

Rainbow Connection Tours (321-453-3233; www.rctours.net) Linda May, Faye Gallant, and a team of travel experts are available to plan and escort customized excursions for visitors—on the Space Coast or throughout the central Florida area. They make all the arrangements. Wedding planning, including cruise ship ceremonies, is one of their specialties.

Sun Touched Weddings (321-258-7122; www.suntouchedweddings.com) Michael Howard, founder of Sun Touched Weddings, is a Cocoa Beach native who specializes in intimate beachside weddings and can provide everything you need for a casual barefoot-on-the-beach event or a formal gathering. Michael is also a professional photographer and offers beach portrait packages for a lasting memory of your vacation.

SunWard Tours (321-453-0704; www.sunwardtours.com) Tour and event coordinators David and Margaret Bodchon serve as your concierges, tailoring an itinerary exactly to your time and budget.

IF TIME IS SHORT A first visit to the Space Coast is sometimes squeezed in around a cruise, a business trip, or a stay in Orlando, and time is limited. The beach, of course, is the star attraction, so enjoy taking in the sunrise or wading in the shallow surf. Beyond that, here is a list of personal favorites, each with something extra special that will make you love the area and impatient to return for a longer stay.

A WEDDING AT THE BREVARD ZOO IS QUITE AN ADVENTURE.

Jim White Photography

Cape Canaveral and Cocoa Beach

LODGING Beach Place Guesthouses (321-783-4045, fax 321-868-2492; www.beachplaceguesthouses.com) 1445 S. Atlantic Avenue, Cocoa Beach 32920. Perfect for a calming retreat even if only for a night, with a nearly private beach and comfortable accommodations; also ideal for hosting an intimate wedding.

Best Western Oceanfront Hotel (321-783-7621, 1-800-962-0028, fax 321-799-4576; www.bestwesterncocoabeach.com) 5500 Ocean Beach Boulevard, Cocoa Beach 32931. One of the best locations on the beach, the hotel is near the Cocoa Beach Pier and within walking distance of several restaurants.

Radisson Resort at the Port (321-784-0000, 1-800-333-3333, fax 321-784-3737; www.radisson.com/capecanaveralfl) 8701 Astronaut Boulevard, Cape Canaveral 32920. An ideal location for a pre-cruise overnight stay where you can relax and play by the pool, have dinner at the Flamingo restaurant, and then board a quick shuttle to the ship the next day.

BEACHES **Cocoa Beach Pier** (321-783-7549; www.cocoabeachpier.com) 401 Meade Avenue, Cocoa Beach 32931. Like a trip to a seaside mall, everything you need for a fun day at the beach is in one convenient location.

Jetty Park 400 E. Jetty Road, Cape Canaveral 32920. If time is extra short but you would like to experience the beach, take a walk on the shore of Jetty Park or on the 1,200-foot fishing pier. Time your visit to catch cruise ships that leave at about 5 most evenings.

RECREATION **Space Coast Kayaking** (321-784-2452; www.spacecoastkayak ing.net) Ramp Road, Cocoa Beach. A leisurely kayak paddle through the Thousand Islands is the best way to get close to wildlife, including manatees, bottlenose dolphins, and birds.

Space Coast River Tours (321-652-1052; www.spacecoastrivertours.com) Relax on the river with this two-hour nature tour that departs from Kelly Park near the Beachline Expressway. The comfortable pontoon boat almost always has room for one or two more so they can usually accommodate last-minute calls.

WHERE TO EAT **Fishlips Waterfront Bar & Grill** (321-784-4533) 610 Glen Cheek Drive, Port Canaveral 32920. This portside seafood restaurant has indoor and outdoor seating, and delicious dishes prepared and presented with style.

Milliken's Reef (321-783-0100) 683 Dave Nisbet Drive, Port Canaveral 32920. Arrive late afternoon to watch the cruise ships depart, and then stay for a great seafood dinner. Outside wrap-around deck and indoor bar with open view of the waterfront ensures a great view and comfortable seat in any weather.

Central Brevard

Cocoa Village is just a short drive from the beach. Visit the galleries and shops, and take a break for breakfast, lunch, or dinner at **Ossorio's** (316 Brevard Avenue), a charming bistro in the heart of the village, or **Café Margaux** (220 Brevard Avenue), a fine dining restaurant with fabulous dishes and great service; resort casual dress is fine. Plan your day around one of these excursions:

Indian River Cruises (321-223-6825; www.indianrivercruises.com) 90 Delannoy Avenue. Guests are treated like old friends along for an unforgettable sail down the Indian River aboard a luxury 47-foot catamaran. Couple a romantic sunset cruise with dinner at Café Margaux.

Twister Airboat Rides (321-632-4199; www.twisterairboatrides.com) FL 520 at St. Johns River, Cocoa. Just a short drive from Cocoa Village, adventurers of all ages will enjoy a uniquely Florida trek, and an almost-guaranteed chance to see alligators, with Twister Airboat Rides, which leave from Lone Cabbage Fish Camp (8199 King Street) in Cocoa.

THEME PARKS Florida's Space Coast is a short drive from of some of the most popular tourist destinations in the world, making day trips a nice complement to a stay in Brevard. Comparable hotels in Cape Canaveral and Cocoa Beach are usually less expensive than those in the Orlando area—and come with a beach! Seasonal visitors and others who have seen most of the attractions will always discover something new. Weather can change quickly so pack a rain poncho and sweater for the evening, along with a change of clothes if you plan to go on water rides.

Daytona 500 Experience Stock car racing was born along the wide, flat beaches of Daytona, and today the Daytona International Speedway is the sport's most treasured venue. The Daytona 500 NASCAR race kicks off the season in February, but fans (including youngsters fascinated by characters from the movie *Cars*) can experience the thrills year-round. Take a 30-minute tram tour around the track and into pit road and the garages. The attraction includes famous cars, video discussions with drivers, and simulators that bring this fast sport to life. From SR 528, take I-95 north to exit 261, US 92, and follow the signs to Daytona International Speedway; estimated 1 hour, 20 minutes drive time. Daytona 500 Experience: (386-681-6800; www.daytona500experience.com) 1801 W. International Speedway Boulevard, Daytona.

Universal Orlando Resort Two movie-based theme parks have a reputation for thrilling rides and edgy shows that appeal to movie fans of every age, including hard-to-impress teens. At the fast-paced **Universal Studios Orlando**, go behind the scenes or jump onto rides that make you part of the action, like the Hollywood Rip Ride Rocket, a high-speed roller coaster where you pick the music you want to hear before you strap in and then can get a customized video of your experience. The Wizarding World of Harry Potter is their newest attraction. At **Islands of Adventure** toddlers will enjoy Seuss Island, a comfortable couch ride through the pages of *The Cat in the Hat* and a spin on the imaginative Caro-Seuss-el. Both parks stage a variety of live shows, and the **City Walk** entertainment complex features the exciting Blue Man Group, along with a rotating line-up of musical performers. Follow SR 528 west to I-4, take I-4 east about 3 miles to Exit 75A and follow the signs to the main parking garage; estimated one hour drive time. Universal Orlando Resort: (407-363-8000; www.universalorlando.com) 6000 Universal Boulevard, Orlando.

Walt Disney World Resort This small city of theme parks, resorts, and entertainment complexes is the most popular tourist destination in the world for one reason—magic. The only way not to have a good time is to try to do too much, so consider picking just one park to visit in a day. Then take advantage of the **Fastpass** ticket option that minimizes ride wait times. When you arrive, check the schedule for character appearances, parades, and fireworks. The annual pass is a great bargain for frequent visitors.

Each theme park has a special appeal. **Magic Kingdom** is the heart of Walt Disney World and best seen through the eyes of a child. Catch a ride on the Walt Disney World Railroad just inside the entrance and travel to Mickey's Toontown Fair, a guaranteed spot to meet some of the most popular characters. A visit to **Epcot** takes you into the future and around the world. Start with a ride inside the iconic Spaceship Earth, and then catch a boat across the lagoon to see the audio-animatronic American Adventure stage show, a moving look at our nation's early history. The park dresses up in bright spring colors for the International Flower & Garden Festival. At **Disney's Hollywood Studios** multiple stages present a changing menu of live shows featuring current movie and television hits, like *High School Musical*, as well as a behind-the-scenes Studio Backlot Tour. **Disney's Animal Kingdom** invites guests to explore the wilds of Asia and Africa on a safari or in exhibits featuring over 500 species of animals, including some small critters in the Affection Section petting zoo.

For fun outside the theme parks, treat children and grandchildren to a meal with the characters, like breakfast or dinner at the Cape May Café in the Beach Club Resort. Celebrate an evening out at **Downtown Disney**, conveniently located at the edge of the property. Pair drinks and dinner with a movie, a concert at House of Blues, or an unforgettable show at *Cirque du Soleil La Nouba*. Follow SR 528 west to I-4, take I-4 west about 4 miles and follow the signs to your destination; estimated one hour drive time. Walt Disney World Resort: (407-939-6244; www.disneyworld.disney.go.com) Lake Buena Vista.

VISITOR RESOURCES Here are some organizations with resources that may be helpful to you during your stay.

Brevard County Parks and Recreation (321-637-5732; www.brevardparks .com) The easy-to-navigate Web site contains a comprehensive listing of parks, current events, and summer camps, and requirements for booking pavilions.

Brevard Cultural Alliance (321-690-6819; www.artsbrevard.org) They maintain a complete listing of current and upcoming events and performances.

Cocoa Beach Area Chamber of Commerce Tourist Information Center (321-454-2022) 8501 Astronaut Boulevard, Suite 4, Cape Canaveral 32920. Features materials and displays on lodging, dining, and activities, including online terminals and assistance with booking hotels. Open 9–4 daily.

Florida Space Coast Office of Tourism (321-433-4470; www.space-coast .com) Check for a schedule of upcoming space launches and information helpful if relocating to the area.

BIBLIOGRAPHY

Aerospace

Anderson, Eric, and Joshua Piven. *The Space Tourists Handbook*. Philadelphia: Quirk Books, 2005. Space adventurers will appreciate this handy reference on preparing for suborbital and orbital flights, including the now-available zero-gravity flights.

Barbree, Jay. *Live from Cape Canaveral*. New York: HarperCollins Publishers, Inc., 2007. For 50 years veteran NBC News reporter and Brevard County resident Jay Barbree has covered America's manned space flight. Now he shares his inside stories about the astronauts, and the events and evolution of the space program.

Faherty, William Barnaby. *Florida's Space Coast: The Impact of NASA on the Sunshine State*. Gainesville, Fla.: University Press of Florida, 2002. The story of America's space exploration told through the recollections of the people who built the spaceport.

Glenn, John, and Nick Taylor. *John Glenn a Memoir*. New York: Bantam Books, 1999. The life story of the man who would be at the center of man's journey into space, becoming the first, and later oldest, to fly into orbit.

Hawking, Stephen. *The Illustrated A Brief History of Time*. New York: Bantam Books, 1996. The best-selling book on the nature of the universe has been updated and combined with amazing visual displays. In 2007 Hawking experienced space on a zero-gravity flight from Cape Canaveral spaceport.

Kranz, Gene. *Failure Is Not an Option: Mission Control from Mercury to Apollo 13 and Beyond*. New York: Berkley Books, 2000. Former flight director for NASA gives a behind-the-scenes account of the people and work critical to the success of space launches, including the successful recovery efforts that saved *Apollo 13*.

Wendt, Guenter, and Russell Still. *The Unbroken Chain*. Burlington, Ontario, Canada: Apogee Books, 2001. This autobiography of the last man seen by crews before lifting into space from Cape Canaveral from 1967 through 1989 provides insight into the culture and challenges of the manned-flight program.

Wolfe, Tom. *The Right Stuff*. New York: Bantam Books, 2001. A look at the first astronauts, space pioneers, and heroes who "were willing to sit on top of an enormous Roman candle" and wait for the fuse to be lit.

Biography and Reminiscence

Lindbergh, Anne Morrow. *Gift from the Sea.* New York: Random House, 1991. This timeless classic of reflection centered on a solitary trip to the seashore and a collection of seashells has been enjoyed and shared by generations of women since it was first published in 1955.

Rawlings, Marjorie Kinnan. *Cross Creek.* New York: Touchstone, 1996. This Pulitzer Prize-winning novelist left New York to settle a homestead in a wild stretch of central Florida. The tale ends with a trip down the St. Johns River and a discussion of man's relationship with the land.

Environment and Natural Sciences

Alden, Peter, Rick Cech, and Gil Nelson. *National Audubon Society Field Guide to Florida.* New York: Alfred A. Knopf, 2004. This fit-in-a-backpack guide provides an overview of Florida's natural history and detailed descriptions of flora and fauna.

Belleville, Bill. *River of Lakes: A Journey on Florida's St. Johns River.* Athens, Ga.: University of Georgia Press, 2000. Central Florida resident and nature writer Belleville rediscovers the wonder and beauty of nature on a paddle trip along the full length of the St. Johns River.

Katz, Cathie. *The Nature of Florida's Beaches.* St. Petersburg, Fla.: Great Outdoors Publishing Co., 2001. This popular book, written and illustrated by a local environmentalist and sea-bean aficionado, is often carried by local bookstores; an enjoyable and easy-to-read guide.

―――. *The Nature of Florida's Waterways.* Melbourne Beach, Fla.: Atlantic Press, 1996. Learn about the birds, marine life, and plant systems of Brevard County's estuaries.

Littler, Mark Masterton, and Diane Scullion Littler. *Waterways & Byways of the Indian River Lagoon: Field Guide for Boaters, Anglers & Naturalists.* Washington, D.C.: Offshore Graphics, Inc., 2005. Boaters, anglers, and naturalists will appreciate the intricate view of each section of the Indian River Lagoon, along with photos and descriptions of plants and animals in the region.

Whitney, Ellie, D. Bruce Means, and Anne Rudloe. *Priceless Florida.* Sarasota, Fla.: Pineapple Press, 2004. A paperback, coffee table reference guide to the state's natural ecosystems and native species includes discussion on coastal estuarine waters, sea floors, and the ocean.

Fiction

Argo, Don. *Canaveral Light.* Cocoa, Fla.: Chapin House Books, 2001. An award-winning and best-selling novel centered around the conflicts and interactions of Florida pioneers and Native Americans during the Seminole Wars.

Dorsey, Tim. *Stingray Shuffle.* New York: HarperCollins, 2003. This laugh-out-loud story blends murder, mayhem, and drugs with the history of Florida and the east coast railroad. Other books by Dorsey are equally irreverent and entertaining.

Gear, Kathleen O'Neal, and W. Michael Gear. *People of the Lightning.* New York: HarperCollins, 2003. The Gears are both writers and archaeologists. This historical novel is set eight thousand years ago in pre-Columbian North America and is woven with fact and fiction from the Windover Pond discovery in north Brevard.

Hemingway, Ernest. *The Old Man & the Sea.* New York: Scribner, 2003. This classic work by Hemingway is the definitive fishing tale.

Hurston, Zora Neale. *Their Eyes Were Watching God.* New York: HarperCollins, 2006. Hurston was born and raised in Eatonville, outside Orlando, and lived in Eau Gallie for several years. Her fictional story of the life of a proud, independent black woman was first published in 1937 and is a classic of African American literature.

Pratt, Theodore. *The Barefoot Mailman.* Port Salerno, Fla.: Florida Classics Library, 1993. A mail carrier in the mid-19th century walks a 100-mile route along the sands of Florida's Atlantic coast.

Rawlings, Majorie Kinnan. *The Yearling.* New York: Simon Pulse, 1988. Pulitzer Prize–winning novel tells the story of a young boy growing up in remote central Florida in the early 20th century.

Smith, Patrick D. *A Land Remembered.* Sarasota, Fla.: Pineapple Press, 1984. Merritt Island resident Smith penned this story, which begins in 1858 and follows three generations of the MacIvey family as they go from dirt-poor Crackers and cowboys to land barons. Winner of the Florida Historical Society's Tebeau Prize as the Most Outstanding Florida Historical Novel.

History

Arnold, Wade. *Cocoa Beach Then & Now.* Charleston, S.C.: Arcadia Publishing, 2008. Historical and contemporary images and stories.

Gannon, Michael. *Florida: A Short History.* Gainesville, Fla.: University Press of Florida, 1996. Since its publication, this comprehensive and easy-to-read book by University of Florida professor Gannon has become a respected and quoted reference of the state's history.

Hiller, Herbert L. *Highway A1A: Florida at the Edge.* Gainesville, Fla.: University Press of Florida, 2005. Take a ride from the past to the present down Florida's famous beachside highway, including a 38-mile stretch through Brevard County.

Mormino, Gary R. *Land of Sunshine, State of Dreams.* Gainesville, Fla.: University Press of Florida, 2005. Mormino weaves the influences of citrus, land development, tourism, technology, and America's continuing fascination with the beach into an entertaining social history of modern Florida.

Osborne, Ray. *Cape Canaveral.* Charleston, S.C.: Arcadia Publishing, 2008. Historical images and stories.

Parrish, Ada Edmiston, A. Clyde Field, and George Leland Harrell. *Images of America: Merritt Island and Cocoa Beach.* Charleston, S.C.: Arcadia Publishing, 2003. Historical images and stories.

Hobbies and Special Interests

Arnov, Boris, and Susan Jyl Feldmann. *Fish Florida: Saltwater.* Houston, Tex.: Gulf Publishing Co., 1998. A guide on where and how to catch more than 35 varieties of sport fish.

Hardister-Heumann, Darlene. *The Southern Sass Cookbook: It's All in the Sass.* Apopka, Fla.: Palm Crews Printing, 2005. Recipes for Southern favorites such as fried chicken, biscuits, and peach cobbler are presented with healthier, but still tasty, ingredients and preparation tips.

Wynne, Nick. *Southern Cooking: A Man's Domain.* Cocoa, Fla.: Chapin House Books, 2006. Recipes for down-home Cracker dishes such as catfish, okra, biscuits, and Hoppin' John, a stew of black-eyed peas and rice.

Pictorial

Gorn, Michael, and Buzz Aldrin. *NASA: The Complete Illustrated History.* London: Merrell Publishers, 2005. The story of space exploration from the early 20th century to the present, told through photographs, personal stories, and technical illustrations.

Monroe, Gary. *The Highwaymen.* Gainesville, Fla.: University Press of Florida, 2001. Learn the history of young African American artists who sold their works on roadsides along the Indian River Lagoon in the 1950s and '60s, and enjoy color photo plates of selected works.

Moran, John. *Journal of Light: The Visual Diary of a Florida Nature Photographer.* Gainesville, Fla.: University Press of Florida, 2004. Prize-winning photographer Moran has beautifully captured the best of Florida; essays weave together philosophical observations and photographic technique.

Young People

Crane, Carol. *S is for Sunshine: A Florida Alphabet.* Chelsea, Mich.: Sleeping Bear Press, 2000. An illustrated alphabet designed to introduce children to the wonders of Florida—like the alligator, which can stay underwater for an hour.

Dunham, Montrew, and Meryl Henderson. *Neil Armstrong: Young Flyer.* New York: Aladdin Paperbacks, 1996. Follow astronaut Armstrong from his days as a young boy to becoming the first man on the moon.

Farndon, John, and Tim Furniss. *1000 Facts on Space.* New York: Barnes & Noble Publishing, Inc., 2006. This complete overview of space, from the big bang theory to a history of space technology, is perfect for curious middle and high school students.

Gamble, Adam, and Red Hansen. *Good Night Florida.* Yarmouth, Mass.: Our World of Books, 2006. A board book for young children that captures highlights of the state.

Hammond, Roger, and Steve Weaver. *Those Peculiar Pelicans.* Sarasota, Fla.: Pineapple Press, 2005. Children are introduced to one of Florida's most familiar birds in an easy-to-read book.

Hixon, Mara Uman, and Steve J. Harris. *Turtles Way: Loggy, Greeny & Leather.* Melbourne Beach, Fla.: Canmore Press, 2005. An accurate and entertaining story of sea turtles perfect for toddlers and preschoolers.

Lithgow, John, and Ard Hoyt. *I'm a Manatee.* New York: Simon & Schuster Books for Young Readers, 2003. Grade school children will enjoy this imaginative and informative book about a young boy's dream of being a manatee.

Check Out from the Local Library

Ball, Jim, Roz Foster, Douglas Hendriksen, and Vera Zimmerman. *History of Brevard County: Photographic Memories.* Stuart, Fla.: Southeastern Printing Co., Brevard County Historical Commission, 2001. Photographs and stories reflect each era of life in Brevard County, from steamboat captains and citrus barons to community leaders.

Kjerulff, Georgiana Greene. *Tales of Old Brevard.* Melbourne, Fla.: The Kellersberger Fund of the South Brevard Historical Society, Inc., 1972. An informal history focused on southern Brevard and based on letters, journals, and interviews with early settlers.

Rabac, Glenn. *The City of Cocoa Beach: The First Sixty Years.* Winona, Minn.: Apollo Books, 1986. Follow along as the author tracks the fast-paced growth of the city and provides insight into the people and times.

TAKING A BREAK AT THE COCOA BEACH LIBRARY.

Sansom, Dixie, Rachel Moehle, and Rosalind Postell. *Staying the Course: Port Canaveral—the First 50 Years.* Cocoa, Fla.: Wolf Jessee Paquin Communications, 2003. Follow along on the evolution of Port Canaveral from a mud bank with a fishing pier to a world-class seaport.

Shofner, Jerrell H. *History of Brevard County: Volume 1.* Stuart, Fla.: Southeastern Printing Co., Brevard County Historical Commission, 1995. A comprehensive look at the history of the area, told in stories and photographs. Volume 2 was published one year later.

Thurm, Ann Hatfield. *History of the City of Cape Canaveral.* Cape Canaveral, Fla.: City of Cape Canaveral, 1994. Thurm, at one time the city's historian, records the early settlement and development of Cape Canaveral from its incorporation in 1962.

Verne, Jules. *From the Earth to the Moon.* Philadelphia, Pa.: Xlibris Corp., 2001. Written in 1865, this early entry to the science fiction genre provides details on designing and launching a space vehicle. Verne's lunar launch pad was based in Florida.

Von Braun, Dr. Wernher. *Space Frontier.* New York: Holt, Rinehart and Winston, 1971. Space buffs will learn about rocketry, man's journey into space, and the future possibilities from the man considered the architect of space exploration.

INDEX

A

AAA Road Service, 22
AAT Taxi Service, 45
ABC Urgent Care, 18
A1A Ocean Drive Transportation & Limo, 43
accommodations. *See* lodging; *and specific accommodations*
Ace of Hearts Ranch, 142
Action Bait & Tackle, 181
Adventure Zone, 75
aerospace. *See* Kennedy Space Center Visitor Complex; NASA; space
African Americans, 33, 159, 170, 182, 184
Air Force Space and Missile Museum, 68–69, 165
air shows, 133, 184
airboat tours, 142, 219
airports, 40–41; shuttles, 43
Ais Indians, 26–27, 30, 140–41, 162
Albatross, 207
alligators, 54, 142, 214–15
ambulances, 17
American Police Hall of Fame and Museum, 169–70
AMTRAK, 44
amusement parks, 220–21
Anacapri Pizzeria, 119

Angy, Jim, 54
Ann Lia Gift Shop, 125–26
Annie's Toy Chest, 154
Antique Emporium Mall (Cocoa Village), 152
antiques, 152, 180, 206–7
A N.Y. Pizza House, 119
Apollo Treasures Gallery, 165
Apollo/Saturn V Center, 165
area codes, 14
Art and Antique Studio (Eau Gallie), 208
Art Expressions (Eau Gallie), 206
art festivals, 133, 182, 184, 212, 213–14
art galleries, 17; Cape Canaveral, 125; Cocoa Beach, 124–25; Cocoa Village, 158–59; Eau Gallie, 206, 208–9, 211; Melbourne, 209; Titusville, 180–82
Art Gallery and Studio LLC (Melbourne), 209
art museum. *See* Brevard Art Museum
Art of Coffee, 116–17
Art of Sand Festival, 131–32
ArtWorks Eau Gallie

Fine Art Festival, 213–14
Astronaut Encounters, 165
Astronaut Hall of Fame Museum, U.S., 23, 166
Astronaut Memorial at Space View Park, 167
Astronaut Memorial Planetarium and Observatory, 23, 136–37
Astronaut Training Experience (ATX), 166
astronauts: books about, 15–16, 222–23; meeting with, 165. *See also specific astronauts*
athletic events, 61
Atlantic Ocean Grille (Cocoa Beach), 101
Atlantic Towing & Service, 22
Atlantis (space shuttle), 165
Atlantis Bar and Grill (Cocoa Beach), 101–2
auto racing, 220
Avenue Viera, 136, 157; eating, 149–50; movie theater, 151; nightlife, 151; shopping, 157
Aviles Building, 139
Avocet Lagoon, 70
Azteca Two, 102

B

Baby Patch, 207
Backcountry Fly Fishing, 56
BadBirds Gallery, 158
Bair's Cove, 171
bald eagles, 53, 60, 141
Bald Strawberry Coffee Shop & Bakery, 117
ballet, 205
Banana Alley Antiques, 180
Banana River, 77, 86–87; boating, 70–71, 73–74; fishing, 56–57; jet skiing, 78; windsurfing, 76, 86
Banana River Bridge, 44, 79
Banana River Marine, 70, 73
Banana River Naval Air Station, 34
Bank of America, 14
banks, 14
Barge Canal, 44, 70–71
Barnes & Noble Booksellers (Merritt Island), 123
Barrier Island Sanctuary, 23, 192–93; turtle walks, 49
Barrier Jack's, 102
bars. See music; nightlife
Barton Avenue Residential Historic District, 139
baseball, 143
Bath Cottage, 154
Beach $ Plus (Cocoa Beach), 127
beach gear: Cocoa Beach, 127–29; Melbourne, 210–11; Titusville, 181–82
Beach Island Resort (Cocoa Beach), 87
Beach Place Guesthouses (Cocoa Beach), 218
Beach Shack Blues Bar (Cocoa Beach), 121
Beach Unlimited (Cocoa Beach), 127
Beach Wave (Cocoa Beach), 127

beaches, 14–15, 46–50; fun and games, 48–50; safety tips, 47–48; lifeguard coverage, 83, 173; Cape Canaveral, 82–83, 219; Cocoa Beach, 82–85, 219; Port Canaveral, 83–84; Sebastian Inlet, 192; Titusville, 173. See also specific beaches
Beachline Transportation, 43
Beachside Gallery (Cocoa Beach), 124
Bellaire Arcade, 139, 154
Belleville, Bill, 16, 145, 223
Bennett Causeway, space launch viewing sites, 166
Best Western Ocean Beach Hotel & Suites, 88, 218
Betty's Antiques, 206
biking, 61, 69–70, 78–79
Bilt Surf and Skate, 69, 127–28
birds, 52–53; bald eagles, 53, 60, 141; brown pelicans, 52, 160; great blue herons, 53, 183; ospreys, 53, 60; photography tips, 54; roseate spoonbills, 53, 130, 170
bird-watching (birding), 24–25, 50, 52; resources, 53; Cocoa Beach, 70, 85–86; Melbourne, 190; Port Canaveral, 70; Titusville, 170; Viera, 141, 145
Black Point Wildlife Drive, 170, 175
Black Tulip, 146–47
Blanton, Captain Doug, 56, 59
Blue Dolphin, 74
Bluepoints Marina, 44, 70
blues music, 20, 121, 204
boat travel and cruises, 44, 54–56, 73–75, 142, 219
boating, 53–54; Cocoa Beach, 70–71, 73–75; Cocoa Village, 141–42; Indian Harbour Beach,

190–91; Melbourne Beach, 190–91; Titusville, 171. See also kayaking
books, recommended, 15–16, 222–27
Books-A-Million, 123
bookstores, on Merritt Island, 123
Boston Beef and Seafood, 102–3
bottlenose dolphins, 42, 70–74, 171
Bottom Dollar Charter Fishing, 57
Bourbeau Memorial Park, 141, 145
Brano's Italian Grill, 103
Brevard Art Museum, 23, 189–90
Brevard Art Museum School, 190
Brevard Community College, 136; Astronaut Memorial Planetarium and Observatory, 23, 136–37; Broadway on Brevard Series, 151–52; Space Coast Birding & Wildlife Festival, 182; television station, 20
Brevard County: Cape Canaveral, Cocoa Beach, and Port Canaveral, 65–134; central, 136–60; maps, 64, 138, 164, 188; north, 162–84; south, 186–215. See also specific destinations
Brevard County Bank & Trust Company, 137
Brevard County Courthouse, 169
Brevard County Historical Commission, 139–40
Brevard County Manatees, 143
Brevard County Parks and Recreation, 221; boating, 71
Brevard County Public Libraries, 68

Brevard Cultural Alliance, 221
Brevard Museum of History & Natural Sciences, 23, 140–41
Brevard Symphony Orchestra, 157, 187, 204
Brevard Symphony Youth Orchestra, 205
Brevard Theatrical Ensemble, 151
Brevard Zoo, 143–44, 171
Brio Italiano, 197
BunJava Coffee Shop, 117
Burnham, Mills, 31
bus travel, 43–44
Busy Traveler Transport, 43

C
cabs, 45
Café Margaux, 147, 219
Café Unique Amish Deli & Coffee Shop, 147, 151
cafés (coffee shops): Cape Canaveral, 117–18; Cocoa Beach, 116–18; Cocoa Village, 150; Melbourne, 202–3; Titusville, 178–79
Caffe Chocolat, 177
Calema Kayak Rentals, 71, 73
Calema Midwinters Windsurfing Festival, 131
Calema Windsurfing & Watersports, 76
Camp Kennedy, 166
Campbell Park, 189
camping (campgrounds), 16, 75, 172, 191
Canaveral Air Station, 35, 66, 165
Canaveral Barge Canal, 44, 70–71
Canaveral Meats and Deli, 120
Canaveral National Seashore, 173; beaches, 173; birding, 170; boating, 171; camping, 172; turtle walks, 49
Canaveral Star, 58–59

Canaveral Towers Resort, 99
Candles by G, 154
candy, 118, 150–51, 182, 203–4
Cape Canaveral, 65–134; activities, 69–87; art galleries, 125; beaches, 82–83, 219; biking, 78–79; birding, 70; boating, 70–71, 73; camping, 75; city hall, 14; eating, 104–11, 116–20; family fun, 76–78; gift stores, 126; golf, 78; historic places, 66; itineraries, 218–19; libraries, 68; lodging, 89, 95–97, 99, 100–101; map, 64; museums, 68–69; music, 121–22; nature parks, 86; nightlife, 121–22; pizzerias, 119; post office, 19; shopping, 125, 126, 128–29, 131; sightseeing, 65–69; space launch viewing sites, 166; special events, 131–32; specialty markets, 120; sporting goods, 128–29; surfing, 79; take-out, 119–20; wildlife, 85–87
Cape Canaveral Air Force Space and Missile Museum, 68–69, 165
Cape Canaveral Fine Arts Show, 131
Cape Canaveral Friday Fest, 131
Cape Canaveral Hospital, 18
Cape Canaveral Lighthouse, 66
Cape Canaveral Public Library, 68
Cape Canaveral Recreation Complex, 76
Cape Codder, The, 119
Cape Marina, 44, 57–58, 70
Cape Winds Resort, 99
Captain Doug Blanton, 56, 59

Captain Ed's Tiki Bar & Grill, 103
Captain Hook's Bait & Tackle, 181
Captain J's Ocean Deck Restaurant, 104
Captains Grill, 104
car rentals, 41, 45
car travel, 43, 44; highways, 40; road services, 22
Cara Mia Riverside Grill, 147–48
Carnival Cruise Lines, 55
Caroline's House of Records, 152
Carolyn Seiler Studios, 158
Casa Coquina Bed & Breakfast, 176
Catri, Dick, 80–81
Cazoni's Pizza, 119
Center Street Park, 66–67
central Brevard, 136–60; map, 138. *See also specific destinations*
Central Brevard Library and Reference Center, 140
Central Florida Shuttle, 43
chambers of commerce, 16–17
Chandlery, The, 207, 210
Chart House Restaurant, 197
charters, 56–59
Cherie Down Park, 82–83
children. *See* family fun and fitness
children's books, recommended, 225–27
Chocolate Salon, 182
Christmas Boat Parade, 134
Christmas Cottage, 210
cinemas. *See* movie theaters
Circle K, 118
city halls, 14
civil rights, 33, 159, 170, 182, 184
Clay Studio, The, 158
clothing stores, 124, 152–54, 207

Coastal Angler Magazine, 61

Coastal Bank, 14

Cocoa (village). *See* Cocoa Village

Cocoa Beach, 65–134; activities, 69–87; art galleries, 124–25; banks, 14; beaches, 82–85, 219; biking, 69–70, 78–79; birding, 70, 85–86; boating, 70–71, 73–75; city hall, 14; clothing, shoes, and accessories, 124; eating, 101–20; entertainment, 120–23; family fun, 75–78; fishing, 56–59; gift stores, 125–27; golf, 78; historic places, 65–68; hospitals, 18; information, 16, 221; itineraries, 218–19; libraries, 68; lodging, 87–101, 218–19; map, 64; museums, 68–69; music, 120–22; nature preserves and parks, 85–87; nightlife, 120–22; pizzerias, 119; post office, 19; shopping, 123–31; sightseeing, 65–69; space launch viewing sites, 166; spas, 79; special events, 131–34; sporting goods, 127–29; surfing, 69, 79–82, 132–34; tennis, 77–78; theater, 122–23; wildlife, 85–87

Cocoa Beach Air Show, 133

Cocoa Beach Aquatic Center, 76

Cocoa Beach Area Chamber of Commerce, 16, 221

Cocoa Beach Beachfest, 132

Cocoa Beach Boardwalk, 102, 121

Cocoa Beach Brewing Company, 122

Cocoa Beach Christmas Boat Parade, 134

Cocoa Beach Club Condominiums, 99–100

Cocoa Beach Community Church, 68

Cocoa Beach Country Club, 78

Cocoa Beach Harley-Davidson, 129

Cocoa Beach Health & Fitness, 77

Cocoa Beach Kayaking, 73

Cocoa Beach Parasail, 77

Cocoa Beach Pier, 83, 219; eating, 101–2, 109–10; fishing, 59; nightlife, 121; special events, 132–33

Cocoa Beach Public Library, 68

Cocoa Beach Skatepark, 77

Cocoa Beach Spa, 79

Cocoa Beach Surf Company, 128

Cocoa Beach Surf Company Beachside, 69, 79, 128

Cocoa Beach Surf Company Surf School, 79–80

Cocoa Beach Surf Museum, 69, 132

Cocoa Beach Taxi Service, 45

Cocoa Village, 136–60; activities, 141–45; birding, 141; boating, 141–42; cafés, 150; camping, 142–43; eating, 146–51, 219; entertainment, 151–52; family fun, 142–44; golf, 144; historic places, 137, 139; horseback riding, 142; ice cream, 150–51; itineraries, 219; libraries, 139–40; lodging, 145–46; map, 138; museums, 140–41; music, 151; nature preserves, 145; nightlife, 151; performing arts, 139, 151–52; shopping, 152–59; sightseeing, 136–41; special events, 157–59; theater, 151–52; transportation, 136

Cocoa Village Marina, 141, 142

Cocoa Village Playhouse, 139, 151–52

Cocoa Village Riverfront Park, 145, 157

Coconuts on the Beach, 104, 121

Coco's, 154

comedy, 121

Comfort Inn & Suites (Cocoa Beach), 88–89

Concepts on Highland, 197–98

condo rentals, 99–101

Contemporary Concepts, 156

Continental Flambé, 198

Cool Beans Fishing Charters, 57

Coombs, Wayne, 95, 125

Cornerstone Plaza, 119, 120, 127

Country Inns & Suites by Carlson, 89

Courage Belle Art Studio and Gallery, 124–25

Courtyard by Marriott Cocoa Beach, 89–90

Cove at Port Canaveral, 121

Crane Creek Inn Waterfront Bed & Breakfast, 194

Crane Creek Promenade, 189

Crane Creek Reserve, 192

Creative Energy, 210

Croissant Chateau Bakery, 203

Crowne Plaza Melbourne Oceanfront Resort & Spa, 145–46; spa, 192

Cruickshank Trail, 175

cruises. *See* boat travel and cruises

Curington, Captain Floyd, 59

CVS (Cocoa Beach), 129

cycling. *See* biking

D

Dairy Queen (Cocoa Beach), 118
Day Away Kayak Tours, A, 171
Days Inn Cocoa Beach, 90
Daytona 500 Experience, 220
Daytona International Speedway, 220
Denham Department Store, 169
Denny's Restaurant (Cocoa Beach), 118
Depot Café, 202–3
DiLorenzo's, 104–5
dining. *See* eating; *and specific restaurants*
Dinosaur Store (Cocoa Beach), 75, 126
dinosaurs, 69, 75, 126
disabled travelers, 17–18
Discovery Beach Resort, 90
Disney Cruise Line, 55
Disney's Animal Kingdom, 221
Disney's Hollywood Studios, 221
Dixie Crossroads, 177–78
Doctors, Lawyers, and Weekend Warriors, 132–33
Dog 'n' Bone, 151
dolphins, 42, 70–74, 171
Dondi's Downtown, 204
Dorsey, Tim, 16, 223–24
Double ShAAfted, 142
Doubletree Oceanfront Hotel, 90–91, 217; eating, 115–16
Downtown Disney, 221
Downtown Divas (Cocoa Village), 152–53; (Melbourne), 207
Downtown Gallery (Titusville), 180
Dream Beach Weddings, 217
driving (car travel), 43, 44;

highways, 40; road services, 22
Dunkin Donuts (Cocoa Beach), 118
Duran Golf Club, 144
Durango Steakhouse, 67–68, 105
Dusty Rose Antique Mall, 180

E

East Coast Surfing Hall of Fame, 69
Easter Extravaganza, 132
eating, 21–22; price codes, 6, 101, 146; Cape Canaveral, 104–11, 116–20; Cocoa Beach, 101–20; Cocoa Village, 146–51, 219; Eau Gallie, 197–98, 201, 202; Melbourne, 197–204; Melbourne Beach, 199–202; Merritt Island, 103; Port Canaveral, 106, 107, 110–12, 120, 219; Satellite Beach, 198–99; Titusville, 177–79; Viera, 148–50
Eau Gallie, 186; art galleries, 206, 208–9, 211; eating, 197–98, 201, 202; historic places, 186–87; lodging, 194; map, 188; shopping, 206; special events, 211, 213–14; transportation, 186
Eau Gallie Arts District, 186, 206, 208–9, 211, 213–14
Eau Gallie Fine Art Festival, 213–14
Eau Gallie Florist, 206
Eddy Creek, 171
808 Art Gallery, 209
emergencies, 17, 18
Emma Parrish Theater, 169, 179
Enchanted Forest Sanctuary, 23, 173–75
Enchanted Spirit, 126

Enigma, 198–99
Epcot, 220–21
Evans, Ben, 74–75
events. *See* special events; *and specific events*
Executive Cigar Shop & Lounge, 204
Exotic Shells and Gifts by Eleanor, 126
Eye of the Universe: The Hubble Telescope, 165

F

Fairfield Inn & Suites (Titusville), 176
Fairvilla, 129, 131
family fun and fitness, 17; Cape Canaveral, 76; Cocoa Beach, 75–78; Cocoa Village, 142–44; Port Canaveral, 77; Titusville, 172
Family Salsa Festival, 212–13
Fat Snook, The, 105–6
Fawlty Towers Resort Motel, 91
Festival of Trees, 214
festivals. *See* special events; *and specific festivals*
Fifth Avenue Art Gallery, 208
Fin Expeditions, 73
fire, 17
First Friday Art Walk at Eau Gallie, 211
Fischer Park, 83
fishing, 56–59, 61; resources, 59, 61
Fishing & Diving Center (Cape Canaveral), 59
Fishing Museum (Sebastian), 195
Fishlips Waterfront Bar & Grill, 106, 121, 219
Five Guys Burgers and Fries (Viera), 148
Flamingos at the Radisson Hotel, 106
Flat Iron Building, 189
Flirt, 124

Flop Shop, The, 207
Florida Books and Gifts, 23, 140
Florida Fish & Wildlife Conservation Commission, 59
Florida Historical Society Library of Florida History, 23, 140
Florida Keys Piano Bar & Cocktail Lounge, 204
Florida Puerto Rican/Hispanic Chamber of Commerce, 16
Florida Space Coast Office of Tourism, 221
Florida State Paddleboard Championships, 132
Florida State Road 520 (SR 520), 78–79
Florida Today, 19–20
Florida's Seafood Bar & Grill, 106
Fly Fisherman, The (Titusville), 61, 181–82
Foo Bar & Lotus Gallery, 204
Four Points by Sheraton Cocoa Beach, 91–92
Fourth of July Concert & Fireworks (Cocoa Village), 157
Fourth of July on the Beach (Cocoa Beach), 132
Freddie Patrick Park, 71
Freida's Kritter Boutique, 156–57
Friday Art Walk at Eau Gallie, 211
Friday Fest (Cape Canaveral), 131; (Melbourne), 211
From My Heart to Yours, 210
From Olives & Grapes, 154
Front Street, 187, 189
Funntasia Fantasy Golf, 77

G
Gabrielle, 207

Gale, Brian, 81
galleries. *See* art galleries
Gannon, Michael, 15, 27, 224
Gauzeway, The, 207
geocaching, 172
Gettin There II Charters, 57–58
getting to and around Brevard County. *See* transportation
gift stores, 125–27, 154–55, 207, 210
Gingerbread House, 154
Gleason House, 187, 194
Glenn, John, 15–16, 40, 222
Goddard, Robert, 23
golf: Cocoa Beach, 78; Cocoa Village, 144; Melbourne, 192; Melbourne Beach, 192; Mims, 172–73; Rockledge, 144; Titusville, 172–73; Viera, 144
Gordon, R. Merrill, 181
Gourmet Garden, The, 210
Grant Seafood Festival, 211
Grasshopper Airboat Eco Tours, 142
great blue herons, 53, 183
Great Florida Birding Trail, 50, 52, 53, 86, 141
Greater Palm Bay Chamber of Commerce, 16–17
Greek Festival, 211
Green Apples, 153
Green Lodging: about, 88
Green Room Café, 117
Green Turtle, The, 204
Greenwood Gallery, 181
Gregory's Comedy Club, 121
Gregory's Steak & Seafood, 107
Greyhound Bus Lines, 43
Grills Seafood Deck, 107–8, 121
Grimaldi Candies, 203
Grissom Memorial Wetlands at Viera, 141, 145

Groucho's Comedy Show, 121

H
Habitat for Humanity Strawberry Festival, 211–12
Hampton Inn Cocoa Beach, 92
Hampton Inn Titusville, 176–77
Handwerk Haus, 154
Harbortown Marina Boatyard, 70–71
Harley-Davidson, 129
Harrell, Speedy, 140
Harry Goode's Outdoor Shop, 210–11
Harry T. & Harriette V. Moore Cultural Center, 170
Harry T. & Harriette V. Moore Heritage Festival of the Arts & Humanities, 182, 184
Harvey's Indian River Groves, 118
Haulover Canal, 31, 175–76; boating, 171; kayaking tour, 171
Hayman, Richard, 206
Health First Physicians Walk-in Clinic, 18
Health First Triathlon, 61
Heidelberg Restaurant, 108
Heidi's Jazz Club, 122
Hemingway, Ernest, 16, 224
Henegar Center for the Arts, 205
Henegar School Complex, 189
Highway Grrls and Studio, 208
hiking, 61, 78–79, 145, 193
Hilton Cocoa Beach Oceanfront, 92–93
Hippodrome Club, 151
Historic Cocoa Village Playhouse, 139, 151–52
historic places, 18; Cocoa

Beach, 65–68; Cocoa Village, 137, 139; Eau Gallie, 186–87; Melbourne, 187, 189; Rockledge, 137; Titusville, 168–69
history, 26–37; books, 224–25; natural, 27–29; social, 30–37
Holiday Inn Express Hotel & Suites (Cocoa Beach), 93
Holiday Inn Melbourne-Viera Conference Center, 146
Holmes Park, 189
Holmes Regional Medical Center, 18
home decor, 126–27, 155–56, 207, 210
Hometown News, 20
Horse Feathers Antiques and Gifts, 152
horseback riding, 142
hospitals, 18
Hotel Indian River, 139
hotels. *See* lodging; *and specific hotels*
Hubble Telescope, 165
Hurston, Zora Neale, 15, 36, 224

I
I Dream of Jeannie Lane, 68, 84
ice cream, 118, 150–51, 203
Ice Cream Junction, 118
Images in Art, 132
IMAX Experience (Kennedy Space Center), 165
Indiafest, 211
Indialantic, 186; city hall, 14; lodging, 196–97; music, 204, 205; spas, 192
Indian Harbour Beach: boating, 190–91; city hall, 14; specialty markets, 204; transportation, 186
Indian River, 136, 172; boat cruises, 142, 219; boating, 171; camping, 191; fishing, 57; kayaking, 171
Indian River Cruises, 142, 219
Indian River Festival, 184
Indian River Lagoon, 28–29, 162, 175–76, 193; boating, 190–91; fishing, 56–59; kayaking, 73, 171
Indian River Lagoon House, 189
Indian River Outfitters, 190–91
Indian River Potters' Guild, 208–9
Indian River Queen, 142
Indian River Soap, 210
Inlet Marina, 190, 191
Inn at Cocoa Beach, 93
International Palms Resort, 93–94, 104
International Sea-Bean Symposium, 133
International Space Station Center, 165
Intracoastal Waterway: boating, 171
Irish Shop, 154, 210
Isabella's Ladies Apparel, 207
Island Boat Lines, 73, 142
Island Pasta Company, 199
Island Watercraft Rentals, 74
Italian Courtyard, 108
itineraries, suggested, 217–21
Izzy's Bistro, 108

J
James G. Bourbeau Memorial Park, 141, 145
James Wadsworth Rossetter House, 187
jazz, 20, 122, 151, 204
Jessup's of Melbourne, 210
Jetty Park, 65–66; beaches, 83–84, 219; biking, 79; birding, 70; campground, 75; fishing, 59
Jetty Park Bait & Tackle Shop, 128
jewelry stores, 156, 210
John and Nannie Lee House, 187, 189
John F. Kennedy Space Center Visitor Complex. *See* Kennedy Space Center Visitor Complex
Jon's Fine Jewelry, 156
Juice N Java, 117, 119
Julia Roberts House, 139
Just for You Estate Jewelry, 210

K
kayaking, 71, 73–74, 128, 144, 171, 190–91
Kayaks by Bo, 171
Kelly Park, 86; boating, 71, 73, 74; windsurfing, 76, 131
Kelsey's Pizzeria, 109
Kennedy Space Center Visitor Complex, 162–66; guided tours, 165; handicapped services, 17; map, 167; space launches, best viewing sites, 166, 167; transportation, 162
Ketcham Park, 59, 71, 79
kids. *See* family fun and fitness
Kilwin's of Melbourne, 203
Kim Bo, 119
King Center for the Performing Arts, 20–21, 205
Kiwi Seeds, 207
Kloiber's Cobbler Eatery, 178
Kurt Zimmerman Gallery & Studio, 158

L
La Bella Spa, 173
La Fiesta Mexican Restaurant, 109
La Quinta Inn (Cocoa Beach), 94
La Quinta Inn & Suites Oceanfront (Cocoa Beach), 94
Lagooner Charters &

Expeditions, 57
LaGrange Church
(Titusville), 169
Laughing Mermaid, 206
Lawndale, 139
Le Bon Cafe, 203
Lea's Bistro, 150
Leroy Wright Recreation
Area, 141, 145
Lexi, 204
libraries, 68, 139–40, 189
Lindbergh, Anne Morrow,
16, 223
live music. *See* music
Lobster Shanty & Wharf-
side, 109
Locklear Studio, 159
lodging, 18–19; price codes,
6, 87; Cape Canaveral,
89, 95–97, 99, 100–101;
Cocoa Beach, 87–101,
218–19; Cocoa Village,
145–46; Eau Gallie, 194;
Indialantic, 196–97; Mel-
bourne, 145–46, 194;
Melbourne Beach,
194–96; Titusville,
176–77. *See also specific
lodgings*
Lone Cabbage Fish Camp,
142, 148
Long Point Cafe, 199–200
Long Point Park, 191
LoPressionism Gallery, 209
Lord Ravenswood Hall,
210
Lori Wilson Park, 84; Maritime Hammock, 70,
85–86
Lou's Blues Upstairs, 204
Luna Sea Bed & Breakfast
Motel, 94–95

M
McCarthy, Kevin, 35
McDonald's Restaurant
(Cape Canaveral), 118;
(Cocoa Beach), 118
McLarty Treasure Muse-
um, 195
McLouth Fishing Pier, 59

magazines, 19–20
Magic Kingdom, 220–21
*Magnificent Desolation:
Walking on the Moon 3D*
(film), 165
Mai Tiki Studio & Gallery,
125
Mai Tiki Studio Apart-
ments, 95
mail, 19
Mainstreet Pub, 204
Malabar: eating, 202
Malcolm E. McLouth Fish-
ing Pier, 59
Manatee Hammock Park,
172
Manatee Observation
Deck, 175
Manatee Sanctuary Park,
77
manatees, 67, 73, 77,
212–13
Mangos Fashion Boutique,
153
Mar Chiquita Swimwear,
124
marathons, 61
Mardi Gras, 157
Marina Park, 171
marinas, 44, 70–71,
141–42, 171, 190
marine services, 22
Maritime Hammock, 70,
85–86
Marlins Good Times Bar
and Grill, 109
Mary Moon's Surf Art
Camp, 80
Matt's Bicycle Center, 128
Matt's Casbah, 200, 204
Maxwell C. King Center
for the Performing Arts,
20–21, 205
media, 19–20
Meg O'Malley's, 200–201
Meg-O-Ween, 213
Melbourne, 186–215; activities, 190–93; antiques,
206–7; art galleries, 209;
cafés, 202–3; city hall, 14;
clothing, shoes, and

accessories, 207; eating,
197–204; golf, 192; his-
toric places, 187, 189;
home decor, 207, 210;
hospitals, 18; ice cream,
203; information, 17;
lodging, 145–46, 194;
map, 188; museums,
189–90; music, 204;
nightlife, 204; performing
arts, 20–21, 204–6; radio,
20; shopping, 206–7,
210–11; sightseeing,
186–90; spas, 192; special
events, 184, 211–15;
sporting goods, 210–11;
transportation, 186; zoo,
143–44, 171
Melbourne Antique
Gallery, 207
Melbourne Area Associa-
tion of Realtors, 21
Melbourne Art Festival,
212
Melbourne Beach, 186;
birding, 190; boating,
190–91; camping, 191;
eating, 199–202; golf,
192; lodging, 194–96;
nature preserves, 192–93
Melbourne Chamber
Music Society, 205
Melbourne Civic Theatre,
205
Melbourne Friday Fest,
211
Melbourne Hotel, 189
Melbourne Independent
Filmmakers Festival,
214–15
Melbourne International
Airport, 40, 43
Melbourne Oktoberfest,
213
Melbourne-Palm Bay Area
Chamber of Commerce,
17
Melting Pot, The, 148
Mercury 7 Foundation,
165–66
Merritt Island, 162; boat-

ing, 70–71, 73–74; bookstores, 123; eating, 103; geocaching, 172; movie theater, 120; nature park, 86; shopping, 123; spas, 173; special events, 131; water sports, 76, 78. *See also* Kennedy Space Center Visitor Complex
Merritt Island First Baptist Church, 205–6
Merritt Island National Wildlife Refuge, 23, 174–75; birding, 170; boating, 171; kayaking tour, 171; turtle walks, 49
Merritt Square 16, 120
Merritt Square Mall, 120, 123
Mezza Luna Italian Restaurant & Bar, 201
Middleton, Girard, 82
Milliken's Reef, 110, 219
Milliken's Sand Bar, 121
Milwaukee Brewers, 143
Mims: camping, 172; golf, 172–73; museums, 170
Minutemen Causeway: beaches, 84–85; biking, 61, 79
Mirabella's, 207
Miss Bailey's Curiosity Shoppe, 159
Miss Cape Canaveral, 58
Moon's (Mary) Surf Art Camp, 80
Moore, Harry and Harriette, 33, 169–70, 182, 184
Moore Heritage Festival of the Arts & Humanities, 182, 184
Mormino, Gary R., 15, 39, 224
Mosquito Beaters, 140
Mosquito Lagoon, 175–76; boating, 171; fishing, 56–59
Mosquito Lagoon Fishing Charters, 57
Mosquito Lagoon Fly-Fishing Unlimited, 57

Mousetrap, 67–68
movie theaters: Merritt Island, 120; Satellite Beach, 151; Viera, 151
Murdock's Bistro and Char Bar, 148–49
Murkshe Memorial Park, 85
Museum of Dinosaurs & Ancient Cultures, 69
museums: Cape Canaveral, 68–69; Cocoa Beach, 68–69; Cocoa Village, 140–41; Melbourne, 189–90; Mims, 170; Titusville, 169–70
music: radio stations, 20; Cape Canaveral, 121–22; Cocoa Beach, 120–22; Cocoa Village, 151; Indialantic, 204, 205; Melbourne, 204

N
NASA (National Aeronautics and Space Administration), 24, 35, 162–66; map, 167. *See also* Kennedy Space Center Visitor Complex
NASCAR, 220
National Kidney Foundation of Florida Pro-Am Surf Festival, 133
Native Rhythms Festival, 215
natural foods, 120
natural history, 27–29
nature preserves and parks, 50; map, 51; Cocoa Beach, 85–87; Cocoa Village, 145; Melbourne Beach, 192–93; Titusville, 173–76. *See also specific preserves and parks*
Nature's Spirit, 157
New Habit, 117, 118
New Look Boutique, 153
newspapers, 19–20
Nex Generation Surf School, 81

nightlife: Cape Canaveral, 121–22; Cocoa Beach, 120–22; Cocoa Village, 151; Melbourne, 204; Viera, 151
905 Café, 203
Nolan's Irish Pub, 122
north Brevard, 162–84; map, 164. *See also* Titusville
North Brevard Historical Museum, 170
North Tidal Pool, 190
Norwegian Cruise Line, 55–56
Nosh & Ganache, 201

O
observatory, 23, 136–37
Obsession Charters, 58
Ocean Club Marina (Port Canaveral), 71
Ocean Landings Resort & Racquet Club (Cocoa Beach), 100
Ocean Reef Spa (Indialantic), 192
Oceanside Cafe (Cape Canaveral), 117–18
Oceansports World (Cocoa Beach), 81–82, 128
Odyssey Charters, 58
Oh Shucks Seafood Bar, 110, 121
Oktoberfest, 213
Ola Grande Condominiums, 100
Old Pineapple Inn, 194
Oleander Village Bakery and Cookie Factory, 150
Oriental Food Mart, 118
Orlando International Airport, 41, 43
Orlando Princess, 58–59
Orlando Sentinel, 20
ospreys, 53, 60
Ossorio, 137, 139, 149, 219

P
paddling. *See* boating; kayaking
Palm Bay, 186; emergen-

cies, 18; information, 16–17; libraries, 189
Palm Bay Area Chamber of Commerce, 17
Palm Bay Community Hospital, 18
Papa Vito's, 119
parasailing, 77
parks. *See* nature preserves and parks
Parrish Medical Center, 18
Parrish Park, 171
Parrish Theater, 169, 179
Patrick Air Force Base Seashore, 79, 85
Patrick Park, 71
Paul's Smokehouse, 178
Pear Tree, 154–55
Peggy Gunnerson Studio & Gallery, 181
pelicans, 52, 160
Perfect Gift and Florist, 126
performing arts: Cocoa Beach, 122–23; Cocoa Village, 139, 151–52; Melbourne, 20–21, 204–6; Titusville, 179
Petite Bakery, 118
photography tips, for birds and wildlife, 54
Pig & Whistle English Pub & Restaurant, 110–11
Pine Island, 66–67
Pizza Gallery & Grill, 149–51
pizzerias (pizza), 119–20, 149–50
Place Guesthouses, 87–88
planetarium, 23, 136–37
Playalinda Beach, 173
Poison Control, 17
police, 17
Police Hall of Fame and Museum, 169–70
Ponce de León, Juan, 26–27
Porcher House, 137
Port Canaveral, 36, 65, 79; beaches, 83–84; biking, 79; birding, 70; boating, 70–71; cruises, 54–56; eating, 106, 107, 110–12, 120, 219; family fun, 77; fishing, 56–59; map, 72; museums, 68–69; nature parks, 86; nightlife, 121; seafood, 120; space launch viewing sites, 166; special events, 133; specialty markets, 120; water sports, 77
Port Canaveral Navigation Lock, 77
Port d'Hiver Bed & Breakfast, 194–95
Port Fest/Pink Ribbon Walk, 133
post offices, 19
Pratt, Theodore, 16, 224
preserves. *See* nature preserves and parks
Pritchard House, 169
Prop'a Place Hobby Shop, 182
Publix Supermarket, 120

Q

Quiet Flight Surf Shop, 82, 128

R

R. L. Lewis Gallery, 159
R. Merrill Gordon, Artist, 181
Race Trac, 118
Racquet Club of Cocoa Beach, 77–78
radio stations, 20
Radisson Resort at the Port, 95–96, 218–19; eating, 106
Rainbow Connection Tours, 217–18
Ralph's Art Supply, 206
Ramp Road Park, 59, 71
Rape Crisis Hotline, 17
Rare Essentials, 153
Rave Motion Pictures Avenue 16, 151
Rawlings, Marjorie Kinnan, 16, 223, 224
RCB Centura Bank, 14
real estate (realtors), 21
recreational activities, 46–61. *See also specific activities*
Reindeer Run, 61
Rendez-Vous, 155
rental properties, 99–101
Residence Inn by Marriott (Cape Canaveral), 96
Resort on Cocoa Beach, 96–97
restaurants. *See* eating; *and specific restaurants*
Revive, 180
Rich Grissom Memorial Wetlands at Viera, 141, 145
Rick Pipers' Big Art Studio, 125
River Road Mercantile, 180
Riverfront Park at Cocoa Village, 145, 157
RJK Studio, 125
road services, 22
Robert P. Murkshe Memorial Park, 85
Roberto's Little Havana, 111
Rockledge, 136, 139; city hall, 14; golf, 144; historic places, 137; hospitals, 18
Rockledge City Hall, 139
Rockledge Drive, 139
Rodney S. Ketcham Park, 59, 71, 79
Roesch House, 187
Ron Jon Cape Caribe Resort, 97
Ron Jon Easter Surfing Festival, 132
Ron Jon Surf Grill, 111
Ron Jon Surf School by Craig Carroll, 82
Ron Jon Surf Shop, 128–29
Ron Jon Watersports, 70, 74, 129
roseate spoonbills, 53, 130, 170
Rossetter House, 187
Royal Caribbean International, 55

Royal Mansions, 100–101
Running Zone, 61
Rusty's Seafood & Oyster Bar, 111–12, 121
Ryan's Village Pizza, 150

S
S. F. Travis Building, 137
St. Gabriel's Episcopal Church (Titusville), 169
St. Johns River, 145; airboat rides, 142, 219; alligators, 214; boating, 141; books about, 16, 223
St. Katherine's Greek Orthodox Church (Melbourne), 211
St. Mark's Episcopal Church (Cocoa Village), 137
St. Patrick's Day Parade & Street Party (Melbourne), 184
Sams House at Pine Island, 66–67
Sand & Sea Gifts & Gallery (Cocoa Village), 155
Sand on the Beach (Melbourne Beach), 201–2
Satellite Beach: city hall, 14; eating, 198–99; movie theaters, 151
Satellite Cinemas, 151
Saturn V, 165
Savannahs Golf Course, 78
Scafidi, Roy, 81–82
Sea Aire Motel, 97–98
Sea Legs, 59
Sea Tow Port Canaveral, 22
Sea Turtle Preservation Society, 49
sea turtles, 38, 49, 193, 195
seafood, 21, 120, 179. *See also specific restaurants*
Seafood Atlantic (Port Canaveral), 120
Seafood Festival (Grant), 211
Seagull Beach Club, 101
Seashell Suites, 195–96

Season Tickets Boutique, 153
seasons, 24
Sebastian Fishing Museum, 195
Sebastian Inlet State Park, 193; beaches, 192; birding, 190; boating, 190; campground, 191; turtle walks, 49
Seiler (Carolyn) Studios, 158
Sendala's, 210
7-11 Food Stores (Cocoa Beach), 119
Sexual Assault Victim Services, 17
Shady Characters Sunglass Emporium, 124
Shamrock Room, 151
Shark Pit Bar and Grill, 112
Shepard, Alan, 85, 192
Shepard Park, 85; special events, 132, 133
shipping, 19
Shobha's Boutique, 124
shoe stores, 124, 152–54, 207
shopping, 22; Cape Canaveral, 125, 126, 128–29, 131; Cocoa Beach, 123–31; Cocoa Village, 152–59; Eau Gallie, 206; Melbourne, 206–7, 210–11; Merritt Island, 123; Titusville, 179–82; Viera, 157
Shuttle Launch Experience, 163
Siam Orchid, 112–13
Sidney Fischer Park, 83
Silvestro's, 113
Simply Delicious Café and Bakery, 113–14
skatepark, 77
Slater Brothers Invitational, 133–34
Slow and Low Barbeque Bar & Grill, 114
Smith, Patrick D., 15, 30, 224

Smokehouse Foods, 120
SoBe Surf, 82
social history, 30–37
Something Different, 155
Sonny's Real Pit Bar-B-Que, 119
South Beach Inn, 98
south Brevard, 186–215; map, 188. *See also specific destinations*
space: about, 22–24; best viewing sites for space launches, 166, 167; books, 15–16, 222–23. *See also* Kennedy Space Center Visitor Complex; NASA
Space Coast Area Transit, 44–45
Space Coast Art Festival, 133
Space Coast Association of Realtors, 21
Space Coast Audubon Society, 53
Space Coast Ballet, 205
Space Coast Birding, 53
Space Coast Birding & Wildlife Festival, 182
Space Coast Business, 20
Space Coast Crafters, 155
Space Coast Geocachers, 172
Space Coast Kayaking, 74, 219
Space Coast Living, 20
Space Coast Mardi Gras, 157
Space Coast Pops, 205–6
Space Coast River Tours, Inc., 74, 219
Space Coast Runners Marathon and Half-Marathon, 61
Space Coast Stadium, 143
Space Coast State Fair, 157
Space Coast Symphony Orchestra, 206
Space Shuttle Plaza, 163
Space View Park, 167; Astronaut Memorial, 167
Space Walk of Fame

Museum, U.S., 23, 167–68
spas: Cocoa Beach, 79;
  Melbourne, 192;
  Titusville, 173
special events: athletic, 61;
  Cocoa Beach, 131–34;
  Cocoa Village, 157–59;
  Eau Gallie, 211, 213–14;
  Melbourne, 184, 211–15;
  Titusville, 182, 184
specialty markets, 120, 179
Spessard Holland, 192
sporting goods: Cocoa
  Beach, 127–29; Mel-
  bourne, 210–11;
  Titusville, 181–82
spring training, 143
Squid Lips Overwater Grill,
  202
Starbucks (Cocoa Beach),
  118
Stone Street Antiques, 152
Sun Shoppe Cafe, 203
Sun Touched Weddings,
  218
Sundancer Gallery, 155
Sunny Side Up Cafe, 150
Sunrise Bank, 14
Sunrise Bread Company,
  178–79
Sunrise Diner, 114
Sunrise Marina, 44, 57–59,
  71
Sunseed Food Co-op, 120
Sunset Café Waterfront
  Bar & Grill, 114
SunTrust Bank, 14
SunWard Tours, 218
Surf & Ski Jet Ski Rentals
  (Merritt Island), 78
Surf Bar and Grill (Cocoa
  Beach), 114–15
Surf Museum (Cocoa
  Beach), 69, 132
surf shops, Cocoa Beach,
  127–29
Surf Studio Beach Resort,
  98
Surf the Sand 8K Beach
  Run, 61
Surfet (Cocoa Beach), 82

surfing: Cocoa Beach, 69,
  79–82, 132–34; Sebastian
  Inlet, 192
surfing festivals, 132–34
Surfing Hall of Fame, 69
Surfside Playhouse, 122–23
Susan's Birkenstock Shoes,
  124
symphonies, 157, 187,
  204–6

T
Taco City, 119
taxis, 45
Taylor Bank Building, 137
television stations, 20
temperatures, average
  monthly, 24
tennis, at Cocoa Beach,
  77–78
Thai Basil Takeout Cuisine,
  119–20
Thai Thai Restaurant &
  Sushi Bar, 120
theater: Cocoa Beach,
  122–23; Cocoa Village,
  139, 151–52; Titusville,
  179
theme parks, 220–21
Thompson, Rodney, 179
Thousand Islands, 86–87;
  boating, 71, 73–75
Three Wishes, 115–16
TICO Warbird Airshow,
  184
Tin Roof Popcorn Compa-
  ny, 203–4
Titusville, 162–84; activities, 170–76; antiques,
  180; art galleries, 180–82;
  beaches, 173; birding,
  170; boating, 171; cafés,
  178–79; camping, 172;
  city hall, 14; eating,
  177–79; entertainment,
  179; family fun, 172; golf,
  172–73; historic places,
  168–69; hospitals, 18;
  information, 17; lodging,
  176–77; map, 164; muse-
  ums, 169–70; nature pre-

serves, 173–76; seafood,
  179; shopping, 179–82;
  sightseeing, 162–70;
  space launch viewing
  sites, 166; spas, 173; special events, 182, 184;
  sporting goods, 181–82;
  transportation, 162
Titusville Area Chamber of
  Commerce, 17
Titusville Art Walk, 182
Titusville Bridge and
  Causeway, 59
Titusville KOA, 172
Titusville Municipal Marina, 171
Titusville Playhouse, 169,
  179
Toy Box, 155
Trafford and Field Real
  Estate Firm, 137, 139
train travel, 44
transportation, 39–45; to
  Brevard County, 40–44;
  within Brevard County,
  44–45
Travelynx, 17, 43
Travis Hardware Store,
  155–56
triathlons, 61
Tuckaway Shores Resort,
  196
Turcot, Captain John, 56
Turtle Creek Golf Club,
  144
Twister Airboat Rides, 142,
  219
Twombly's Nautical Furni-
  ture, 126–27

U
Ulysses' Prime Steakhouse,
  150
Unique Treasures, 207
Universal Orlando Resort,
  220
UPS Store, 19
U.S. Astronaut Hall of
  Fame Museum, 23, 166
U.S. Space Walk of Fame
  Museum, 23, 167–68

V

vacation rentals, 99–101
Valencia Historic District, 139
Valiant Air Command Warbird Museum, 168
Ventana al Mundo, 156
VernaFlora Boutique, 153–54
Vessels in Stoneware, 181
Viera, 136; baseball, 143; birding, 141, 145; eating, 148–50; golf, 144; movie theater, 151; nightlife, 151; shopping, 157
Village Home, A (Cocoa Village), 154
Village Ice Cream and Sandwich Shop (Cocoa Village), 150–51

W

Wakulla Suites, 98–99
Walgreens (Cocoa Beach), 129
Walkabout Golf & Country Club, 172–73

Walt Disney World Resort, 220–21
Washington Hotel, 168–69
Washington Nationals, 143
Waterman's Challenge Surf Contest Weekend, 132
weather, 24
weddings, 217–18
What You Love to Do, 157
Wild Ocean Seafood Market, 120, 179
Wild Side Tours, 74–75
wildlife: about, 24–25; photography tips, 54. *See also* alligators; birds; bottlenose dolphins; manatees; nature preserves and parks; sea turtles
William H. Gleason House, 187, 194
Winchester Symphony House, 187
Windemere Inn by the Sea, 196–97
windsurfing, 76, 86, 131
Wolfe, Tom, 15, 222–23
World of Beer, 151

World Skin Cancer Foundation Slater Brothers Invitational, 133–34
Wuesthoff Medical Center-Melbourne, 18
Wuesthoff Medical Center-Rockledge, 18

X

Xtreme Fun at Jungle Village, 78
Xtreme Surf Shop, 127

Y

Yapa, 207
Yellow Cab, 45
Yellow Dog Café, 202
Yen-Yen, 116

Z

Zachary's Family Restaurant, 116
Zero G Weightless Flights, 168
Zimmerman (Kurt) Gallery & Studio, 158
zip codes, 25
Zoo, Brevard, 143–44, 171